VOLUME FORTY EIGHT

INTERNATIONAL REVIEW OF RESEARCH IN DEVELOPMENTAL DISABILITIES

VOLUME FORTY EIGHT

INTERNATIONAL REVIEW OF RESEARCH IN DEVELOPMENTAL DISABILITIES

Health Disparities and Intellectual Disabilities

Edited by

CHRIS HATTON

Centre for Disability Research (CeDR),
C/O Division of Health Research,
Lancaster University, Lancaster, Lancashire, UK

ERIC EMERSON

Centre for Disability Research and Policy,
University of Sydney, NSW, Australia;
Centre for Disability Research,
Lancaster University, Lancaster, Lancashire, UK

ELSEVIER

AMSTERDAM • BOSTON • HEIDELBERG • LONDON
NEW YORK • OXFORD • PARIS • SAN DIEGO
SAN FRANCISCO • SINGAPORE • SYDNEY • TOKYO
Academic Press is an imprint of Elsevier

Academic Press is an imprint of Elsevier
225 Wyman Street, Waltham, MA 02451, USA
525 B Street, Suite 1800, San Diego, CA 92101-4495, USA
125 London Wall, London EC2Y 5AS, UK
The Boulevard, Langford Lane, Kidlington, Oxford OX5 1GB, UK

First edition 2015

ISBN: 978-0-12-802291-7
ISSN: 2211-6095

For information on all Academic Press publications
visit our website at http://store.elsevier.com

CONTENTS

CONTRIBUTORS

R.S. Balogh
University of Ontario Institute of Technology, Oshawa; Physical Therapy Department, University of Toronto, Toronto, ON, Canada

M. Bayley
Brain and Spinal Cord Rehabilitation Program – UHN Toronto Rehabilitation Institute; Division of Physical Medicine and Rehabilitation, Faculty of Medicine, University of Toronto, Toronto, ON, Canada

Alexandra Bonardi
Center for Developmental Disabilities Evaluation and Research (CDDER), E.K. Shriver Center, University of Massachusetts Medical School, Boston; Human Services Research Institute (HSRI), Cambridge, MA, USA

K. Dobranowski
University of Ontario Institute of Technology, Oshawa, ON, Canada

Eric Emerson
Centre for Disability Research and Policy, University of Sydney, NSW, Australia; Centre for Disability Research, Lancaster University, Lancaster, Lancashire, UK

D. Fehlings
Holland Bloorview Kids Rehabilitation Hospital, Department of Paediatrics, University of Toronto, Toronto, ON, Canada

Michael H. Fox
National Center for Birth Defects and Developmental Disabilities, Centers for Disease Control and Prevention, Atlanta, GA, USA

Gyles Glover
Learning Disabilities Team, Public Health England, UK

Chris Hatton
Centre for Disability Research, Lancaster University, Lancaster, Lancashire, UK

Pauline Heslop
Norah Fry Research Centre, School for Policy Studies, University of Bristol, Bristol, UK

Matthew Hoghton
Clevedon Medical Centre, Clevedon Riverside Group, Clevedon, UK

Gloria L. Krahn
College of Public Health and Human Sciences, Oregon State University, Corvallis, OR, USA

J.K. Lake
Centre for Addiction and Mental Health, Toronto, ON, Canada

Emily Lauer
Center for Developmental Disabilities Evaluation and Research (CDDER), Eunice Kennedy Shriver Center, University of Massachusetts Medical School, Charlestown, MA, USA

Gwynnyth Llewellyn
Centre for Disability Research and Policy, University of Sydney, NSW, Australia

Y. Lunsky
Centre for Addiction and Mental Health, Toronto, ON, Canada

Lynn Martin
Department of Health Sciences, Lakehead University, Thunder Bay, ON, Canada

C. McGarry
Centre for Addiction and Mental Health, Toronto, ON, Canada

Katherine McKenzie
Department of Public Health Sciences, Queen's University, Kingston, ON, Canada

C. McMorris
Centre for Addiction and Mental Health, Toronto; Psychology Department, York University, Toronto, ON, Canada

Hélène Ouellette-Kuntz
Department of Public Health Sciences, Queen's University; Ongwanada, Kingston, ON, Canada

Nick Spencer
Division of Mental Health and Wellbeing, Warwick Medical School, University of Warwick, Coventry, UK

Sue Turner
National Development Team for Inclusion, Bath, UK

Cathy Vaughan
Centre for Health Equity, Melbourne School of Population and Global Health, University of Melbourne, Parkville, VIC, Australia

PREFACE

I would like to start by congratulating editors, Professors Chris Hatton and Eric Emerson, and all of the contributors, for this extremely important and valuable special issue of the *International Review of Research in Developmental Disabilities*. The World Health Organization (WHO) has, at least since the Declaration of Alma-Ata in 1978,[1] focused considerable attention generally on the issue of health inequalities around the globe. In particular, and of concern for me as Coordinator of the unit on disability, WHO has highlighted the urgency of dealing with health inequities involving persons with intellectual, developmental, and other disabilities. The *World Report on Disability*, jointly produced by the WHO and the World Bank in 2011,[2] relying on the best worldwide evidence, documented the profound health disparities that people with disabilities experience around the world. Study after study has shown that people with disabilities in general have a greater vulnerability to secondary conditions, comorbid conditions, age-related conditions, and higher rates of premature death than people without disabilities. Although this is particularly true in low and medium resource countries, it is also the case in the highest resource countries of the world.

More significantly, as editors Hatton and Emerson remark and as many of the collected papers demonstrate, although persons with intellectual and developmental disabilities experience poorer health associated with their underlying impairments and sometimes as well experience "premature aging,"[3] health disparities are primarily the result of unjust and unequal distribution of basic health resources. These fundamental health services are often not available, accessible, or affordable for people with disabilities; health-care workers do not always have the skills and knowledge needed to properly serve clients with disabilities; and health promotion and prevention activities rarely target people with disabilities. Significantly as well, people with disabilities are more directly and adversely impacted by social

1 Declaration of Alma-Ata. International Conference on Primary Health Care, Alma-Ata, USSR, 6–12 September 1978. Accessible at http://www.who.int/publications/almaata_declaration_en.pdf.

2 WHO. *World Report on Disability*. Geneva: WHO. 2011 and WHO Health and Disability Fact Sheet Number 352. Accessible at http://www.who.int/mediacentre/factsheets/fs352/en/.

3 Havercamp, S. M., Scandlin, D., Roth, M. (2004). Health disparities among adults with developmental disabilities, adults with other disabilities, and adults not reporting disability in North Carolina. *Public Health Reports, 119*, 418–426 and *Disability and ageing: Australian population patterns and implications*. (2000). Canberra: Australian Institute of Health and Welfare.

determinants of ill-health such as poverty and violence, and tend to have a higher exposure to lifestyle-related risk factors such as smoking and alcohol abuse, lack of exercise, and poor nutrition.

But since these major causes of health inequity are more social than biological, society at large is responsible for the inequity. The moral urgency of this is reinforced by Article 25 of the United Nations *Convention on the Rights of Persons with Disabilities* that makes it a human right that all societies ensure that persons with disabilities attain the highest standard of health care, without discrimination.[4] Despite the enormity and persistence of health disparities, there is a great deal that we can do to effectively respond to them. WHO's *World Report on Disability* sets out explicit and concrete recommendations for change: reforming policy and legislation to identify gaps and priorities in order to reduce health inequalities and plan improvements for access and inclusion; addressing barriers to financing and affordability to ensure universal health coverage; removing barriers to service delivery to ensure accessibility; educating health-care professionals in the specific requirements of persons with disabilities; and filling in gaps in data and research for continued, evidence-based policy change. All of these recommendations are grounded in the best evidence, and have been shown in practice to have positive impact.

What makes this special issue both timely and of particularly importance is that only relatively recently has research made it abundantly clear that persons with intellectual disabilities are one of the most deeply affected by these health disparities. The important study *Equality treatment: Closing the gap* in 2006 by the Disability Rights Commission in the United Kingdom[5] and the 2009 White Paper by the United States Centers for Disease Control and Prevention,[6] produce staggering statistics on the higher prevalence of chronic health conditions and higher rates of morbidity and mortality experience by individuals with developmental and intellectual disabilities, as compared with other persons with disabilities and the general population.

4 *Convention on the Rights of Persons with Disabilities*, G.A. Res. 61/106 (2007). Accessible at http://www.un.org/esa/socdev/enable/rights/convtexte.htm.

5 *Equality treatment: closing the gap: a formal investigation into the physical health inequalities experiences by people with learning disabilities and/or mental health problems.* (2006). London: Disability Rights Commission. Accessible at http://disability-studies.leeds.ac.uk/files/library/DRC-Health-FI-main.pdf.

6 Centers for Disease Control and Prevention, National Center on Birth Defects and Developmental Disabilities Health Surveillance Work Group. (2009). U.S. surveillance of health of people with intellectual disabilities a white paper. Accessible at http://www.cdc.gov/ncbddd/disabilityandhealth/pdf/209537-a_idmeeting-short-version12-14-09.pdf.

Research on persons with intellectual disabilities has lagged behind, and continues to, for two major reasons. First, it has only been in the last couple decades that this group has come "out of the shadows" of institutions, or hidden away out of public sight within the home. Their needs have therefore not received the attention they deserve. Secondly, long held assumptions about the longevity of persons with intellectual disabilities have been challenged and, although the facts are not all in, it appears that these individuals age similarly to the general population, and so are increasingly experiencing higher prevalence of age-related chronic health conditions. As we begin to get a better epidemiological picture of the population of persons with intellectual disabilities we get an ever more disturbing portrait of health inequity.

Although there are many social strategies that need to be implemented in the coming years to respond to the needs of this underserved population, the key is *accessible inclusion*: ensuring that people with intellectual and developmental disabilities are included in all health surveillance and public health interventions offered to the general public and fully including in all health-care services, while at the same time making sure that these services and interventions respond to incorporate the specific needs of this population.[7]

The work represented in the seven chapters of this special issue is of exceptionally high quality and moves us ever closer, not only to a better understanding of health disparities experienced by persons with developmental and intellectual disabilities, but also how we can effectively respond to these disparities. From my perspective at WHO, it is remarkable that this work reported in this special issue accords so well with WHO's *Disability Action Plan, 2014–2020*. The three objectives of the Plan focus on improving access to health-care services and programs, strengthening and extending rehabilitation services, and supporting the collection of appropriate and internationally comparable data on disability, and promote multidisciplinary research on disability.[8] It is therefore with great pleasure that I welcome the opportunity to congratulate the editors and contributors to this vitally important and timely special issue, which represents the kind of research that constitute an essential first step toward evidence-based action and

7 Heller, T., Fisher, D., Marks, B., Hsieh, K. (2014). Interventions to promote health: crossing networks of intellectual and developmental disabilities and aging. *Disability and Health Journal*, 7, S24–S32.

8 *WHO disability action plan 2014–2021 – better health for persons with disabilities*. Accessible at http://apps.who.int/gb/ebwha/pdf_files/WHA67/A67_16-en.pdf?ua=1.

evidence-informed policy that can effectively address the health disparities of persons with developmental and intellectual disabilities.

Alarcos Cieza
Blindness and Deafness Prevention, Disability and Rehabilitation,
World Health Organization

CHAPTER ONE

Introduction: Health Disparities, Health Inequity, and People with Intellectual Disabilities

Chris Hatton*, Eric Emerson*,§,1
*Centre for Disability Research, Lancaster University, Lancaster, Lancashire, UK
§Centre for Disability Research and Policy, University of Sydney, NSW, Australia
[1]Corresponding author: e-mail address: eric.emerson@lancaster.ac.uk

Content

Abstract

In this chapter, we provide a brief overview of what is known about disparities in the health of people with intellectual disabilities when compared to those in their non-intellectual disabled peers and current approaches to conceptualizing the causes of these differences. We then provide an overview of the six chapters that form the core of this edited volume on the health disparities (and inequities) experienced by people with intellectual disabilities.

Extensive evidence from high-income countries in Europe, North America, and Australasia indicates that people with intellectual disabilities experience substantially poorer health outcomes than their nonintellectually disabled peers (Anderson et al., 2013; Emerson & Hatton, 2014; Krahn & Fox, 2014; Krahn, Hammond, & Turner, 2006; O'Hara, McCarthy, & Bouras, 2010; Oeseburg, Dijkstra, Groothoff, Reijneveld, & Jansen, 2011; Prasher & Janicki, 2003; Scheepers, Kerr, O'Hara, Bainbridge, & Cooper, 2005; Sutherland, Couch, & Iacono, 2002; Taggart & Cousins, 2014; Van Schrojenstein Lantman-de Valk, 2005). They are more likely to die at an earlier age (e.g., Bittles et al., 2002; Emerson, Glover, Hatton, & Wolstenholme, 2014; Glover & Ayub, 2010; Heslop et al., 2014; Hollins, Attard, van Fraunhofer, McGuigan, & Sedgwick, 1998; McGuigan, Hollins, & Attard, 1995), to have poor rated general health (e.g., Emerson & Hatton, 2007a, 2007c; Emerson, Hatton, Robertson, & Baines, 2014; Haider, Ansari, Vaughan, Matters, & Emerson, 2013; Havercamp & Scott, 2015; Larson,

International Review of Research in Developmental Disabilities, Volume 48
ISSN 2211-6095
http://dx.doi.org/10.1016/bs.irrdd.2015.04.001

Lakin, Anderson, & Kwak, 2001), and to live with a wide range of complex health conditions such as,

- epilepsy (e.g., Beange, McElduff, & Baker, 1995; Cardoza & Kerr, 2010; Schieve et al., 2012; Straetmans, van Schrojenstein Lantman-de Valk, Schellevis, & Dinant, 2007);
- sensory impairments (e.g., Beange et al., 1995; Nielsen, Skov, & Jensen, 2007; Oeseburg et al., 2011; van Splunder, Stilma, Bernsen, & Evenhuis, 2006);
- respiratory disorders (e.g., Oeseburg et al., 2011; Schieve et al., 2012; Straetmans et al., 2007);
- obesity (e.g., Beange et al., 1995; Melville, Hamilton, Hankey, Miller, & Boyle, 2007);
- diabetes (e.g., Straetmans et al., 2007);
- oral health problems (e.g., Davies, 2012; Morgan et al., 2012);
- disorders of the digestive system (e.g., Böhmer et al., 1999; Davis, 2010; Schieve et al., 2012; Straetmans et al., 2007);
- osteoporosis (e.g., Center, Beange, & McElduff, 1998; Jaffe, Timell, & Gulanski, 2001);
- mental health problems (e.g., Cooper, Smiley, Morrison, Williamson, & Allan, 2007; Einfeld, Ellis, & Emerson, 2011; Emerson, 2011).

Historically, the poorer health of people with intellectual disabilities has been primarily understood as being caused by the biological bases of syndromes or conditions associated with intellectual disability. More recently, these disparities in health status have begun to be conceptualized as examples of health inequity, differences in health status that, being caused by environmental factors beyond the control of individuals concerned, are avoidable, unfair, and unjust (Emerson & Durvasula, 2005; Emerson & Hatton, 2014; Graham, 2005; Krahn et al., 2006; Ouellette-Kuntz, 2005). Evidence that supports an inequity perspective has emerged from disparate sources including investigations by government agencies on the health and healthcare of people with intellectual disabilities (e.g., Disability Rights Commission, 2006; Michael, 2008; NHS Health Scotland, 2004; Parliamentary and Health Service Ombudsman and Local Government Ombudsman, 2009; US Department Health & Human Services, 2002) and research studies that have investigated such issues as

- access to appropriate healthcare and health promotion programs (Alborz, McNally, & Glendinning, 2005; Hayden, Kim, & DePaepe, 2005; Norwood & Slayton, 2013; Osborn et al., 2012; Parish & Saville, 2006) and the quality of management of health conditions among people with intellectual disabilities (Balogh, Brownell, Ouellette-Kuntz, & Colantonio, 2010; Bowley & Kerr, 2000; Janicki et al., 2002; Jensen, Taylor, & Davis, 2013; Lunsky et al., 2014; McDermott et al., 2005);

- lifestyle factors (e.g., lack of exercise and poor nutrition) associated with poorer health among people with intellectual disabilities (Bartlo & Klein, 2011; Robertson, Emerson, Baines, & Hatton, 2014; Robertson et al., 2000);
- exposure to environmental factors (e.g., poverty and violence) associated with poorer health among people with intellectual disabilities (Emerson, 2010, 2013; Emerson & Hatton, 2007b, 2007c, 2007d; Emerson, Hatton et al., 2014);

The aim of this volume of *International Review of Research in Developmental Disabilities* is to summarize what is known (and what needs to be known) about the impact of this "cascade of disparities" (Krahn et al., 2006) on the health and well-being of people with intellectual disabilities.

In Chapter 2, Emerson and Spencer review the existing knowledge about the determinants ofhealth inequities experienced by children with intellectual disabilities. They argue that the limited evidence that is available indicates that children with intellectual disabilities are at an increased risk of exposure to all of the major categories of social determinants of poorer physical and mental health. They are more likely to live in households characterized by low socioeconomic position and poverty, and to be exposed to recurrent poverty. They are more likely to be exposed to a wide range of material and psychosocial hazards that are detrimental to their health, including inadequate nutrition, poor housing conditions, exposure to environmental toxins, family, peer and community violence, poor parenting and family instability. They are also less likely to have access to the resources necessary to build resilience in the face of adversity. However, the literature in this area is highly variable in its scope and quality. In order to better identify and understand health inequities in this group of children, they suggest three priorities for future research: (1) longitudinal studies using the extensive network of cohort studies in high-income countries to elucidate pathways and mechanisms in the association of low family socioeconomic position with childhood intellectual disability and to strengthen the evidence base on the combined impact of socioeconomic position and intellectual disability on health and well-being across the life course; (2) cross-sectional and longitudinal studies in different country settings to strengthen the evidence base in areas where it is weak; (3) controlled interventions designed to test approaches to reducing discrimination and strengthening resilience at both an individual and societal level.

In Chapter 3, Lauer, Heslop, and Hoghton present a comprehensive review of premature mortality among people with intellectual disabilities, with a particular focus on data from the United States and the United Kingdom. They highlight some of the major challenges to obtaining mortality data concerning people with intellectual disabilities, including reliably identifying people with intellectual disabilities in administrative information systems (see also Chapter 4), and obtaining consistent and valid information on the cause of death. Whilst life expectancy is increasing for people with intellectual disabilities, it is not approaching the life expectancy for the rest of the population, with median age of death at least 20 years younger for people with intellectual disabilities compared to that for the general population. The major causes of death are similar to those for the general population but more diverse among people with intellectual disabilities. Furthermore, much of the excess mortality associated with many causes of death for people with intellectual disabilities is preventable through better access to effective healthcare and support, or amenable through better public health measures to improve healthy lifestyles. The authors conclude with priorities for ensuring better mortality data, and its effective use to drive improvements in healthcare for people with intellectual disabilities.

In Chapter 4, Hatton and colleagues use case studies from the United States, Canada, and England to frame a discussion of key conceptual and methodological issues associated with health surveillance programs for people with intellectual disabilities. These include the challenges associated with (1) identifying people with intellectual disabilities in administrative databases; (2) identifying people with intellectual disabilities in population-based surveys through data linkage and cognitive testing and self- or informant report; (3) sampling issues; (4) the use of specific intellectual disability surveys; and (5) challenges in measuring health. They conclude with a discussion of the relationship between health surveillance and health policy.

In Chapter 5, Balogh and colleagues present a comprehensive review of the physical and mental health status and healthcare usage of people with cerebral palsy, comparing people with cerebral palsy with and without intellectual disabilities. The review identified a number of chronic physical and mental health issues that were more common among people with cerebral palsy, such as bladder issues, musculoskeletal problems, chronic pain, depression and self-injurious behavior, and early mortality compared to the general population. However, the research was limited in its identification of people with intellectual disabilities and in its examination of the range of possible determinants of health problems among people with cerebral palsy. Despite increased health needs and early mortality, the research about service utilization (and the effectiveness of service utilization) is sparse and inconsistent, with some evidence of increased hospitalizations. The authors conclude that more work is needed to understand health disparities between children and adults with cerebral palsy, the role of intellectual disability in the health status of people with cerebral palsy, and health disparities between people with cerebral palsy and the general population.

In Chapter 6, Oullette-Kuntz and colleagues review and highlight the importance of health surveillance for the growing population of older people with intellectual and developmental disabilities, using both international evidence and more detailed health surveillance data in Ontario, Canada. The authors review the major physical and mental health issues associated with aging among people with intellectual and developmental disabilities, noting patterns of similarities and differences to the aging general population. The consequences of deinstitutionalization for designing (cost-) effective health-care systems for more dispersed populations of older people with intellectual and developmental disabilities are also comprehensively discussed.

Finally, in Chapter 7, Llewellyn and colleagues note that increasing attention is being paid within general health inequity research to the impact of discrimination on the health of oppressed groups. In their chapter, they review the impact of the personal experience of discrimination on the health and well-being of people with intellectual disabilities. They begin by addressing conceptual and methodological issues facing research on links between discrimination and health and then review (1) research that has addressed the impact of the personal experience of discrimination on the health of oppressed groups; (2) what is known about the extent to which people with intellectual disabilities experience personal discrimination; (3) the literature that has attempted to address the impact of the personal experience of discrimination on the health of people with intellectual disabilities; (4) the literature on interventions aimed at reducing the exposure to or impact of discrimination among people with intellectual disabilities. Finally, they provide suggestions and recommendations for future research in this area.

While the chapters in this volume acknowledge continuing challenges in getting comprehensive information relevant to the public health of people with intellectual and developmental disabilities, the chapters in this volume also demonstrate the great strides that have been made during 1995–2015. The number of areas with ongoing health surveillance programs specifically concerning people with intellectual and developmental disabilities, well embedded within broader public health systems, is increasing. Major research initiatives to shed light on the health inequalities experienced by people with intellectual and developmental disabilities, including premature mortality, are leading to international collaborations that illustrate important crossnational similarities in the health experiences of people with intellectual and developmental disabilities. Taken together, the evidence base is beginning to demonstrate the range of health inequalities experienced by people with intellectual and developmental disabilities, and to highlight priorities for health and service systems improvement. The next challenge is to use this evidence to reduce or eliminate these health inequities.

REFERENCES

Alborz, A., McNally, R., & Glendinning, C. (2005). Access to health care for people with learning disabilities in the UK: mapping the issues and reviewing the evidence. *Journal of Health Services Research & Policy, 10*, 173–182.

Anderson, L. L., Humphries, K., McDermott, S., Marks, B., Sisarak, J., & Larson, S. (2013). The state of the science of health and wellness for adults with intellectual and developmental disabilities. *Intellectual & Developmental Disabilities, 51*, 385–398.

Balogh, R., Brownell, M., Ouellette-Kuntz, H., & Colantonio, A. (2010). Hospitalisation rates for ambulatory care sensitive conditions for persons with and without an intellectual disability—a population perspective. *Journal of Intellectual Disability Research, 54*, 820–832.

Bartlo, P., & Klein, P. J. (2011). Physical activity benefits and needs in adults with intellectual disabilities: systematic review of the literature. *American Journal of Intellectual and Developmental Disabilities, 116*, 220–232.

Beange, H., McElduff, A., & Baker, W. (1995). Medical disorders of adults with mental retardation: a population study. *American Journal on Mental Retardation, 99*, 595–604.

Bittles, A. H., Petterson, B. A., Sullivan, S. G., Hussain, R., Glasson, E. J., & Montgomery, P. (2002). The influence of intellectual disability on life expectancy. *Journal of Gerontology, 57*, 470–472.

Böhmer, C. J., Niezen-de Boer, M. C., Klinkenberg-Knol, E. C., Deville, W. L., Nadorp, J. H., & Meuwissen, S. G. (1999). The prevalence of gastroesophageal reflux disease in institutionalized intellectually disabled individuals. *American Journal of Gastroenterology, 94*, 804–810.

Bowley, C., & Kerr, M. (2000). Epilepsy and intellectual disability. *Journal of Intellectual Disability Research, 44*, 529–543.

Cardoza, B., & Kerr, M. (2010). Diseases of the nervous system I: epilepsy, hydrocephalus and nervous system malformations. In J. O'Hara, J. E. McCarthy, & N. Bouras (Eds.), *Intellectual disability and ill health : A review of the evidence* (pp. 190–202). Cambridge: Cambridge University Press.

Center, J., Beange, H., & McElduff, A. (1998). People with mental retardation have an increased prevalence of osteoporosis: a population study. *American Journal on Mental Retardation, 103*, 19–28.

Cooper, S. A., Smiley, E., Morrison, J., Williamson, A., & Allan, L. (2007). Mental ill-health in adults with intellectual disabilities: prevalence and associated factors. *British Journal of Psychiatry, 190*, 27–35.

Davies, G. (2012). Oral health among adults with learning disabilities in England 2010/11. *Paper presented at the better dental services for people with learning disabilities, Birmingham.*

Davis, R. W. (2010). Digestive system diseases. In J. O'Hara, J. E. McCarthy, & N. Bouras (Eds.), *Intellectual disability and ill health: A review of the evidence* (pp. 88–97). Cambridge: Cambridge University Press.

Disability Rights Commission. (2006). *Equal treatment—closing the gap*. London Disability Rights Commission.

Einfeld, S., Ellis, L., & Emerson, E. (2011). Comorbidity of intellectual disability and mental disorder: a systematic review. *Journal of Intellectual & Developmental Disability, 36*, 137–143.

Emerson, E. (2010). Self-reported exposure to disablism is associated with poorer self-reported health and wellbeing among adults with intellectual disabilities in England: cross sectional survey. *Public Health, 124*, 682–689.

Emerson, E. (2011). Health status and health risks of the 'hidden majority' of adults with intellectual disability. *Intellectual & Developmental Disabilities, 49*, 155–165.

Emerson, E. (2013). Commentary: childhood exposure to environmental adversity and the well-being of people with intellectual disabilities. *Journal of Intellectual Disabilities Research, 57*, 589–600. http://dx.doi.org/10.1111/j.1365-2788.2012.01577.x.

Emerson, E., & Durvasula, S. (2005). Health inequalities and people with intellectual disabilities: an introduction to the special issue. *Journal of Applied Research in Intellectual Disabilities, 18*(2), 95–96.

Emerson, E., Glover, G., Hatton, C., & Wolstenholme, J. (2014). Trends in age-standardised mortality rates and life expectancy of people with learning disabilities in Sheffield over a 33-year period. *Tizard Learning Disability Review, 19*, 90–95.

Emerson, E., & Hatton, C. (2007a). The contribution of socio-economic position to the health inequalities faced by children and adolescents with intellectual disabilities in Britain. *American Journal on Mental Retardation, 112*, 140–150.

Emerson, E., & Hatton, C. (2007b). The mental health of children and adolescents with intellectual disabilities in Britain. *British Journal of Psychiatry, 191*, 493–499.

Emerson, E., & Hatton, C. (2007c). Poverty, socio-economic position, social capital and the health of children and adolescents with intellectual disabilities in Britain: a replication. *Journal of Intellectual Disability Research, 51*, 866–874.

Emerson, E., & Hatton, C. (2007d). The socio-economic circumstances of children at risk of disability in Britain. *Disability and Society, 22*, 563–580.

Emerson, E., & Hatton, C. (2014). *Health inequalities and people with intellectual disabilities*. Cambridge: Cambridge University Press.

Emerson, E., Hatton, C., Robertson, J., & Baines, S. (2014). Perceptions of neighbourhood quality, social and civic participation and the self rated health of British adults with intellectual disability: cross sectional study. *BMC Public Health, 14*, 1252. 1210.1186/1471-2458-1214-1252.

Glover, G., & Ayub, M. (2010). *How people with learning disabilities die*. Durham: Improving Health & Lives: Learning Disabilities Observatory.

Graham, H. (2005). Intellectual disabilities and socioeconomic inequalities in health: an overview of research. *Journal of Applied Research in Intellectual Disabilities, 18*, 101–111.

Haider, S. I., Ansari, Z., Vaughan, L., Matters, H., & Emerson, E. (2013). Health and well-being of Victorian adults with and without an intellectual disability. *Research in Developmental Disabilities, 34*, 4034–4042.

Havercamp, S. M., & Scott, H. M. (2015). National health surveillance of adults with disabilities, adults with intellectual and developmental disabilities, and adults with no disabilities. *Disability and Health Journal, 8*, 165–172.

Hayden, M. F., Kim, S., & DePaepe, P. (2005). Health status, utilization patterns, and outcomes of persons with intellectual disabilities: review of the literature. *Mental Retardation, 43*, 175–195.

Heslop, P., Blair, P. S., Fleming, P., Hoghton, M., Marriott, A., & Russ, L. (2014). The confidential inquiry into premature deaths of people with intellectual disabilities in the UK: a population-based study. *Lancet, 383*, 889–895.

Hollins, S., Attard, M., van Fraunhofer, N., McGuigan, S. M., & Sedgwick, P. (1998). Mortality in people with learning disability: risks causes, and death certification findings in London. *Developmental Medicine and Child Neurology, 40*, 50–56.

Jaffe, J. S., Timell, A. M., & Gulanski, B. I. (2001). Prevalence of low bone density in women with developmental disabilities. *Journal of Clinical Densitometry, 4*, 25–29.

Janicki, M. P., Davidson, P. W., Henderson, C. M., McCallion, P., Taets, J. D., & Force, L. T. (2002). Health characteristics and health services utilization in older adults with intellectual disability living in community residences. *Journal of Intellectual Disability Research, 46*, 287–298.

Jensen, K. M., Taylor, L. C., & Davis, M. M. (2013). Primary care for adults with down syndrome: adherence to preventive healthcare recommendations. *Journal of Intellectual Disabilities Research, 57*, 409–421.

Krahn, G., & Fox, M. H. (2014). Health disparities of adults with intellectual disabilities: what do we know? What do we do? *Journal of Applied Research in Intellectual Disability, 27*, 431–446. http://dx.doi.org/10.1111/jar.12067.

Krahn, G. L., Hammond, L., & Turner, A. (2006). A cascade of disparities: health and health care access for people with intellectual disabilities. *Mental Retardation and Developmental Disabilities Research Reviews, 12*, 70–82.

Larson, S., Lakin, C., Anderson, L., & Kwak, N. (2001). *Characteristics of and service use by persons with MR/DD living in their own homes or with family members: NHIS-D analysis*. Minneapolis, MN: Research and Training Center on Community Living, Institute on Community Integration, University of Minnesota.

Lunsky, Y., Lake, J. K., Durbin, J., Perry, A., Bullock, H., & Morris, S. (2014). Understanding and improving care for individuals with intellectual and developmental disabilities in the emergency department. *International Review of Research in Developmental Disabilities, 47*, 1–37.

McDermott, S., Moran, R., Platt, T., Wood, H., Isaac, T., & Dasari, S. (2005). Prevalence of epilepsy in adults with mental retardation and related disabilities in primary care. *American Journal on Mental Retardation, 110*, 48–56.

McGuigan, S. M., Hollins, S., & Attard, M. (1995). Age-specific standardized mortality rates in people with learning disability. *Journal of Intellectual Disability Research, 39*(Pt 6), 527–531.

Melville, C., Hamilton, S., Hankey, C., Miller, S., & Boyle, S. (2007). The prevalence and determinants of obesity in adults with intellectual disabilities. *Obesity Reviews, 8*, 223–230.

Michael, J. (2008). *Healthcare for all: Report of the independent inquiry into access to healthcare for people with learning disabilities*. London: Independent Inquiry into Access to Healthcare for People with Learning Disabilities.

Morgan, J. P., Minihan, P. M., Stark, P. C., Finkelman, M. D., Yantsides, K. E., & Park, A. (2012). The oral health status of 4,732 adults with intellectual and developmental disabilities. *Journal of the American Dental Association, 143*, 838–846.

NHS Health Scotland. (2004). *People with learning disabilities in Scotland: Health needs assessment report*. Glasgow: NHS Health Scotland.

Nielsen, L. S., Skov, L., & Jensen, H. (2007). Visual dysfunctions and ocular disorders in children with developmental delay. II. Aspects of refractive errors, strabismus and contrast sensitivity. *Acta Opthalmologica Scandinavica, 85*, 419–426.

Norwood, K. W., & Slayton, R. L. (2013). Oral health care for children with developmental disabilities. *Pediatrics, 131*, 614–619.

O'Hara, J., McCarthy, J. E., & Bouras, N. (2010). *Intellectual disability and ill health: A review of the evidence*. Cambridge: Cambridge University Press.

Oeseburg, B., Dijkstra, G. J., Groothoff, J. W., Reijneveld, S. A., & Jansen, D. E. M. C. (2011). Prevalence of chronic health conditions in children with intellectual disability: a systematic literature review. *Intellectual & Developmental Disabilities, 49*, 59–85.

Osborn, D. P. J., Horsfall, L., Hassiotis, A., Petersen, I., Walters, K., & Nazareth, I. (2012). Access to cancer screening in people with learning disabilities in the UK: cohort study in the health improvement network, a primary care research database. *PLoS One, 7*. http://dx.doi.org/10.1371/journal.pone.0043841.

Ouellette-Kuntz, H. (2005). Understanding health disparities and inequities faced by individuals with intellectual disabilities. *Journal of Applied Research in Intellectual Disabilities, 18*, 113–121.

Parish, S. L., & Saville, A. W. (2006). Women with cognitive limitations living in the community: evidence of disability-based disparities in health care. *Mental Retardation, 44*, 249–259.

Parliamentary and Health Service Ombudsman and Local Government Ombudsman. (2009). *Six lives: The provision of public services to people with learning disabilities*. London: Parliamentary and Health Service Ombudsman and Local Government Ombudsman.

Prasher, V., & Janicki, M. P. (Eds.). (2003). *Physical health of adults with intellectual disabilities*. Oxford: Blackwell.

Robertson, J., Emerson, E., Baines, S., & Hatton, C. (2014). Obesity and health behaviours of British adults with self-reported intellectual impairments: cross sectional survey. *BMC Public Health, 14*, 219.

Robertson, J., Emerson, E., Gregory, N., Hatto, C., Turner, S., & Kessissoglou, S. (2000). Lifestyle related risk factors for poor health in residential settings for people with intellectual disabilities. *Research in Developmental Disabilities, 21*(6), 469–486. S0891422200000536 [pii].

Scheepers, M., Kerr, M., O'Hara, D., Bainbridge, D., & Cooper, S. A. R. D. (2005). Reducing health disparity in people with intellectual disabilities: a report from the Health Issues Special Interest Research Group of the International Association for the Scientific Study of Intellectual Disabilities. *Journal of Policy and Practice in Intellectual Disabilities, 2*, 249–255.

Schieve, L. A., Gonzalez, V., Boulet, S. L., Visser, S. N., Rice, C. E., & Braun, K. V. N. (2012). Concurrent medical conditions and health care use and needs among children with learning and behavioral developmental disabilities, National Health Interview Survey, 2006–2010. *Research in Developmental Disabilities, 33*, 467–476.

van Splunder, J., Stilma, J. S., Bernsen, R. M. D., & Evenhuis, H. M. (2006). Prevalence of visual impairments in adults with intellectual disabilities in the Netherlands: cross-sectional study. *Eye, 20*, 1004–1010.

Straetmans, J. M. J. A. A., van Schrojenstein Lantman-de Valk, H. M. J., Schellevis, F. G., & Dinant, G.-J. (2007). Health problems of people with intellectual disabilities: the impact for general practice. *British Journal of General Practice, 57*, 64–66.

Sutherland, G., Couch, M. A., & Iacono, T. (2002). Health issues for adults with developmental disability. *Research in Developmental Disabilities, 23*, 422–445.

Taggart, L., & Cousins, W. (Eds.). (2014). *Health promotion for people with intellectual and developmental disabilities*. Maidenhead, UK: McGraw Hill.

US Department Health & Human Services. (2002). *Report of the surgeon general's conference on health disparities and mental retardation*. Rockville: Closing the Gap.

Van Schrojenstein Lantman-de Valk, H. (2005). Health in people with intellectual disabilities: current knowledge and gaps in knowledge. *Journal of Applied Research in Intellectual Disabilities, 18*, 325–333.

CHAPTER TWO

Health Inequity and Children with Intellectual Disabilities

Eric Emerson[*,§,1], **Nick Spencer**[¶]
[*]Centre for Disability Research and Policy, University of Sydney, NSW, Australia
[§]Centre for Disability Research, Lancaster University, Lancaster, Lancashire, UK
[¶]Division of Mental Health and Wellbeing, Warwick Medical School, University of Warwick, Coventry, UK
[1]Corresponding author: e-mail address: eric.emerson@lancaster.ac.uk

Contents

International Review of Research in Developmental Disabilities, Volume 48
ISSN 2211-6095
http://dx.doi.org/10.1016/bs.irrdd.2015.03.001

Abstract

The limited evidence that is available indicates that children with intellectual disabilities are at increased risk of exposure to all of the major categories of social determinants of poorer physical and mental health. They are more likely to live in households characterized by low socioeconomic position (SEP) and poverty, and to be exposed to recurrent poverty. Over time they are more likely to become poor and less likely to escape from poverty. They are more likely to be exposed to a wide range of material and psychosocial hazards that are detrimental to their health, including inadequate nutrition; poor housing conditions; exposure to environmental toxins; family, peer, and community violence; poor parenting; and family instability. They are also less likely to have access to the resources necessary to build resilience in the face of adversity. However, the published literature in this area is highly variable in its scope and quality. In order to better identify and understand health inequities in this particularly vulnerable group of children, we suggest the following priorities for future research: (1) longitudinal studies using the extensive network of cohort studies in high-income countries to elucidate pathways and mechanisms in the association of low family SEP with childhood intellectual disability and to strengthen the evidence base on the combined impact of SEP and intellectual disability on health and well-being across the life course; (2) cross-sectional and longitudinal studies in different country settings to strengthen the evidence base in areas where it is weak; (3) controlled interventions designed to test approaches to reducing discrimination and strengthening resilience at both an individual and societal level.

1. INTRODUCTION

People with intellectual disabilities have significantly poorer health and increased age-adjusted mortality than their nondisabled peers (Emerson & Hatton, 2014; Heslop et al., 2014; Krahn & Fox, 2014). It is clear that this difference in health status is, to an extent, preventable and unjust (Centers for Disease Control and Prevention (CDC) & National Center on Birth Defects and Developmental Disabilities (NCBDDD) Health Surveillance Work Group, 2009; Disability Rights Commission, 2006; Emerson & Hatton, 2014; Heslop et al., 2014; Mencap, 2007, 2012; Michael, 2008; Ouellette-Kuntz, 2005; US Department of Health & Human Services, 2002a, 2002b). As such, it represents an example of health inequity. We use the term "inequity" rather than "inequality" in this chapter to describe socially determined differences in health among children with intellectual disabilities and between children with and without intellectual disabilities.

The WHO glossary of terms (http://www.who.int/hia/about/glos/en/index1.html) explains the important distinction between these terms as follows: "Health inequalities can be defined as differences in health status or in the distribution of health determinants between different population groups. It is important to distinguish between inequality in health and inequity. Some health inequalities are attributable to biological variations or free choice and others are attributable to the external environment and conditions mainly outside the control of the individuals concerned. In the first case it may be impossible or ethically or ideologically unacceptable to change the health determinants and so the health inequalities are unavoidable. In the second, the uneven distribution may be unnecessary and avoidable as well as unjust and unfair, so that the resulting health inequalities also lead to inequity in health."

Some inequalities in health associated with intellectual disability, such as the increased risk of congenital abnormalities among those with moderate to profound intellectual impairment, are unavoidable given current knowledge (Tyrer & McGrother, 2009). Similarly, a number of syndromes associated with intellectual disabilities are also associated with some specific health risks (Arron, Oliver, Moss, Berg, & Burbidge, 2011; Batshaw, Pellegrino, & Roizen, 2007; Dykens, Hodapp, & Finucane, 2000; Emerson & Einfeld, 2011; Harris, 2005; Jacobson et al., 2010; McCarthy et al., 2010; Melville, Cooper, McGrother, Thorp, & Collacott, 2005; Proto et al., 2007; Stinton, Elison, & Howlin, 2010; Stinton, Tomlinson, & Estes, 2012; Torr & Lee, 2010). These include: congenital heart disease among people with Down's syndrome and Williams syndrome; early onset dementia and immune system disorders in people with Down's syndrome (Torr & Lee, 2010); hypothalamic disorders and obesity among people with Prader—Willi syndrome; mental health problems and challenging behaviors among people with autism spectrum disorders and a range of specific syndromes.

The increased health risks associated with specific syndromes cannot, at present, be prevented. As the WHO glossary indicates if these are not amenable to change they cannot be characterized as unjust. However, given that many of these health conditions are treatable, inequity would arise if health care systems were less likely to identify and/or treat these health conditions among children with intellectual disabilities. For example, surgical interventions for congenital heart abnormalities have been denied to children with Down's syndrome due to prevailing cultural beliefs about the value or the quality of life of living with Down's syndrome (Amark & Sunnergardh, 1999; Irving & Chaudhari, 2012). In this instance, the increased infant and child mortality rates of children with Down's syndrome is a clear example of health inequity. Similarly, the association of intellectual disability with low socioeconomic position (SEP) and the consequences that this has for health, one of the primary foci of this chapter, is inequitable as it is unjust and amenable to change.

Current knowledge suggests that while action to address health inequities needs to take place across the life course, intervening during childhood may bring particular benefits (The Marmot Review, 2010; World Health Organization, 2008; World Health Organization Regional Office for Europe, 2013; World Health Organization and the World Bank, 2011). Our aims in this chapter, therefore, are: (1) to summarize current knowledge about the determinants of health inequities experienced by children with intellectual disabilities; and (2) to identify key issues for further research in this area.

To do this we will draw on three sources of evidence. First, we will use key research reviews and policy documents to summarize what is known about the determinants of health inequities among children in general. Knowledge from this source will be used to structure this chapter. Second, we will review research reports that provide information on the extent to which children with intellectual disabilities are exposed to these determinants of health inequities. Finally, we will review research studies that have investigated the association between exposure to key social determinants and the health on the well-being of children with intellectual disabilities. In all three areas, we have prioritized research studies that have employed sampling strategies that allow generalization to national populations. We stress, however, that this is not a systematic review of research in this area. Rather, it is a conceptual review that uses existing research to illustrate the issues raised.

2. THE NATURE AND EXTENT OF HEALTH INEQUITIES EXPERIENCED BY CHILDREN WITH INTELLECTUAL DISABILITIES

Over the last decade, numerous review papers, reports, and books have summarized what is known about the (generally poorer) health of people with intellectual disabilities (Emerson & Hatton, 2014; Graham, 2005; Haveman et al., 2010; Krahn & Fox, 2014; Krahn, Hammond, & Turner, 2006;

NHS Health Scotland, 2004; O'Hara, McCarthy, & Bouras, 2010; Oeseburg, Dijkstra, Groothoff, Reijneveld, & Jansen, 2011; Ouellette-Kuntz, 2005; Perry, Hammond, Marston, Gaskell, & Eva, 2011; Prasher & Janicki, 2003; Scheepers et al., 2005; Sutherland, Couch, & Iacono, 2002; US Department of Health & Human Services, 2002b; Van Schrojenstein Lantman-de Valk, 2005). The vast majority of this research has focused on the health of adults with intellectual disability.

It is clear, however, the available evidence suggests that: (1) people with intellectual disabilities have increased age-specific mortality rates across all ages (Bittles et al., 2002; Glover & Ayub, 2010; Heslop et al., 2014; Hollins, Attard, van Fraunhofer, McGuigan, & Sedgwick, 1998; McGuigan, Hollins, & Attard, 1995); and (2) children with intellectual disability have significantly poorer mental and physical health than their nondisabled peers (Einfeld, Ellis, & Emerson, 2011; Emerson & Hatton, 2014; Oeseburg et al., 2011; Schieve et al., 2012).

3. THE DETERMINANTS OF INEQUITIES IN CHILD HEALTH

Health inequities arise from the societal conditions in which people are born, grow, live, work and age, referred to as social determinants of health. These include early years' experiences, education, economic status, employment and decent work, housing and environment, and effective systems of preventing and treating ill health.
Preamble to the Rio Political Declaration on Social Determinants of Health, *adopted by UN Member States in October 2011*

World Health Organization (2011)

There are extensive (and at times disparate) literatures on the nature and determinants of health inequities experienced by children globally and, more specifically, within high-income countries (Anda et al., 2006; Arseneault, Bowes, & Shakoor, 2010; Black et al., 2008; Black, Morris, & Bryce, 2003; Bolte, Tamburlini, & Kohlhuber, 2010; Braubach & Fairburn, 2010; Bzostek & Beck, 2011; Carpenter & Stacks, 2009; Conger & Donnellan, 2007; Currie et al., 2012; Department of Health, 2010, 2013; Fowler, Tompsett, Braciszewski, Jacques-Tiura, & Baltes, 2009; Gilbert et al., 2009; Graham, 2007; Grantham-McGregor et al., 2007; Hertzman & Boyce, 2010; Irish, Kobayashi, & Delahanty, 2010; Leventhal & Newman, 2010; Marmot & on behalf of the Commission on Social Determinants of Health, 2007; Marmot & Wilkinson, 2006; McEwen & Gianaros, 2010; Pickett &

Wilkinson, 2007; Rough, Goldblatt, Marmot, & Nathanson, 2013; Shonkoff, 2010; Shonkoff, Boyce, & McEwen, 2009; Spencer, 2012; The Marmot Review, 2010; Turner, Finkelhor, & Ormrod, 2006; Viner et al., 2012; Waldfogel, Craigie, & Brooks-Gunn, 2010; Walker et al., 2007, 2011; Wilkinson & Pickett, 2009; World Health Organization, 2008; World Health Organization Regional Office for Europe, 2013; World Health Organization and the World Bank, 2011). Most approaches to synthesizing this body of knowledge focus on the extent to which **social stratification** leads to: (1) differential rates of **exposure** to material and psychosocial hazards that are detrimental to well-being; and (2) differential **vulnerability or resilience** to the impact of such exposures on health and subsequent well-being (Bartley, 2004; Diderichsen, Evans, & Whitehead, 2001; Graham, 2007; Kreiger, 2011; Marmot, 2005; Spencer, 2012; Viner et al., 2012). We will use this simple framework to structure this chapter.

3.1 Social Stratification and SEP

All societies are hierarchically structured in relation to access to wealth, power, and status. These hierarchies result from the interaction between the impact of powerful social institutions (such as the labor market, education, and legal systems) in stratifying the social order and people's active involvement in recreating and maintaining the social hierarchy through cultural and social practices (Graham, 2007). SEP refers to the position occupied in a social hierarchy by an individual or family. There exists a very extensive literature documenting the association between family SEP and the health of children (Department of Health, 2010, 2013; Graham, 2007; Marmot & on behalf of the Commission on Social Determinants of Health, 2007; Marmot & Wilkinson, 2006; Rough et al., 2013; Spencer, 2000, 2012; The Marmot Review, 2010; Wilkinson & Pickett, 2009; World Health Organization Regional Office for Europe, 2013).

3.2 Differential Exposure

The association between family SEP and the health of children appears to be, in part, attributable to the association between low family SEP and the increased risk of children being exposed to a wide range of material and psychosocial hazards that are detrimental to their health. These hazards include, but are not limited to, inadequate nutrition; poor housing conditions; environmental toxins; family, peer, and community violence; poor parenting; and family instability (Anda et al., 2006; Arseneault et al., 2010;

Black et al., 2008; Bolte et al., 2010; Braubach & Fairburn, 2010; Bzostek & Beck, 2011; Carpenter & Stacks, 2009; Currie et al., 2012; Fowler et al., 2009; Gilbert et al., 2009; Graham, 2007; Hertzman & Boyce, 2010; Irish et al., 2010; Leventhal & Newman, 2010; Patel, Ioannidis, Cullen, & Rehkopf, 2015; Rough et al., 2013; Shonkoff, 2010; Shonkoff et al., 2009; Spencer, 2012; Turner et al., 2006; Waldfogel et al., 2010; Walker et al., 2011). While none of these hazards are unique to low-SEP families, the risk of exposure to all of them are socially patterned, with risk increasing at lower levels of SEP. Further, children in low-SEP households are at risk of exposure to multiple hazards (Evans & English, 2002).

3.3 Differential Vulnerability and Resilience

The association between family SEP and the health of children also appears to be, in part, attributable to the association between low family SEP and increased vulnerability (or decreased resilience) to the effects of exposure. The terms vulnerability and resilience are often misused to refer solely to the attributes and characteristics of individuals (e.g., personality or temperament) that may make them more or less susceptible to the impact of exposure to material or psychosocial hazards. However, a contemporary approach to the study of resilience also includes consideration of a wide range of environmental protective factors that make children less susceptible to the impact of such exposures (Buck & Gregory, 2013; Friedli, 2009; Luthar, 2003, 2006; Masten, 2001; Public Health England, 2014; Ungar, 2008). These include access to such resources as wealth, social connections, and timely access to appropriate health and welfare services (Buck & Gregory, 2013; Davydov, Stewart, Ritchie, & Chaudieu, 2010; Friedli, 2009; Goldstein & Brooks, 2006; Jenkins, 2008; Luthar, 2003; Masten, 2001; MIND & Mental Health Foundation, 2013; Public Health England, 2014; Schoon, 2006; Seccombe, 2002; Ungar, 2008).

4. SEP AND CHILDREN WITH INTELLECTUAL DISABILITIES

4.1 The Association between SEP and Intellectual Disabilities

Disabled children are significantly more likely than their peers to live in low-SEP households that are characterized by poverty and material hardship (Blackburn, Read, & Spencer, 2010, 2013; Emerson & Hatton,

2007c; Parish & Cloud, 2006; Parish, Rose, Andrews, Grinstein-Weiss, & Richman, 2008; Parish, Rose, & Swaine, 2010; World Health Organization and the World Bank, 2011). The association between low SEP and child disability is particularly strong for children with intellectual disabilities, especially children with less severe intellectual disabilities (Chapman, Scott, & Stanton-Chapman, 2008; Emerson, 2004, 2007, 2012; Fryers, 1993; Fujiura, 1998; Heber, 1970; Leonard et al., 2011, 2005; Leonard & Wen, 2002; Maulik, Mascarenhas, Mathers, Dua, & Saxena, 2011; Roeleveld, Zielhuis, & Gabreels, 1997) and is evident from an early age (Emerson & Brigham, 2015; Emerson & Einfeld, 2010; Emerson et al., 2009). For example, a recent systematic review of the association between SEP and the prevalence of intellectual disabilities reported pooled estimates of 6.8 (6.3, 7.4) for mild intellectual disabilities and 2.2 (1.9, 2.4) for moderate/severe intellectual disabilities (Spencer, Blackburn, & Read, submitted for publication).

In addition to children with intellectual disabilities being at greater risk of poverty at any particular point in time, they are also, in common with disabled children more generally, more likely over time to become poor, remain poor, experience longer spells of poverty, and less likely over time to escape from poverty (Emerson, Shahtahmasebi, Lancaster, & Berridge, 2010; Shahtahmasebi, Emerson, Berridge, & Lancaster, 2011). For example, recent research in the United Kingdom has suggested that, while the majority (53%) of children without intellectual disabilities were not exposed to poverty at any of five waves of data collection from age 9 months to 11 years, the majority (59%) of children with intellectual disabilities were exposed to income poverty at three or more waves of data collection (Public Health England, 2015). At every transition point between waves of data collection, children with intellectual disabilities were significantly more likely than their peers to become poor and significantly less likely than their peers to escape from poverty (Public Health England, 2015).

4.2 The Association between SEP and Health among Children with Intellectual Disabilities

As noted above, there exists an extensive literature documenting the association between family SEP and the health of children generally (Graham, 2007; Marmot & on behalf of the Commission on Social Determinants of Health, 2007; Marmot & Wilkinson, 2006; Rough et al., 2013; Spencer, 2012; Wilkinson & Pickett, 2009; World Health Organization Regional

Office for Europe, 2013). However, few studies have examined the association between family SEP and the health of children with intellectual disabilities (Emerson & Hatton, 2014). Key findings from those studies that have addressed this issue are summarized below.

4.3 Physical Health

Analysis of data from the UK's Millennium Cohort Study (MCS) indicated no statistically significant relationship between exposure to material hardship or indicators of area-level deprivation and risk of obesity at age five. These relationships were, however, significant among children without intellectual disabilities (Emerson, 2009). Analysis of data from the *Longitudinal Study of Australian Children* indicated that exposure to income poverty at ages 4/5 and 6/7 was associated with increased risk of obesity at age 6/7. These associations were stronger for children with intellectual disabilities than other children (Emerson & Robertson, 2010). More recently, analysis of MCS data has indicated little relationship between either exposure to income poverty or material hardship and multiple indicators of the general physical health of children with intellectual disability at age 11 (Public Health England, 2015).

4.4 Mental Health

Analysis of the UK's 1999 and 2004 *ONS Child and Adolescent Mental Health Surveys* revealed a cross-sectional dose-dependent relationship between breadth of exposure to indicators of low SEP and the risk of conduct disorders, emotional disorders, and ADHD among British children with intellectual disabilities. For all three disorders, the strength of the relationship between exposure and risk was higher among children with intellectual disabilities than among other children (Emerson & Hatton, 2007a). Analysis of the 1999 *Survey* revealed cross-sectional associations between: (1) lower social class and increased rates of conduct disorder and hyperkinesis among children with intellectual disabilities; and (2) living in lower-income households and increased rates of any diagnosed disorder, emotional disorder, depression, and conduct disorder among children with intellectual disabilities (Emerson, 2003b).

Analysis of data from the MCS has indicated a dose-dependent relationship between breadth of exposure to indicators of low SEP at ages 9 months and 3 years and: (1) the risk of conduct difficulties at age three; (2) the persistence of conduct difficulties from age three to ages five and seven. In both cases, the strength of the relationship between exposure and risk was higher among children with intellectual disabilities than among other children (Emerson et al., 2014). More recently, analysis of MCS data has indicated positive relationships between exposure to income poverty and/or material hardship and multiple indicators of the poorer mental health of children at age 11, relationships that were particularly strong for conduct difficulties (Public Health England, 2015).

Analysis of data from MCS and the *Longitudinal Study of Australian Children* indicated a cross-sectional dose-dependent relationship between exposure to adverse socioeconomic circumstances and risk of mental health problems at age three among UK and Australian children with intellectual disabilities. However, only the association for UK children was statistically significant. For all comparisons, the strength of the associations between exposure and risk was weaker for children with intellectual disabilities than for other children (Emerson & Einfeld, 2010). Finally, analysis of data from the *Longitudinal Study of Australian Children* indicated a dose-dependent relationship between exposure to SEP-related adversity at age four/five and the risk of conduct difficulties at that age and the persistence of conduct difficulties to ages six/seven and eight/nine among children with borderline intellectual disabilities. For prevalence at age four/five, the strength of the association between exposure and risk was greater for children with intellectual disabilities than for other children (Emerson, Einfeld, & Stancliffe, 2011).

Analysis of health visitor records in three areas of SW England indicated a significant relationship between low SEP and increased risk of behavior problems in young children with developmental delay (Emerson & Brigham, 2015). A number of smaller scale studies, often relying on administratively defined convenience samples, have also reported an association between exposure to general indicators of low SEP and poorer mental health among children with intellectual disabilities (Emerson, Robertson, & Wood, 2005, 2007; Taggart, Taylor, & McCrum-Gardner, 2010).

4.5 Health Behaviors

Analysis of data from the 1999 ONS *Child and Adolescent Mental Health Survey* indicated that the odds of 11- to 15-year old children with intellectual disability being current smokers was 5.2 times greater if they lived in poverty (Emerson & Turnbull, 2005). More recently, analysis of MCS data has indicated positive relationships between exposure to income poverty and/or material hardship and multiple indicators of risky health behaviors at age 11 among children with intellectual disabilities (Public Health England,

2015). For example, exposure to income poverty was associated with a 6.1 increase in the odds of having tried cigarettes, a 3.1 increase in the odds of not eating fruit each day, a 2.4 increase in the odds of having tried alcohol, a 2.3 increase in the odds of not eating breakfast every day, a 2.1 increase in the odds of never cycling, a 1.8 increase in the odds of never participating in sport, a 1.7 increase in the odds of not cleaning teeth twice a day, and a 1.5 increase in the odds of having sweetened drinks more than once a day.

5. RISK OF EXPOSURE TO SPECIFIC MATERIAL AND PSYCHOSOCIAL HAZARDS

As noted above, the association between family SEP and the health of children appears to be, in part, attributable to the association between low family SEP and the increased risk of children being exposed to a wide range of specific material and psychosocial hazards that are detrimental to their health. In this section, we will review evidence relating to the risk of children with intellectual disabilities being exposed to specific material and psychosocial hazards and the impact that this may have on their health.

5.1 Nutrition

Analysis of MCS data has indicated that infants with intellectual disabilities were less likely than their peers to have been ever breast-fed, breast-fed exclusively or at all at 3 months or breast-fed at all at 6 months (Gore, Emerson, & Brady, 2015). Similar results have been reported in a US study (Burd et al., 1988). More recently, analysis of MCS data has indicated that 11-year-old children with intellectual disability are significantly more likely than their peers to have a poorer diet (skipping breakfast, lower rates of consumption of fruit, higher rates of consumption of sweetened drinks, eating crisps (potato chips), biscuits and sweets (candy) between meals) (Public Health England, 2015).

5.2 Housing Conditions

Analysis of data from the UK's *Families and Children Study* indicated that children with intellectual disabilities were significantly more likely than their peers to live in rented housing, overcrowded housing, housing in a poor state of repair, and housing that was too cold in winter (Emerson & Hatton, 2005). Similar results have been reported for disabled children in general (Beresford & Oldman, 2002; Beresford & Rhodes, 2008; Emerson & Hatton, 2007c; Oldman & Beresford, 1998). More recently, analysis of

MCS data has indicated that 11-year-old children with intellectual disability are significantly more likely than their peers to have been homeless and to live in damp housing (Public Health England, 2015).

5.3 Environmental Toxins

There exists an extensive literature on the impact of exposure to environmental toxins and teratogens on the health and development of children, including the impact of exposure on cognitive development (Gavidia et al., 2011; Landrigan & Etzel, 2014). Very few studies have examined rates of exposure among children with and without intellectual disabilities to environmental toxins and teratogens beyond the limited literature that has investigated whether exposure to specific agents may cause intellectual disabilities (Davidson, Myers, & Weiss, 2005; Diav-Citrin, 2011). However, given the association between poverty and risk of exposure (Claudio, 2015; Patel et al., 2015) and the association between intellectual disabilities and poverty (see above), it is likely that children with intellectual disabilities are more likely to be exposed to a range of potentially harmful environmental risks. More recently, analysis of MCS data has indicated that 11-year-old children with intellectual disability are significantly more likely than their peers to be exposed to tobacco smoke (Public Health England, 2015).

5.4 Violence

A recent systematic review has reported that disabled children, and especially children with intellectual disabilities, are at increased risk of exposure to violence (Jones et al., 2012), including physical, sexual, emotional abuse, or neglect (Benedict, Zurvain, Somerfield, & Brandt, 1996; Hobbs, Hobbs, & Wynne, 1999; Jonson-Reid, Drake, Kim, Porterfield, & Han, 2004; van der Put, Asscher, Wissink, & Stams, 2014; Reiter, Bryen, & Shachar, 2007; Spencer et al., 2005; Sullivan & Knutson, 2000; Vig & Kaminer, 2002). For example, a population-based study undertaken in West Sussex indicated that children with intellectual disabilities, when compared with their nondisabled peers, were 8.0 times more likely to be registered for sexual abuse, 5.9 times more likely to be registered for neglect, 4.0 times more likely to be registered for emotional abuse, and 3.9 times more likely to be registered for physical abuse (Spencer et al., 2005).

Analysis of data from the *Longitudinal Study of Young People in England* has indicated that adolescents with mild/moderate intellectual disabilities were significantly more likely that their nondisabled peers to be bullied (Naylor,

Dawson, Emerson, & Tantam, 2011). Other UK- and US-based studies have reported similar results (Carter & Spencer, 2006; Christensen, Fraynt, Neece, & Baker, 2012; Norwich & Kelly, 2004). A small-scale study undertaken in Northern Ireland has reported that being bullied and being exposed to community violence was associated with higher rates of behavioral/emotional disorders among young people with intellectual disabilities (Taggart et al., 2010). More recently, analysis of MCS data has indicated that 11-year-old children with intellectual disabilities are significantly more likely than their peers to be exposed to domestic violence, to be bullied, to feel unsafe, and to be exposed to physical chastisement (Public Health England, 2015).

5.5 Parental Well-Being, Parenting, and Family Functioning

There exists an extensive literature on the associations between child health and parental, and especially maternal, well-being, parenting, and family functioning (Center on the Developing Child at Harvard University, 2009; Klebanov & Travis, 2015; Landry & Cooper, 2014; National Scientific Council on the Developing Child, 2012; Shonkoff, 2010; Stein, Ramchandani, & Murray, 2008). There also exists a relatively robust evidence base on parental well-being, parenting, and family functioning in relation to children with intellectual disabilities (Families Special Interest Research Group of IASSIDD, 2014).

Analysis of data from the MCS has indicated that: (1) mothers, and to a lesser extent, fathers of 3- and 5-year-old children with intellectual disabilities were at significantly increased risk of mental health problems when compared to other parents (Emerson, McCulloch, et al., 2010); (2) mothers of 3-year-old children with intellectual disabilities had a less close relationship and more conflict with their child when compared to other mothers and having a less close relationship and more conflict predicted concurrent and future child behavior problems (Totsika, Hastings, Vagenas, & Emerson, 2014); (3) at 9 months and 3 years of age mothers of children with intellectual disabilities showed significantly higher rates of inconsistent and harsh parenting than mothers of "typically developing" children and that higher rates of inconsistent and harsh parenting were associated with increased rates of conduct difficulties among children with intellectual disabilities (Emerson et al., 2014); (4) children with intellectual disabilities were significantly less likely than other children to be living in households with both biological parents or in households where the mother was married, including at the time of the child's birth, and more likely than families with a typically developing child to experience changes in both family composition and marital status over the first 5 years of the child's life (Hatton, Emerson, Graham, Blacher, & Llewellyn, 2010).

Analysis of data from the 1999 *ONS Child and Adolescent Mental Health Survey* indicated that among mothers of children with intellectual disabilities, mental health problems were associated with the child's difficulties having a greater social impact, the child experiencing more than one potentially stressful life event, poverty, receipt of means-tested welfare benefits, and "unhealthy" family functioning (Emerson, 2003a). Analysis of data from the combined 1999 and 2004 *ONS Child and Adolescent Mental Health Surveys* indicated that mothers of children with intellectual disabilities were at significantly increased risk of emotional problems when compared to other parents and that this risk was higher among children with intellectual disabilities with behavior problems (Totsika, Hastings, Emerson, Lancaster, & Berridge, 2011).

Analysis of data from the UK's *Families and Children Study* indicated that mothers of children with intellectual disabilities reported lower levels of happiness, self-esteem, and self-efficacy than mothers of children without intellectual disabilities (Emerson, Hatton, Blacher, Llewellyn, & Graham, 2006). These results are consistent with those from the wider literature which indicates that children with intellectual disabilities are more likely than other children to be exposed to a wide range of indicators associated with low maternal, and to a lesser extent paternal, well-being, less positive parenting practices, and family functioning (Families Special Interest Research Group of IASSIDD, 2014; Public Health England, 2015).

5.6 Life Events

There exists an extensive literature on the association between exposure to general "life events" or "acute life stresses" (including those discussed above) and the well-being of children (Sandberg & Rutter, 2008). Very little of this research has focused on children with intellectual disabilities (Hulbert-Williams & Hastings, 2008).

Analysis of the 1999 *ONS Child and Adolescent Mental Health Survey* indicated that British children with intellectual disabilities were more likely to be exposed to a greater number and wider range of potentially adverse life events than their peers, and that exposure was related to poorer mental health, especially emotional disorders, among children with intellectual disabilities (Emerson, 2003b; Hatton & Emerson, 2004). A small-scale study undertaken in Northern Ireland has reported that exposure to a greater number of potentially adverse life events was associated with higher rates of behavioral/emotional disorders among young people with intellectual disabilities (Taggart et al., 2010). Similar results have been reported in a US-based study (Coe et al., 1999).

5.7 Summary

Children with intellectual disabilities are at increased risk of being exposed to a wide range of specific material and psychosocial hazards that are detrimental to health. These include, but are not limited to: inadequate nutrition; poor housing conditions; environmental toxins; family, peer, and community violence; poor parenting; and family instability. This increased risk of exposure is likely to result from the combined effects of the link between child intellectual disability and poverty and systemic and overt discrimination faced by people with intellectual disabilities.

6. VULNERABILITY AND RESILIENCE

> *Resilience is not an innate feature of some people's personalities. Resilience and adversity are distributed unequally across the population, and are related to broader socioeconomic inequalities which have common causes — the inequities in power, money and resources that shape the conditions in which people live and their opportunities, experiences and relationships. Those who face the most adversity are least likely to have the resources necessary to build resilience. This "double burden" means that inequalities in resilience are likely to contribute to health inequalities.*
>
> Local action on health inequalities: Building children and young people's resilience in schools, *Public Health England*
>
> ***Public Health England (2014)***

Health inequities also arise due to the inequitable distribution of resources that promote resilience (or decrease vulnerability) in the face of exposure to low family SEP and associated material and psychosocial hazards. Historically, resilience was often used to refer solely to the attributes and characteristics of individuals (e.g., temperament) that may make them more or less susceptible to the impact of exposure. A more contemporary approach, however, also includes consideration of a wide range of environmental protective factors that make children less susceptible to the impact of exposure (Buck & Gregory, 2013; Davydov et al., 2010; Friedli, 2009; Goldstein & Brooks, 2006; Jenkins, 2008; Luthar, 2003; Masten, 2001;

MIND & Mental Health Foundation, 2013; Public Health England, 2014; Sapienza & Masten, 2011; Seccombe, 2002; Ungar, 2008). These include:

- Individual capabilities such as intelligence, self-regulation, and problem-solving skills
- Individual characteristics such as faith, hope, spirituality (with associated beliefs that life has meaning), perceived efficacy, having a sense of control, having a sense of belonging
- Positive relationships with caring adults, acquaintances, friends, and romantic partners
- Access to resources such as effective caregiving and parenting, teachers and schools, health and welfare services, social capital, wealth and power.

Little research has been undertaken on the resilience of people, and especially children, with intellectual disabilities (Broberg, Blacher, & Emerson, 2009; Gilmore, Campbell, Shochet, & Roberts, 2013; Murray & Doren, 2013).

6.1 Individual Capabilities

Children with intellectual disabilities are defined in terms of their impaired intellectual ability (Einfeld & Emerson, 2008), an impairment which is associated with problems relating to executive functioning, self-regulation, and problem solving (Hartman, Houwen, Scherder, & Visscher, 2010; Memisevic & Sinanovic, 2014; Whitman, 1990). As such, they are likely to be less resilient than their nondisabled peers when exposed to adversity.

6.2 Individual Characteristics

Individual characteristics/beliefs such as faith, hope, spirituality (with associated beliefs that life has meaning), perceived efficacy, having a sense of control, and having a sense of belonging have been associated with greater resilience among children in general. We are only aware of one small-scale Australian study which has investigated the extent to which children with intellectual disabilities are more or less likely than their peers to possess such characteristics or hold such beliefs (Buchanan & Lopez, 2013; Gaventa, 2013; Rand & Shea, 2013). This study reported that while adolescents with mild intellectual disabilities showed similar levels of optimism and self-esteem to their peers, they reported lower levels of tolerance and higher levels of sensitivity (Gilmore et al., 2013). An additional exploratory US-based study has reported that hope and optimism were associated with greater life satisfaction among adolescents with intellectual disabilities (Shogren, Lopez, Wehmeyer, Little, & Pressgrove, 2006).

6.3 Positive Relationships

The majority of research on the quality of relationships between young people with intellectual disabilities and their parents and/or peers has collected information from informants rather than the child with intellectual disabilities. For example, as noted above analysis of data from the MCS has indicated that mothers of 3-year-old children with intellectual disabilities reported that they had a less close relationship with their child when compared to other mothers (Totsika et al., 2014).

The existing evidence on friendships, social networks, and social support indicates that, when compared with their nondisabled peers, people (primarily adults) with intellectual disabilities: (1) tend to have fewer friends, smaller social networks, and receive less social support; (2) show similar patterns of association between having friends, more extensive social networks and social support, and more positive indicators of well-being (Gilmore et al., 2013; Jahoda & Pownall, 2014; Kersh, Corona, & Siperstein, 2013). For example, a recent US-based study reported that adolescents with intellectual disabilities had friendships characterized by significantly lower levels of warmth/closeness and positive reciprocity than their typically developing peers and that adolescents with intellectual disabilities spent less time with friends outside of school and were less likely to have a cohesive group of friends (Tipton, Christensen, & Blacher, 2013). More recently, analysis of MCS data has indicated that 11-year-old children with intellectual disability are significantly less likely than their peers to have at least one good friend, spend time with their friends outside school, enjoy playing with their friends, and enjoy school (Public Health England, 2015).

6.4 Access to Resources

In previous sections, we have reviewed the evidence which suggests that families supporting children with intellectual disabilities are significantly less likely than other families to have access to such resources as wealth and power, and that children with intellectual disabilities are significantly less likely than other children to have access to such resources as positive parenting. In this section, we will review the available evidence on access to a key resource for health; access to health care.

A number of reports have highlighted the disadvantages faced by people with intellectual disabilities in accessing timely, effective, and appropriate health care (Department of Health, 2001, 2009; Disability Rights Commission, 2006; Mencap, 2007, 2012; Michael, 2008; US Department of Health & Human Services, 2002a, 2002b). Each of these reports, and the vast majority of the limited research that has been undertaken in this area, has focused on the situation of adults with intellectual disabilities (Alborz, McNally, & Glendinning, 2005; Alborz, McNally, & Swallow, 2003; Backer, Chapman, & Mitchell, 2009; Iacono, Bigby, Unsworth, Douglas, & Fitzpatrick, 2014). As a result, little robust evidence is available on the extent to which children with intellectual disabilities are also significantly disadvantaged in accessing timely, effective, and appropriate health care. Given that consultation with parents of children with intellectual disabilities commonly elicits concerns about access to health care (Alborz et al., 2003), and the plethora of concerns raised by independent inquiries (Disability Rights Commission, 2006; Michael, 2008), it appears reasonable to assume that the discrimination faced by adults with intellectual disabilities in accessing health care systems may also extend to children. However, analysis of the 2004 *ONS Child and Adolescent Mental Health Survey* indicated that among British children with a diagnosable mental health condition, children with intellectual disabilities had similar rates of access to child and adolescent mental health services and primary health care services as children without intellectual disabilities (Emerson & Hatton, 2007b).

More recently, analysis of MCS data has indicated that 11-year-old children with intellectual disability are significantly less likely than their peers to access preventative health interventions on 65% of 23 indicators associated with access to hearing tests, dental screening, and immunizations. Of the statistically significant differences in uptake, 75% were associated with reduced uptake among children with intellectual disabilities. Of the differences with moderate or larger effect sizes, 85% were associated with reduced uptake among children with intellectual disabilities (Public Health England, 2015).

6.5 Differential Resilience?

The evidence in the preceding sections suggests that children with intellectual disabilities may be less resilient than their nondisabled peers when exposed to adversity. Very few studies have sought to test this proposition. All of the available evidence relates to mental health and behavioral outcomes and the results of these studies are somewhat mixed.

Analysis of the 1999 and 2004 *ONS Child and Adolescent Mental Health Surveys* revealed a cross-sectional dose-dependent relationship between breadth of exposure to indicators of low SEP and the risk of conduct disorders, emotional disorders, and ADHD among British children with intellectual disabilities. For all three disorders, the strength of the relationship between exposure and risk was higher among children with intellectual disabilities than among other children (Emerson & Hatton, 2007a). Analysis of MCS data indicated a dose-dependent relationship between breadth of exposure to indicators of low SEP at ages 9 months and 3 years and: (1) the risk of conduct difficulties at age three; (2) the persistence of conduct difficulties from age three to ages five and seven. In both cases, the strength of the relationship between exposure and risk was higher among children with intellectual disabilities than among typically developing children (Emerson et al., 2014). Analysis of data from the *Longitudinal Study of Australian Children* indicated a dose-dependent relationship between exposure to SEP-related adversity at age four/five and the risk of conduct difficulties at that age and the persistence of conduct difficulties to ages six/seven and eight/nine among children with borderline intellectual disabilities. For prevalence at age four/five, the strength of the association between exposure and risk was greater for children with intellectual disabilities than for other children (Emerson et al., 2011). Analysis of data from Waves 1–3 of the MCS and the *Longitudinal Study of Australian Children* indicated a cross-sectional dose-dependent relationship between exposure to adverse socioeconomic circumstances and risk of mental health problems at age three among UK and Australian children with intellectual disabilities. For all comparisons, the strength of the associations between exposure and risk was weaker for children with intellectual disabilities than for other children (Emerson & Einfeld, 2010). A recent US-based study has reported that maltreatment had a stronger association with subsequent sexual and violent offending among adolescents with intellectual disabilities than their peers (van der Put et al., 2014).

7. CONCLUSIONS

The association of childhood intellectual disabilities with low family SEP is now well established and is consistently shown in different countries (Spencer et al., submitted for publication). A small number of studies based on longitudinal data (Emerson, Shahtahmasebi, Berridge, & Lancaster, 2010; Public Health England, 2015; Shahtahmasebi et al., 2011) have shown that families with children with intellectual disabilities are not only at higher risk of being poor but also of becoming poor and are less likely to escape from poverty. The paucity of studies based on longitudinal data is a significant weakness of the existing literature on the association of SEP with childhood intellectual disability. Although the association of low family SEP with childhood intellectual disability is well known, there are no data from longitudinal studies to distinguish cause and consequence in the association and a very limited literature on life course economic and social trajectories of these children.

The available evidence suggests that children with intellectual disabilities are at increased risk of exposure to all of the major categories of social determinants of poorer physical and mental health. As noted above, they are more likely to live in households characterized by low socioeconomic position and poverty. They are also more likely to be exposed to a wide range of material and psychosocial hazards that are detrimental to their health, including inadequate nutrition; poor housing conditions; exposure to environmental toxins; family, peer, and community violence; poor parenting; and family instability. This increased risk of exposure is likely to result from the combined effects of the link between child intellectual disability and poverty and systemic and overt discrimination faced by people with intellectual disabilities. They are less likely to have access to the resources necessary to build resilience in the face of adversity. However, in many of these areas, the evidence is sparse and of variable quality.

The available evidence also suggests that exposure of children with intellectual disabilities to low family SEP is associated with poorer child mental health and increased engagement with more risky health behaviors (e.g., sedentary lifestyle, poorer diet, substance use). Similar patterns are, of course, evident among children who do not have intellectual disabilities.

With regard to other aspects of general and physical health, the evidence of an association among children with intellectual disabilities between exposure to low family SEP and poorer health is highly inconsistent. This may be due to a masking effect resulting from the association between family SEP and risk of child intellectual disabilities of different severity. As noted above, while low family SEP is associated with increased risk of intellectual disabilities, this is particularly the case for mild/moderate intellectual disabilities (Emerson, 2012; Leonard et al., 2011, 2005). As a result, children with less severe intellectual disabilities will be overrepresented in the population of children with intellectual disabilities living in low SEP families when compared with high SEP families. Given the association between increased severity of intellectual disabilities and poorer general health (Emerson & Hatton, 2014), we would (all other things being equal) expect children with intellectual disabilities in higher SEP families to have poorer health as they contain a greater *proportion* of children with more severe intellectual disabilities. We are not aware of any research on the association between family SEP and the health of children with intellectual disabilities that has taken differences in severity of intellectual disabilities into account.

Indeed, the majority of research undertaken in this area has largely been unable to examine the association between severity of intellectual disability or specific syndromes associated with intellectual disability and either risk exposure or the impact of exposure on the health of children with intellectual disability. Population-based studies of children with intellectual disability are, given the distribution of intelligence within population cohorts, primarily studies of children with mild and moderate intellectual disabilities. Existing epidemiological research clearly indicates that the association between low family SEP and child intellectual disability is strongest for children with mild and moderate intellectual disabilities, with relatively weak associations for children with profound multiple intellectual disabilities and children with autism (Emerson, 2012; Leonard et al., 2011, 2005). If the increased risk of exposure to a wider range of material and psychosocial hazards results from the combined effects of the link between child intellectual disability and low family SEP and the systemic and overt discrimination faced by people with intellectual disabilities, it is possible that risk exposure to this wider range of hazards may be lower among children with profound multiple intellectual disabilities and children with autism. It is also possible that severity of intellectual disability and/or the presence of specific syndromes associated with intellectual disabilities may moderate the relationship between exposure and health. There is, for example, some limited evidence that the relationship between exposure and mental health is considerably weaker among children with autism when compared to children with intellectual disabilities (Emerson et al., 2014; Gray et al., 2012).

Overall the published literature on health inequities among children with intellectual disabilities is variable, with some robust evidence but many areas in which evidence is weak. In order to better identify and understand health inequities in this particularly vulnerable group of children, we suggest the following four priorities for future research:

- Longitudinal studies using the extensive network of cohort studies in high-income countries (http://www.chicosproject.eu/) to elucidate pathways and mechanisms in the association of low family SEP with childhood intellectual disabilities and to strengthen the evidence base on the combined impact of SEP and intellectual disabilities on health and well-being across the life course. The availability of data from new birth cohort studies with significantly larger samples (e.g., the UK's new Life Study project which plans to follow up a cohort of 80–90,000 children, http://www.esrc.ac.uk/research/surveys/life-study.aspx) will also open up possibilities of exploring possible moderation effects associated with severity of intellectual disabilities;

- Cross-sectional and longitudinal studies in different countries, especially low- and middle-income countries, to strengthen the evidence base in those areas, highlighted above, where it is weak;
- Cross-sectional and longitudinal studies that examine the association between severity of intellectual disabilities and/or the presence of specific syndromes associated with intellectual disabilities and both risk exposure and the impact of exposure on the health of children;
- Controlled interventions and well-constructed qualitative studies designed to test approaches to reducing discrimination and strengthening resilience at both an individual and societal level.

ACKNOWLEDGMENTS

This chapter draws on a report written by the first author and colleagues, and funded through Public Health England's intellectual disability work programme, for Public Health England (Public Health England, 2015). However, the views expressed are those of the authors and should not be taken to necessarily represent the views of Public Health England.

REFERENCES

Alborz, A., McNally, R., & Glendinning, C. (2005). Access to health care for people with learning disabilities in the UK: mapping the issues and reviewing the evidence. *Journal of Health Services Research & Policy, 10*, 173–182.

Alborz, A., McNally, R., & Swallow, A. (2003). *From the cradle to the grave: A literature review of access to health care for people with learning disabilities across the lifespan*. London: National Co-ordinating Centre for NHS Service Delivery and Organisation.

Amark, K., & Sunnergardh, J. (1999). The effect of changing attitudes to Down's syndrome in the management of complete atrioventricular septal defects. *Archive of Diseases of Childhood, 81*, 4.

Anda, R. F., Felitti, V. J., Bremner, J. D., Walker, J. D., Whitfield, C., Perry, B. D., et al. (2006). The enduring effects of abuse and related adverse experiences in childhood: a convergence of evidence from neurobiology and epidemiology. *European Archives of Psychiatry and Clinical Neuroscience, 256*, 174–186.

Arron, K., Oliver, C., Moss, J., Berg, K., & Burbidge, C. (2011). The prevalence and phenomenology of self-injurious and aggressive behaviour in genetic syndromes. *Journal of Intellectual Disability Research, 55*, 109–120.

Arseneault, L., Bowes, L., & Shakoor, S. (2010). Bullying victimization in youths and mental health problems: "Much ado about nothing"? *Psychological Medicine, 40*, 717–729.

Backer, C., Chapman, M., & Mitchell, D. (2009). Access to secondary healthcare for people with intellectual disabilities: a review of the literature. *Journal of Applied Research in Intellectual Disabilities, 22*(6), 514–525. http://dx.doi.org/10.1111/j.1468-3148.2009.00505.x.

Bartley, M. (2004). *Health inequality*. Cambridge: Polity Press.

Batshaw, M. L., Pellegrino, L., & Roizen, N. J. (Eds.). (2007). *Children with disabilities* (6th ed.). Baltimore: P H Brookes.
Benedict, M., Zurvain, S., Somerfield, M., & Brandt, D. (1996). The reported health and functioning of children maltreated while in family foster care. *Child Abuse & Neglect, 20*, 561–571.
Beresford, B., & Oldman, C. (2002). *Housing matters: National evidence relating to disabled children and their housing*. Bristol: Policy Press.
Beresford, B., & Rhodes, D. (2008). *Housing and disabled children*. York: Joseph Rowntree Foundation.
Bittles, A. H., Petterson, B. A., Sullivan, S. G., Hussain, R., Glasson, E. J., & Montgomery, P. (2002). The influence of intellectual disability on life expectancy. *Journal of Gerontology, 57*, 470–472.
Black, R. E., Allen, L. H., Bhutta, Z. A., Caulfield, L. E., de Onis, M., Ezzati, M., et al. (2008). Maternal and child undernutrition: global and regional exposures and health consequences. *Lancet, 371*, 243–260.
Black, R. E., Morris, S. S., & Bryce, J. (2003). Where and why are 10 million children dying every year? *Lancet, 361*, 2226–2234.
Blackburn, C., Read, J., & Spencer, N. (2010). Prevalence of childhood disability and the characteristics and circumstances of disabled children in the UK: secondary analysis of the family resources survey. *BMC Pediatrics, 10*(21).
Blackburn, C., Read, J., & Spencer, N. (2013). Children with neurodevelopmental disabilities. In Department of Health (Ed.), *Annual report of the chief medical officer 2012. Our children deserve better: Prevention pays*. London: Department of Health.
Bolte, G., Tamburlini, G., & Kohlhuber, M. (2010). Environmental inequalities among children in Europe: evaluation of scientific evidence and policy implications. *European Journal of Public Health, 20*, 14–20.
Braubach, M., & Fairburn, J. (2010). Social inequities in environmental risks associated with housing and residential location: a review of evidence. *European Journal of Public Health, 20*, 36–42.
Broberg, M., Blacher, J., & Emerson, E. (2009). Editorial: resilience. *Journal of Intellectual Disability Research, 53*, 955–956.
Buchanan, C. L., & Lopez, S. J. (2013). Understanding hope in individuals with disabilities. In M. L. Wehmeyer (Ed.), *The Oxford handbook of positive psychology and disability* (pp. 154–165). Oxford: Oxford University Press.
Buck, D., & Gregory, S. (2013). *Improving the public's health. A resource for local authorities*. London: The King's Fund.
Burd, L., FisBurd, L., Fisher, W., Kerbeshian, J., Veslely, B., Durgin, B., et al. (1988). A comparison of breastfeeding rates among children with pervasive developmental disorder and controls. *Developmental and Behavioural Paediatrics, 9*, 247–251.
Bzostek, S. H., & Beck, A. N. (2011). Familial instability and young children's physical health. *Social Science & Medicine, 73*, 282–292.
Carpenter, G. L., & Stacks, A. M. (2009). Developmental effects of exposure to intimate partner violence in early childhood: a review of the literature. *Children and Youth Services Review, 31*, 831–839.
Carter, B. B., & Spencer, V. G. (2006). The fear factor: bullying and students with disabilities. *International Journal of Special Education, 21*, 11–23.
Center on the Developing Child at Harvard University. (2009). *Maternal depression can undermine the development of young children*. Working paper no. 8. Cambridge, MS: Center on the Developing Child at Harvard University http://www.developingchild.harvard.edu.
Centers for Disease Control and Prevention (CDC) & National Center on Birth Defects and Developmental Disabilities (NCBDDD) Health Surveillance Work Group. (2009). *U.S. Surveillance of health of people with intellectual disabilities*. Atlanta: CDC/NCBDDD.

Chapman, D., Scott, K., & Stanton-Chapman, T. (2008). Public health approach to the study of mental retardation. *American Journal on Mental Retardation, 113*(2), 102–116.

Christensen, L. L., Fraynt, R. J., Neece, C. L., & Baker, B. L. (2012). Bullying adolescents with intellectual disability. *Journal of Mental Health Research in Intellectual Disabilities, 5*, 49–65.

Claudio, L. (2015). The impact of poverty, disparity, and injustice on children's environmental health. In P. J. Landrigan, & R. A. Etzel (Eds.), *Textbook of children's environmental health*. Oxford: Oxford University Press.

Coe, D. A., Matson, J. L., Russell, D. W., Slifer, K. J., Capone, G., & Baglio, C. (1999). Behavior problems of children with Down syndrome and life events. *Journal of Autism and Developmental Disorders, 29*, 149–156.

Conger, R. D., & Donnellan, M. B. (2007). An interactionist perspective on the socioeconomic context of human development. *Annual Review of Psychology, 58*, 175–199.

Currie, C., Zanotti, C., Morgan, A., Currie, D., de Looze, M., Roberts, C., et al. (2012). *Social determinants of health and well-being among young people. Health behaviour in school-aged children (HBSC) study: International report from the 2009/2010 survey*. Copenhagen: WHO Regional Office for Europe.

Davidson, P. W., Myers, G. J., & Weiss, B. (Eds.). (2005). *International review of research in mental retardation: Neurotoxicity and developmental disabilities*. Elsevier.

Davydov, D., Stewart, R., Ritchie, K., & Chaudieu, I. (2010). Resilience and mental health. *Clinical Psychology Review, 30*, 479–495.

Department of Health. (2001). *Valuing people: A new strategy for learning disability for the 21st century*.

Department of Health. (2009). *Valuing people now: A new three-year strategy for people with learning disabilities*. London: Department of Health.

Department of Health. (2010). *Healthy lives, healthy people: Our strategy for public health in England*. London: Department of Health.

Department of Health. (2013). *Annual report of the chief medical officer 2012: Our children deserve better, prevention pays*.

Diav-Citrin, O. (2011). Prenatal exposures associated with neurodevelopmental delay and disabilities. *Developmental Disabilities Research Reviews, 17*, 71–84.

Diderichsen, F., Evans, T., & Whitehead, M. (2001). The social basis of disparities in health. In T. Evans, M. Whitehead, F. Diderichsen, A. Bhuiya, & M. Wirth (Eds.), *Challenging inequities in health: From ethics to action*. Oxford: Oxford University Press.

Disability Rights Commission. (2006). *Equal treatment – closing the gap*. London: Disability Rights Commission.

Dykens, E. M., Hodapp, R. M., & Finucane, B. M. (2000). *Genetics and mental retardation syndromes: A new look at behavior and interventions*. Baltimore: Paul H. Brookes Publishing.

Einfeld, S., Ellis, L., & Emerson, E. (2011). Comorbidity of intellectual disability and mental disorder: a systematic review. *Journal of Intellectual & Developmental Disability, 36*, 137–143.

Einfeld, S., & Emerson, E. (2008). Intellectual disability. In M. Rutter, D. Bishop, D. Pine, S. Scott, J. Stevenson, E. Taylor, et al. (Eds.), *Rutter's child and adolescent psychiatry* (5th ed.). Oxford: Blackwell.

Emerson, E. (2003a). Mothers of children and adolescents with intellectual disability: social and economic situation, mental health status, and the self-assessed social and psychological impact of the child's difficulties. *Journal of Intellectual Disability Research, 47*(Pt 4–5), 385–399.

Emerson, E. (2003b). Prevalence of psychiatric disorders in children and adolescents with and without intellectual disability. *Journal of Intellectual Disability Research, 47*, 51–58.

Emerson, E. (2004). Poverty and children with intellectual disabilities in the world's richer countries. *Journal of Intellectual & Developmental Disability, 29*, 319–337.

Emerson, E. (2007). Poverty and people with intellectual disability. *Mental Retardation and Developmental Disabilities Research Reviews, 13*, 107–113.
Emerson, E. (2009). Overweight and obesity in 3 and 5 year old children with and without developmental delay. *Public Health, 123*, 130–133.
Emerson, E. (2012). Household deprivation, neighbourhood deprivation, ethnicity and the prevalence of intellectual and developmental disabilities. *Journal of Epidemiology and Community Health, 66*, 218–224.
Emerson, E., Blacher, J., Einfeld, S., Hatton, C., Robertson, J., & Stancliffe, R. (2014). Environmental risk factors associated with the persistence of conduct difficulties in children with and without intellectual disabilities or autistic spectrum disorders. *Research in Developmental Disabilities, 35*, 3508–3517.
Emerson, E., & Brigham, P. (2015). Exposure of children with developmental delay to social determinants of poor health: cross sectional study. *Child: Care, Health & Development, 41*, 249–257. http://dx.doi.org/10.1111/cch.12144.
Emerson, E., & Einfeld, S. (2010). Emotional and behavioural difficulties in young children with and without developmental delay: a bi-national perspective. *Journal of Child Psychology and Psychiatry, 51*, 583–593.
Emerson, E., & Einfeld, S. (2011). *Challenging behaviour* (3rd ed.). Cambridge: Cambridge University Press.
Emerson, E., Einfeld, S., & Stancliffe, R. J. (2011). Predictors of the persistence of conduct difficulties in children with cognitive delay. *Journal of Child Psychology and Psychiatry and Allied Disciplines, 52*, 1184–1194.
Emerson, E., Graham, H., McCulloch, A., Blacher, J., Hatton, C., & Llewellyn, G. (2009). The social context of parenting three year old children with developmental delay in the UK. *Child: Care, Health & Development, 35*(1), 63–70.
Emerson, E., & Hatton, C. (2005). *The socio-economic circumstances of families supporting a child at risk of disability in Britain in 2002*. Lancaster: Institute for Health Research, Lancaster University.
Emerson, E., & Hatton, C. (2007a). The mental health of children and adolescents with intellectual disabilities in Britain. *British Journal of Psychiatry, 191*, 493–499.
Emerson, E., & Hatton, C. (2007b). *The mental health of children and adolescents with learning disabilities in Britain*. London: Foundation for People with Learning Disabilities.
Emerson, E., & Hatton, C. (2007c). The socio-economic circumstances of children at risk of disability in Britain. *Disability and Society, 22*, 563–580.
Emerson, E., & Hatton, C. (2014). *Health inequalities and people with intellectual disabilities*. Cambridge: Cambridge University Press.
Emerson, E., Hatton, C., Blacher, J., Llewellyn, G., & Graham, H. (2006). Socio-economic position, household composition, health status and indicators of the well-being of mothers of children with and without intellectual disability. *Journal of Intellectual Disability Research, 50*(12), 862–873.
Emerson, E., McCulloch, A., Graham, H., Blacher, J., Llewellyn, G., & Hatton, C. (2010). The mental health of parents of young children with and without developmental delays. *American Journal on Intellectual and Developmental Disabilities, 115*, 30–42.
Emerson, E., & Robertson, J. (2010). Obesity in young children with intellectual disabilities or borderline intellectual functioning. *International Journal of Pediatric Obesity, 5*(4), 320–326.
Emerson, E., Robertson, J., & Wood, J. (2005). The mental health needs of children and adolescents with intellectual disabilities in an urban conurbation. *Journal of Intellectual Disability Research, 49*, 16–24.
Emerson, E., Robertson, J., & Wood, J. (2007). The association between area-level indicators of social deprivation and the emotional and behavioural needs of black and South Asian children with intellectual disabilities in a deprived urban environment. *Journal of Applied Research in Intellectual Disabilities, 20*, 420–429.

Emerson, E., Shahtahmasebi, S., Berridge, D., & Lancaster, G. (2010). Factors associated with poverty transitions among families supporting a child with intellectual disability. *Journal of Intellectual & Developmental Disability, 35*, 224–234.

Emerson, E., Shahtahmasebi, S., Lancaster, G., & Berridge, D. (2010). Poverty transitions among families supporting a child with intellectual disability. *Journal of Intellectual & Developmental Disability, 35*, 224–234.

Emerson, E., & Turnbull, L. (2005). Self-reported smoking and alcohol use by adolescents with and without intellectual disabilities. *Journal of Intellectual Disabilities, 9*, 58–69.

Evans, G., & English, K. (2002). The environment of poverty: multiple stressor exposure, psychophysiological stress and socio-emotional adjustment. *Child Development, 73*, 1238–1248.

Families Special Interest Research Group of IASSIDD. (2014). Families supporting a child with intellectual or developmental disabilities: the current state of knowledge. *Journal of Applied Research in Intellectual Disabilities, 27*, 420–430. http://dx.doi.org/10.1111/jar.12078.

Fowler, P. J., Tompsett, C. J., Braciszewski, J. B., Jacques-Tiura, A. J., & Baltes, B. B. (2009). Community violence: a meta-analysis on the effect of exposure and mental health outcomes of children and adolescents. *Development and Psychopathology, 21*, 227–259.

Friedli, L. (2009). *Mental health, resilience and inequalities*. Copenhagen: World Health Organization, Europe.

Fryers, T. (1993). Epidemiological thinking in mental retardation: issues in taxonomy and population frequency. In N. W. Bray (Ed.), *International review of research in mental retardation* (Vol. 19). San Diego CA: Academic Press.

Fujiura, G. T. (1998). Demography of family households. *American Journal on Mental Retardation, 103*, 225–235.

Gaventa, W. (2013). Forgiveness, gratitude and spirituality. In M. L. Wehmeyer (Ed.), *The Oxford handbook of positive psychology and disability* (pp. 226–238). Oxford: Oxford University Press.

Gavidia, T., Bruné, M. N., McCarty, K. M., Pronczuk, J., Etzel, R., Neira, M., et al. (2011). Children's environmental health – from knowledge to action. *Lancet, 377*(9772), 1134–1136.

Gilbert, R., Widom, C. S., Browne, K., Fergusson, D., Webb, E., & Janson, S. (2009). Burden and consequences of child maltreatment in high-income countries. *Lancet, 373*, 68–81.

Gilmore, L., Campbell, M., Shochet, I., & Roberts, C. (2013). Resiliency profiles of children with intellectual disability and their typically developing peers. *Psychology in the Schools, 50*, 1032–1043.

Glover, G., & Ayub, M. (2010). *How people with learning disabilities die*. Durham: Improving Health & Lives: Learning Disabilities Observatory.

Goldstein, S., & Brooks, R. B. (Eds.). (2006). *Handbook of resilience in children*. New York: Springer.

Gore, N., Emerson, E., & Brady, S. (2015). Rates of breastfeeding and exposure to socio-economic adversity amongst children with intellectual disability. *Research in Developmental Disabilities, 39*, 12–19.

Graham, H. (2005). Intellectual disabilities and socioeconomic inequalities in health: an overview of research. *Journal of Applied Research in Intellectual Disabilities, 18*, 101–111.

Graham, H. (2007). *Unequal lives: Health and socioeconomic inequalities*. Maidenhead: Open University Press.

Grantham-McGregor, S., Cheung, Y. B., Cueto, S., Glewe, P., Richter, L., Strupp, B., &, International Child Development Steering Group. (2007). Developmental potential in the first 5 years for children in developing countries. *Lancet, 369*, 60–70.

Gray, K., Keating, C., Taffe, J., Brereton, A., Einfeld, S., & Tonge, B. J. (2012). Trajectory of behavior and emotional problems in autism. *American Journal on Intellectual and Developmental Disabilities, 117*, 121–133.

Harris, J. C. (2005). *Intellectual disability: Understanding its development, causes, evaluation, and treatment*. Oxford: Oxford University Press.

Hartman, E., Houwen, S., Scherder, E., & Visscher, C. (2010). On the relationship between motor performance and executive functioning in children with intellectual disabilities. *Journal of Intellectual Disability Research, 54*, 468–477.

Hatton, C., & Emerson, E. (2004). The relationship between life events and psychopathology amongst children with intellectual disabilities. *Journal of Applied Research in Intellectual Disabilities, 17*(2), 109–118.

Hatton, C., Emerson, E., Graham, H., Blacher, J., & Llewellyn, G. (2010). Changes in family composition and marital status in families with a young child with cognitive delay. *Journal of Applied Research in Intellectual Disabilities, 23*, 14–26.

Haveman, M., Heller, T., Lee, L., Maaskant, M., Shooshtari, S., & Strydom, A. (2010). Major health risks in aging persons with intellectual disabilities: an overview of recent studies. *Journal of Policy and Practice in Intellectual Disabilities, 7*, 59–69.

Heber, R. (1970). *Epidemiology of mental retardation*. Springfield, IL: Charles C. Thomas.

Hertzman, C., & Boyce, T. (2010). How experience gets under the skin to create gradients in developmental health. *Annual Review of Public Health, 31*, 329–347.

Heslop, P., Blair, P. S., Fleming, P., Hoghton, M., Marriott, A., & Russ, L. (2014). The confidential inquiry into premature deaths of people with intellectual disabilities in the UK: a population-based study. *Lancet, 383*, 889–895.

Hobbs, G. F., Hobbs, C. J., & Wynne, J. M. (1999). Abuse of children in foster and residential care. *Child Abuse & Neglect, 23*, 1239–1252.

Hollins, S., Attard, M., van Fraunhofer, N., McGuigan, S. M., & Sedgwick, P. (1998). Mortality in people with learning disability: risks causes, and death certification findings in London. *Developmental Medicine and Child Neurology, 40*, 50–56.

Hulbert-Williams, L., & Hastings, R. P. (2008). Life events as a risk factor for psychological problems in individuals with intellectual disabilities: a critical review. *Journal of Intellectual Disability Research, 52*, 883–895.

Iacono, T., Bigby, C., Unsworth, C., Douglas, J., & Fitzpatrick, P. (2014). A systematic review of hospital experiences of people with intellectual disability. *BMC Health Services Research, 14*, 505.

Irish, L., Kobayashi, I., & Delahanty, D. L. (2010). Long-term physical health consequences of childhood sexual abuse: a meta-analytic review. *Journal of Pediatric Psychology, 35*, 450–461.

Irving, C. A., & Chaudhari, M. P. (2012). Cardiovascular abnormalities in Down's syndrome: spectrum, management and survival over 22 years. *Archive of Diseases of Childhood, 97*, 5.

Jacobson, C., Shearer, J., Habel, A., Kane, F., Tsakanikos, E., & Kravariti, E. (2010). Core neuropsychological characteristics of children and adolescents with 22q11.2 deletion. *Journal of Intellectual Disability Research, 54*, 701–713.

Jahoda, A., & Pownall, J. (2014). Sexual understanding, sources of information and social networks; the reports of young people with intellectual disabilities and their non-disabled peers. *Journal of Intellectual Disability Research, 58*, 430–441.

Jenkins, J. (2008). Psychosocial adversity and resilience. In M. Rutter, D. Bishop, D. Pine, S. Scott, J. Stevenson, E. Taylor, et al. (Eds.), *Rutter's child and adolescent psychiatry* (5th ed.). (pp. 377–391). Oxford: Blackwell.

Jones, L., Bellis, M. A., Wood, S., Hughes, K., McCoy, E., Eckley, L., et al. (2012). Prevalence and risk of violence against children with disabilities: a systematic review and meta-analysis of observational studies. *Lancet, 380*(9845), 899–907.

Jonson-Reid, M., Drake, B., Kim, J., Porterfield, S., & Han, L. (2004). A prospective analysis of the relationship between reported child maltreatment and special education eligibility among poor children. *Child Maltreatment, 9*, 382–394.

Kersh, J., Corona, L., & Siperstein, G. (2013). Social wellbeing and friendship of people with intellectual disability. In M. L. Wehmeyer (Ed.), *The Oxford handbook of positive psychology and disability* (pp. 60–81). Oxford: Oxford University Press.

Klebanov, M. S., & Travis, A. D. (2015). *The critical role of parenting in human development.* New York, NY: Routledge/Taylor & Francis Group.

Krahn, G., & Fox, M. H. (2014). Health disparities of adults with intellectual disabilities: what do we know? what do we do? *Journal of Applied Research in Intellectual Disabilities, 27*, 431–446. http://dx.doi.org/10.1111/jar.12067.

Krahn, G., Hammond, L., & Turner, A. (2006). A cascade of disparities: health and health care access for people with intellectual disabilities. *Mental Retardation and Developmental Disabilities Research Reviews, 12*, 70–82.

Kreiger, N. (2011). *Epidemiology and the people's health: Theory and context.* Oxford: Oxford University Press.

Landrigan, P. J., & Etzel, R. A. (Eds.). (2014). *Textbook of children's environmental health.* Oxford: Oxford University Press.

Landry, S. H., & Cooper, C. L. (Eds.). (2014). *Wellbeing in children and families* (Vol. I). Wiley–Blackwell.

Leonard, H., Glasson, E., Nassar, N., Whitehouse, A., Bebbington, A., Bourke, J., et al. (2011). Autism and intellectual disability are differentially related to sociodemographic background at birth. *PLoS One, 6*(3), e17875. http://dx.doi.org/10.11371/journal.pone.0017875.

Leonard, H., Petterson, B., De Klerk, N., Zubrick, S. R., Glasson, E., Sanders, R., et al. (2005). Association of sociodemographic characteristics of children with intellectual disability in Western Australia. *Social Science & Medicine, 60*, 1499–1513.

Leonard, H., & Wen, X. (2002). The epidemiology of mental retardation: challenges and opportunities in the new millennium. *Mental Retardation and Developmental Disabilities Research Reviews, 8*, 117–134.

Leventhal, T., & Newman, S. (2010). Housing and child development. *Children and Youth Services Review, 32*, 1165–1174.

Luthar, S. S. (Ed.). (2003). *Resilience and vulnerability: Adaptation in the context of childhood adversities.* Cambridge: Cambridge University Press.

Luthar, S. S. (2006). Resilience in development: a synthesis of research across five decades. In D. Cicchetti, & D. J. Cohen (Eds.), *Risk, disorder, and adaptation: Vol. 3. Developmental psychopathology* (pp. 739–795). Hoboken, NJ: John Wiley & Sons.

Marmot, M. (2005). Social determinants of health inequalities. *Lancet, 365*, 1099–1104.

Marmot, M., &, on behalf of the Commission on Social Determinants of Health. (2007). Achieving health equity: from root causes to fair outcomes. *Lancet, 370*, 1153–1163.

Marmot, M., & Wilkinson, R. G. (Eds.). (2006). *Social determinants of health* (2nd ed.). Oxford: Oxford University Press.

Masten, A. S. (2001). Ordinary magic: resilience processes in development. *American Psychologist, 56*, 227–238.

Maulik, P. K., Mascarenhas, M. N., Mathers, C. D., Dua, T., & Saxena, S. (2011). Prevalence of intellectual disability: a meta-analysis of population-based studies. *Research in Developmental Disabilities, 32*, 419–436.

McCarthy, J., Hemmings, C., Kravariti, E., Dworzynski, K., Holt, G., Bouras, N., et al. (2010). Challenging behavior and co-morbid psychopathology in adults with intellectual disability and autism spectrum disorders. *Research in Developmental Disabilities, 31*, 362–366.

McEwen, B. S., & Gianaros, P. J. (2010). Central role of the brain in stress and adaptation: links to socioeconomic status, health, and disease. *Annals of the New York Academy of Sciences, 1186*, 190–222.

McGuigan, S. M., Hollins, S., & Attard, M. (1995). Age specific standardised mortality rates in people with learning disability. *Journal of Intellectual Disability Research, 39*, 527–531.

Melville, C. A., Cooper, S. A., McGrother, C. W., Thorp, C. F., & Collacott, R. (2005). Obesity in adults with Down syndrome: a case-control study. *Journal of Intellectual Disability Research, 49*, 125–133.

Memisevic, H., & Sinanovic, O. (2014). Executive function in children with intellectual disability—the effects of sex, level and aetiology of intellectual disability. *Journal of Intellectual Disability Research, 58*, 830–837.

Mencap. (2007). *Death by indifference*. London: Mencap.

Mencap. (2012). *Death by indifference: 74 deaths and counting. A progress report 5 years on*. London: Mencap.

Michael, J. (2008). *Healthcare for all: Report of the independent inquiry into access to healthcare for people with learning disabilities*. London: Independent inquiry into access to healthcare for people with learning disabilities.

MIND & Mental Health Foundation. (2013). *Building resilient communities: Making every contact count for public mental health*. London: MIND & the Mental Health Foundation.

Murray, C. J. L., & Doren, B. (2013). Resilience and disability: concepts, examples, cautions and prospects. In M. L. Wehmeyer (Ed.), *The Oxford handbook of positive psychology and disability* (pp. 182–197). Oxford: Oxford University Press.

National Scientific Council on the Developing Child. (2012). *The science of neglect: The persistent absence of responsive care disrupts the developing brain: Working Paper 12*. Cambridge, MS: Centre on the Developing Child, Harvard University. http://www.developingchild.harvard.edu.

Naylor, P., Dawson, J., Emerson, E., & Tantam, D. (2011). *Prevalence of bullying in secondary school by SEN type: Analysis of combined NPD and LSYPE data files*. End of award report to ESRC. Swindon: ESRC.

NHS Health Scotland. (2004). *People with learning disabilities in Scotland: Health needs assessment report*. Glasgow: NHS Health Scotland.

Norwich, B., & Kelly, N. (2004). Pupils' views on inclusion: moderate learning difficulties and bullying in mainstream and special schools. *British Educational Research Journal, 30*, 43–65.

O'Hara, J., McCarthy, J. E., & Bouras, N. (2010). *Intellectual disability and ill health: A review of the evidence*. Cambridge: Cambridge University Press.

Oeseburg, B., Dijkstra, G. J., Groothoff, J. W., Reijneveld, S. A., & Jansen, D. E. M. C. (2011). Prevalence of chronic health conditions in children with intellectual disability: a systematic literature review. *Intellectual & Developmental Disabilities, 49*, 59–85.

Oldman, C., & Beresford, B. (1998). *Homes unfit for children: Housing, disabled children and their families*. Bristol: Policy Press.

Ouellette-Kuntz, H. (2005). Understanding health disparities and inequities faced by individuals with intellectual disabilities. *Journal of Applied Research in Intellectual Disabilities, 18*, 113–121.

Parish, S. L., & Cloud, J. M. (2006). Financial well-being of young children with disabilities and their families. *Social Work, 51*(3), 223–232.

Parish, S. L., Rose, R. A., Andrews, M. E., Grinstein-Weiss, M., & Richman, E. L. (2008). Material hardship in US families raising children with disabilities. *Exceptional Children, 75*(1), 71–92.

Parish, S. L., Rose, R. A., & Swaine, J. G. (2010). Financial well-being of US parents caring for co-resident children and adults with developmental disabilities: an age cohort analysis. *Journal of Intellectual & Developmental Disabilities, 35*, 235–243.

Patel, C. J., Ioannidis, J. P. A., Cullen, M. R., & Rehkopf, D. H. (2015). Systematic assessment of the correlations of household income with infectious, biochemical, physiological, and environmental factors in the United States, 1999–2006. *American Journal of Epidemiology, 181*, 171–179.

Perry, D., Hammond, L., Marston, G., Gaskell, S., & Eva, J. (2011). *Caring for the physical and mental health of people with learning disabilities*. London: Jessica Kingsley.

Pickett, K. E., & Wilkinson, R. G. (2007). Child wellbeing and income inequality in rich societies: ecological cross sectional study. *British Medical Journal, 335*, 1080–1086.

Prasher, V., & Janicki, M. P. (Eds.). (2003). *Physical health of adults with intellectual disabilities*. Oxford: Blackwell.

Proto, C., Romualdi, D., Cento, R. M., Romano, C., Campagna, G., & Lanzone, A. (2007). Free and total leptin serum levels and soluble leptin receptors levels in two models of genetic obesity: the Prader–Willi and the Down syndromes. *Metabolism: Clinical and Experimental, 56*, 1076–1080.

Public Health England. (2014). *Local action on health inequalities: Building children and young people's resilience in schools*. London: Public Health England.

Public Health England. (2015). *The determinants of health inequalities experienced by children with learning disabilities*. London: Public Health England.

van der Put, C. E., Asscher, J. J., Wissink, I. B., & Stams, G. J. J. M. (2014). The relationship between maltreatment victimisation and sexual and violent offending: differences between adolescent offenders with and without intellectual disability. *Journal of Intellectual Disability Research, 58*, 979–991.

Rand, K. L., & Shea, A. M. (2013). Optimism within the context of disability. In M. L. Wehmeyer (Ed.), *The Oxford handbook of positive psychology and disability* (pp. 48–59). Oxford: Oxford University Press.

Reiter, S., Bryen, D. N., & Shachar, I. (2007). Adolescents with intellectual disabilities as victims of abuse. *Journal of Intellectual Disabilities, 11*, 371–387.

Roeleveld, N., Zielhuis, G. A., & Gabreels, F. (1997). The prevalence of mental retardation: a critical review of recent literature. *Developmental Medicine and Child Neurology, 39*, 125–132.

Rough, E., Goldblatt, P., Marmot, M., & Nathanson, V. (2013). Inequalities in child health. In BMA Board of Science (Ed.), *Growing up in the UK: Ensuring a healthy future for our children*. London: BMA Board of Science.

Sandberg, S., & Rutter, M. (2008). Acute life stresses. In M. Rutter, D. Bishop, D. Pine, S. Scott, J. Stevenson, E. Taylor, et al. (Eds.), *Rutter's child and adolescent psychiatry* (pp. 392–408). Oxford: Blackwell.

Sapienza, J. K., & Masten, A. S. (2011). Understanding and promoting resilience in children and youth. *Current Opinion in Psychiatry, 24*, 267–273.

Scheepers, M., Kerr, M., O'Hara, D., Bainbridge, D., Cooper, S. A., Davis, R., et al. (2005). Reducing health disparity in people with intellectual disabilities: a report from the Health Issues Special Interest Research Group of the International Association for the Scientific Study of Intellectual Disabilities. *Journal of Policy and Practice in Intellectual Disabilities, 2*, 249–255.

Schieve, L. A., Gonzalez, V., Boulet, S. L., Visser, S. N., Rice, C. E., Braun, K. V. N., et al. (2012). Concurrent medical conditions and health care use and needs among children with learning and behavioral developmental disabilities, National Health Interview Survey, 2006–2010. *Research in Developmental Disabilities, 33*, 467–476.

Schoon, I. (2006). *Risk and resilience: Adaptations in changing times*. Cambridge: Cambridge University Press.

Seccombe, K. (2002). "Beating the Odds" versus "Changing the Odds": poverty, resilience, and family policy. *Journal of Marriage and the Family, 64*, 384–394.

Shahtahmasebi, S., Emerson, E., Berridge, D., & Lancaster, G. (2011). Child disability and the dynamics of family poverty, hardship and financial strain: evidence from the UK. *Journal of Social Policy, 40*, 653–673.
Shogren, K. A., Lopez, S., Wehmeyer, M., Little, T. D., & Pressgrove, C. L. (2006). The role of positive psychology constructs in predicting life satisfaction in adolescents with and without cognitive disabilities: an exploratory study. *Journal of Positive Psychology, 1*, 37–52.
Shonkoff, J. P. (2010). Building a new biodevelopmental framework to guide the future of early childhood policy. *Child Development, 81*, 357–367.
Shonkoff, J. P., Boyce, W. T., & McEwen, B. S. (2009). Neuroscience, molecular biology, and the childhood roots of health disparities: building a new framework for health promotion and disease prevention. *JAMA, 301*, 2252–2259.
Spencer, N. J. (2000). *Poverty and child health* (2 ed.). Oxford: Radcliffe Medical Press.
Spencer, N. (2012). Social determinants of child health: some thoughts on mechanisms and pathways. In M. McKee (Ed.), *For the sake of children: Social paediatrics in action*. Karlstad: Karlstad university.
Spencer, N. J., Devereux, E., Wallace, A., Sundrum, R., Shenoy, M., Bacchus, C., et al. (2005). Disabling conditions and registration for child abuse and neglect: a population-based study. *Pediatrics, 116*, 609–613.
Stein, A., Ramchandani, P., & Murray, L. (2008). Impact of parental psychiatric disorder and physical illness. In M. Rutter, D. Bishop, D. Pine, S. Scott, J. Stevenson, E. Taylor, et al. (Eds.), *Rutter's child and adolescent psychiatry* (pp. 407–420). Oxford: Blackwell.
Stinton, C., Elison, S., & Howlin, P. (2010). Mental health problems in adults with Williams syndrome. *American Journal on Intellectual and Developmental Disabilities, 115*, 3–18.
Stinton, C., Tomlinson, K., & Estes, Z. (2012). Examining reports of mental health in adults with Williams syndrome. *Research in Developmental Disabilities, 33*, 144–152.
Sullivan, P. M., & Knutson, J. F. (2000). Maltreatment and disabilities: a population-based epidemiological study. *Child Abuse & Neglect, 24*, 1257–1273.
Sutherland, G., Couch, M. A., & Iacono, T. (2002). Health issues for adults with developmental disability. *Research in Developmental Disabilities, 23*, 422–445.
Taggart, L., Taylor, D., & McCrum-Gardner, E. (2010). Individual, life events, family and socio-economic factors associated with young people with intellectual disability and with and without behavioural/emotional problems. *Journal of Intellectual Disabilities, 14*, 267–288.
The Marmot Review. (2010). *Fair society, healthy lives: Strategic review of health inequalities in England post-2010*. London: The Marmot Review.
Tipton, L. A., Christensen, L., & Blacher, J. (2013). Friendship quality in adolescents with and without an intellectual disability. *Journal of Applied Research in Intellectual Disabilities, 26*, 522–532.
Torr, J., & Lee, L. (2010). Immune system diseases. In J. O'Hara, J. E. McCarthy, & N. Bouras (Eds.), *Intellectual disability and ill health: A review of the evidence* (pp. 47–60). Cambridge: Cambridge University Press.
Totsika, V., Hastings, R. P., Emerson, E., Lancaster, G. A., & Berridge, D. M. (2011). A population-based investigation of behavioural and emotional problems and maternal mental health: associations with autism spectrum disorder and intellectual disability. *Journal of Child Psychology and Psychiatry and Allied Disciplines, 52*, 91–99.
Totsika, V., Hastings, R. P., Vagenas, D., & Emerson, E. (2014). Parenting and the behaviour problems of young children with an intellectual disability: concurrent and longitudinal relationships in a population-based study. *American Journal of Intellectual & Developmental Disabilities, 119*, 422–435.
Turner, H. A., Finkelhor, D., & Ormrod, R. (2006). The effect of lifetime victimization on the mental health of children and adolescents. *Social Science & Medicine, 62*, 13–27.

Tyrer, F., & McGrother, C. (2009). Cause-specific mortality and death certificate reporting in adults with moderate to profound intellectual disabilities. *Journal of Intellectual Disability Research, 53*(11), 898–904.

Ungar, M. (2008). Resilience across cultures. *British Journal of Social Work, 38*, 218–235.

US Department of Health & Human Services. (2002a). *Closing the gap: A national blueprint to improve the health of persons with mental retardation.* Rockville, MD: US Department of Health and Human Services.

US Department of Health & Human Services. (2002b). *Report of the surgeon general's conference on health disparities and mental retardation.* Rockville: Closing the gap.

Van Schrojenstein Lantman-de Valk, H. (2005). Health in people with intellectual disabilities: current knowledge and gaps in knowledge. *Journal of Applied Research in Intellectual Disabilities, 18*, 325–333.

Vig, S., & Kaminer, R. (2002). Maltreatment and developmental disabilities in children. *Journal of Developmental and Physical Disabilities, 14*, 371–386.

Viner, R. M., Ozer, E. M., Denny, S., Marmot, M., Resnick, M., Fatusi, A., et al. (2012). Adolescence and the social determinants of health. *Lancet, 379*, 1641–1652.

Waldfogel, J., Craigie, T., & Brooks-Gunn, J. (2010). Fragile families and child wellbeing. *The Future of Children, 20*, 87–112.

Walker, S. P., Wachs, T. D., Gardner, J. M., Lozoff, B., Wasserman, G. A., Pollitt, E., &, International Child Development Steering Group. (2007). Child development: risk factors for adverse outcomes in developing countries. *Lancet, 369*, 145–157.

Walker, S. P., Wachs, T. D., Grantham-McGregor, S., Black, M. M., Nelson, C. A., Huff man, S. L., et al. (2011). Inequality in early childhood: risk and protective factors for early child development. *Lancet, 378*, 1325–1338.

Whitman, T. L. (1990). Self-regulation and intellectual disability. *American Journal on Intellectual Disabilities, 94*, 347–362.

Wilkinson, R. G., & Pickett, K. E. (2009). *The spirit level: Why more equal societies almost always do better.* London: Penguin.

World Health Organization. (2008). *Closing the gap in a generation: Health equity through action on the social determinants of health.* Final report of the Commission on the Social Determinants of Health. Geneva: World Health Organization.

World Health Organization. (2011). *Rio political declaration on social determinants of health.* Geneva: World Health Organization. http://www.who.int/sdhconference/declaration/en/.

World Health Organization Regional Office for Europe. (2013). *Report on social determinants and the health divide in the WHO European region: Final report.* Copenhagen: World Health Organization Regional Office for Europe.

World Health Organization and the World Bank. (2011). *World report on disability.* Geneva: World Health Organization.

CHAPTER THREE

Discrimination and the Health of People with Intellectual Disabilities

Gwynnyth Llewellyn[*,1], **Cathy Vaughan**[§], **Eric Emerson**[*,¶]
[*]Centre for Disability Research and Policy, University of Sydney, NSW, Australia
[§]Centre for Health Equity, Melbourne School of Population and Global Health, University of Melbourne, Parkville, VIC, Australia
[¶]Centre for Disability Research, Lancaster University, Lancaster, Lancashire, UK
[1]Corresponding author: e-mail address: gwynnyth.llewellyn@sydney.edu.au

Contents

International Review of Research in Developmental Disabilities, Volume 48
ISSN 2211-6095
http://dx.doi.org/10.1016/bs.irrdd.2015.03.005

Abstract

Increasing attention is being paid to the impact of discrimination on the health of oppressed groups. In this chapter, we review the impact of the personal experience of discrimination on the health and well-being of people with intellectual disabilities. We begin by addressing conceptual and methodological issues facing research on links between discrimination and health. We then review: (1) research that has addressed the impact of the personal experience of discrimination on the health of oppressed groups; (2) what is known about the extent to which people with intellectual disabilities experience personal discrimination; (3) the literature that has attempted to address the impact of the personal experience of discrimination on the health of people with intellectual disabilities; (4) the literature on interventions aimed at reducing the exposure to or impact of discrimination among people with intellectual disabilities. Finally, we provide some suggestions and recommendations for future research in this area.

Discrimination is a socially structured and sanctioned phenomenon, justified by ideology and expressed in interactions among and between individuals and institutions, that maintains privileges for members of dominant groups at the cost of deprivation for others.

Krieger (2014, p. 650)

1. INTRODUCTION

The last two decades have witnessed a resurgence in understanding and addressing the "social determinants" of health, especially with regard to the inequities in the distribution of health between and within countries (Berkman, Kawachi, & Glymour, 2014; Braveman, Egerter, & Williams, 2011; World Health Organization, 2008; World Health Organization Regional Office for Europe, 2013). As specified in the preamble to the *Rio Political Declaration on Social Determinants of Health* (a declaration adopted by all UN Member States in October 2011) social determinants refer to "the societal conditions in which people are born, grow, live, work and age, … [including] early years" experiences, education, economic status, employment and decent work, housing and environment, and effective systems of preventing and treating ill health' (World Health Organization, 2011).

Within this movement the majority of research has focused on the association between social stratification and health, in particular social stratification related to access to economic resources (Berkman et al., 2014; Diderichsen, Evans, & Whitehead, 2001; Marmot & Wilkinson, 1999, 2006; Wilkinson & Pickett, 2009). More recently, increasing attention has been paid to the impact of discrimination on health and health inequity (Braveman et al., 2011; Hatzenbuehler, Phelan, & Link, 2013; Krieger, 1999, 2014). Our aim in the present chapter is to review what is known about the impact of the personal experience of discrimination on the health of people with intellectual disabilities. The chapter is organized in six main sections: First, we will address a number of conceptual and methodological issues facing research on the link between discrimination and health; Second, we will provide a brief summary of research that has addressed the impact of the personal experience of discrimination on the health of people more generally; Third, we will review what is known about the extent to which people with intellectual disabilities experience personal discrimination; Fourth, we will review the very limited literature that has attempted to address the impact of the personal experience of discrimination on the health of people with intellectual disabilities; Fifth, we will review the limited literature on interventions aimed at reducing the exposure to or impact of discrimination among people with intellectual disabilities; Finally, we will provide some suggestions and recommendations for future research in this area.

2. CONCEPTUAL AND METHODOLOGICAL ISSUES

Most approaches to conceptualizing and studying the impact of discrimination make a distinction between: (1) the ways in which *institutional, systemic, or structural discrimination* serve to exclude people with particular characteristics from taking advantage of the opportunities provided by key social institutions (e.g., education systems, labor markets, legal systems) and thereby increase the social disadvantage and marginalization experienced by oppressed groups; and (2) the existence of stigmatizing attitudes toward people with particular characteristics and the impact this has on interactions between members of the dominant and oppressed groups (e.g., avoidance, staring, ridicule, victimization). The latter is often referred to as *interpersonal or individual discrimination* (Krieger, 1999, 2014) or *enacted or public stigma* (Jones & Corrigan, 2014; Link & Phelan, 2001; Scambler, 2012). These two approaches are, of course, interlinked aspects of discrimination as it is often assumed that stigmatizing attitudes arise from and serve to maintain the operation of institutional, systemic, or structural discriminatory processes. However, our aim in the present chapter is to focus on the extent to which the experience of *interpersonal discrimination* contributes to the health inequities experienced by people with intellectual disabilities.

This is not to deny the importance of institutional, systemic, or structural discrimination as important determinants of the health inequities experienced by people with intellectual disabilities (Emerson & Hatton, 2014). Indeed, there is strong evidence that institutional, systemic, or structural discrimination seriously impairs the social and economic participation and access to health care of people with intellectual and other disabilities (Disability Rights Commission, 2006; Krahn & Fox, 2014; Krahn, Hammond, & Turner, 2006; Michael, 2008; Shakespeare, 2013; Thomas, 2007; Watson, Thomas, & Roulstone, 2012; World Health Organization and World Bank, 2011). It is our contention, however, that the impact of *interpersonal discrimination* on the well-being of people with intellectual disabilities is less well understood.

2.1 Conceptualizing Interpersonal or Individual Discrimination

Efforts to measure exposure to discrimination are undermined by the lack of precision in the conceptualization of what constitutes interpersonal or individual discrimination. Typically, discrimination is understood as a social process driven by adverse social judgments about individuals or groups of individuals, which result in exclusion, rejection, blame, and devaluation (Link & Phelan, 2001). Therefore, investigating exposure to discrimination requires an understanding of what constitutes exclusion, rejection, blame, and devaluation and how these processes occur for and are experienced by particular individuals or groups of individuals with disabilities.

Studies of social stigma related to particular health conditions (e.g., Livingston & Boyd, 2010; on living with mental illness; Parker & Aggleton, 2003; on HIV and AIDS-related stigma and discrimination) and investigations in cross-cultural settings (Angermeyer, Buyantugs, Kenzine, & Matschinger, 2004; Kingori et al., 2013) have shown that discrimination takes many forms and operates in multiple contexts, both of which are likely to be specific to particular cultures at particular points in time and the nature of the oppressed and oppressing group. Discriminatory interactions experienced by people with disabilities, for example, may include staring, infantilizing, avoidance, distancing, insulting, bullying, harassment, and physical violence (Garland-Thomson, 2009; Herek, 2014; Imrie, 2000; Roulstone

& Mason-Bish, 2012; Shakespeare, 2006, 2013; Sherry, 2010), and may take place at home, at school, in the workplace, in disability service/care settings on public transport, in the street, in local shopping centers, and in cyberspace (Wedgwood, Smith, Shuttleworth, & Llewellyn, 2013). However, whether an interaction is experienced as discriminatory may depend on the context in which it occurs, with conceptualizations of the interpersonal discrimination experienced by people with disabilities therefore needing to take factors such as place, culture, and period into account.

The specificity of interpersonal discrimination associated with disability, impairment type, and care experienced by people with disabilities is, as yet, poorly understood. For example, Atkinson and Ward (2012) in developing an instrument to assess interpersonal violence for individuals with intellectual and developmental disabilities suggest extending instances of discrimination and violence to include instances such as "the destruction or denial of assistive technology, the manipulation of medication or the refusal to assist with activities of daily living" (p. 302).

Adverse social judgments may be "endorsed," "accepted," or "enacted." Peters et al. (2014), building on the model developed by Weiss, Ramakrishna, and Somma (2006), suggest that endorsed stigma refers to "justifying and supporting exclusion but refraining from being actively engaged in it, while 'accepted' means not endorsing, but nevertheless not speaking out against the process." Any attempts to reduce the stigma experienced by people with intellectual disabilities would require a full understanding of endorsed and accepted social stigma as well as that which is enacted. Conceptualizations of interpersonal discrimination rarely consider endorsed and accepted social stigma.

While there is now an evidence base on discriminatory interactions for people with certain disabling health conditions such as leprosy and other tropical diseases (Sermrittirong & van Brakel, 2014), surprisingly little is known about the prevalence (or impact) of specific forms of discrimination that occur in specific contexts for people with disabilities and in particular for people with intellectual disabilities. As a result, studies typically tend to focus on: (1) general forms of discrimination regardless of context (Williams, Yu, Jackson, & Anderson, 1997); (2) the frequency of unspecified forms of discrimination in different contexts (Krieger, Smith, Naishadham, Hartman, & Barbeau, 2005); (3) very specific forms of discrimination such as peer victimization/bullying (Sentenac et al., 2013) or hate crime (Emerson & Roulstone, 2014); or (4) very general indicators of having been treated unfairly (Emerson, Robertson, Baines, & Hatton, 2014).

2.2 Methodological Issues

The majority of quantitative epidemiological studies that have investigated the association between discrimination and health have used "indirect" methods in which the existence of discrimination is assumed, rather than directly measured (Krieger, 2014). The basic model adopted by "indirect" studies involves: (1) comparing the health outcomes of dominant and oppressed groups; then (2) estimating the extent to which any between-group differences in health outcomes could be accounted for by between-group differences in exposure to risk factors that may plausibly be linked to the impact of discrimination (structural or interpersonal). For example, numerous studies have reported that between-group differences "in current and cumulative impoverishment ... contribute substantially to explaining racial/ethnic inequities in disease occurrence, survival, and mortality" (Krieger, 2014, p. 661). Given the robust evidence that institutional and interpersonal discrimination contribute importantly to ethnic inequities in income and wealth, such studies can provide powerful (if only circumstantial) evidence of the impact of discrimination on health outcomes. The primary benefits of such studies are that: (1) they allow for the exploitation of large well-constructed data sets that typically do not contain direct measures of discrimination; and (2) they avoid some of the complex methodological challenges associated with the direct measurement of discrimination (see below). The obvious weakness of indirect studies is, of course, that discrimination can only be assumed as a critical determinant of between-group differences in exposure to the measured risk factors.

Since the 1980s an increasing number of studies have used self-report measures to estimate levels of exposure to discrimination. The development of such measures faces a number of significant challenges.

2.2.1 Self-Reporting of Discrimination Requires an Understanding of What Is "Fair"

Notions of interpersonal discrimination at the individual level require either an understanding of what constitutes "fair" treatment, or knowledge about what others have experienced (Krieger, 2014). Self-report measures, for example on social inclusion and community participation (van Brakel et al., 2006), have reported difficulties for people with restricted life circumstances in making judgments about their own lives in relation to others without similar life restrictions in their community (Kelders, Van Brakel, Beise, & Irwanto, 2012). These judgments involve reasonably complex cognitive operations that will be beyond the capacity of some people with intellectual disabilities, posing a further challenge for the measurement of interpersonal discrimination against people with intellectual disabilities.

It should be noted, however, that some people with intellectual disabilities are able to describe instances of unfair treatment. Exploratory qualitative studies in which people with intellectual disabilities are interviewed about their experiences of socially validated life events (such as intimate relationships, sexuality, marriage, and parenting) are beginning to reveal participants' understanding of the interpersonal discrimination they experience compared to the population more generally. For example, qualitative interview studies over the last two decades in Australia, Sweden, and England exploring the lived experience of women with intellectual disability becoming pregnant and rearing their children, have identified mostly negative reactions of disbelief or dismay by those close to women with intellectual disabilities when they reveal they are pregnant. This signals to mothers-to-be the suspicions of others regarding their capacity to care adequately for the child. Many women face pressure from family and professionals to abort the baby they carry; they report being blamed, rejected, and constantly devalued for being pregnant, and observe that these are not experiences shared by their nondisabled siblings or friends for whom pregnancy is typically regarded as a joyous event (Booth & Booth, 1995; Hoglund & Larsson, 2013; Llewellyn & McConnell, 2010; Mayes & Llewellyn, 2012; Mayes, Llewellyn, & McConnell, 2006, 2011).

2.2.2 Other Factors Influence Self-Reporting

How questions are asked can have a significant impact on responses. Krieger describes two main approaches to asking about experiences of discrimination: (1) those that ask explicitly about discrimination in the stem of the question and (2) those that first ask about specific acts that may be related to unfair treatment (e.g., assault), followed up with questions about whether the respondent considered the experience to be discriminatory or related to a personal characteristic of theirs (e.g., disability, ethnicity) that may suggest discrimination. Evidence suggests that the latter format results in overall higher reported rates of exposure and less variation by ethnic group than the former (Krieger, 2014). Whether similar findings pertain with people with intellectual disabilities are unknown given the absence of empirical studies investigating the use of different questioning approaches with people with intellectual disabilities.

Finally, there exists some evidence to suggest that people in lower socioeconomic positions may underreport their exposure to discrimination (Krieger, 2014). This may reflect a process of adaptation to the realities of belonging to a persistently marginalized or deprived group. As the Nobel Laureate Amartya Sen argues: "Our desires and pleasure-taking abilities adjust to circumstances, especially to make life bearable in adverse situations. ...deprived people tend to come to terms with their deprivation ... [therefore] the deprivation of the persistently deprived may look muffled and muted [when assessed through measures based on subjective appraisal]" (Sen, 2001).

2.2.3 Limitations to the Qualitative Evidence Base

The methodological difficulties that are associated with quantitative measurement of the relationship between interpersonal discrimination and health outcomes suggest an important role for qualitative research. Qualitative approaches have been used in research on stigma and discrimination with people with intellectual disabilities in a range of settings (Gibbs, Brown, & Muir, 2008; Jahoda & Markova, 2004; Jahoda, Wilson, Stalker, & Cairney, 2010). Qualitative methods can provide valuable insight into what people with intellectual disability perceive to be discrimination. They also allow researchers to explore the contexts (physical, temporal, and social) in which this discrimination occurs, participants' perceptions of factors influencing discriminatory interactions, and allow researchers to examine people's stories of how discriminatory interactions have affected their lives and in particular their health and well-being (Jahoda & Pownall, 2014).

However, there are clear limitations to the current corpus of qualitative studies relevant to understanding relationships between interpersonal discrimination and health for people with intellectual disabilities. Qualitative researchers often aim to document and share the perspectives of people with intellectual disabilities, in their own words, about issues such as discrimination (Beail & Williams, 2014). However, participants with intellectual disability (and most others) would rarely describe their experiences using language such as "interpersonal discrimination" or "structural discrimination," but rather talk about experiences that were unfair, unjust, hurtful, and so on. If qualitative researchers are aiming to understand their participants' perspectives in general, rather than through a theoretical framework that distinguishes between different forms of discrimination, then there may not be efforts to probe with participants their perceptions of the forms and drivers of the discriminatory experiences they describe. Subsequently, there will be insufficient data available for analysis to enable researchers to meaningfully examine interpersonal discrimination specifically.

The potentially central contribution of qualitative research to understandings of the relationship between interpersonal discrimination and health, from the perspective of people with intellectual disability themselves, is yet to be realized (Beail & Williams, 2014). Available studies provide rich description of people's experiences in particular settings and time. However, they are usually small scale, and have not been consolidated with further investigations to form a substantial and cohesive body of work that could examine variance and consistency in the range of contextual factors that underpin discriminatory interactions experienced by people with intellectual disability. They are also largely interview and text-based, and have rarely taken advantage of the broader range of qualitative approaches such as ethnography, oral life history, and visual media, which are relevant to people without formal language skills as well as the utilization of graphic and photographic supplementary materials in narrative and text-based methods (Atkinson, McCarthy, & Walmsley, 2000; Bogdan & Taylor, 1994; Booth & Booth, 2003; Foley et al., 2012).

3. DISCRIMINATION AND HEALTH

The first epidemiological review article on the association between discrimination and health was published just 16 years ago (Krieger, 1999). In her seminal paper, Nancy Krieger identified just 20 studies in the public health literature that employed instruments to measure self-reported experiences of discrimination. Of these, all were undertaken in the United States with 75% focusing on racial discrimination and only one addressing discrimination based on disability (Li & Moore, 1998). Since then, research in this area has burgeoned with the number of published empirical studies exceeding 500 (Krieger, 2014). A review of reviews up to mid-2013 identified 67 published reviews including three review papers focusing on the impact of discrimination on the well-being of people with a disability (Burns, 2009; Emerson et al., 2012; Thornicroft, Rose, & Kassam, 2007). However, the majority of the 67 reviews identified (40, 60%) and the majority of primary research papers continue to focus on the impact of racism, particularly in the United States (Krieger, 2014).

Krieger summarizes the existing evidence base in the following terms (see also, Dolezsar, McGrath, Herzig, & Miller, 2014; Hatzenbuehler et al., 2013; Institute of Medicine & National Research Council, 2014; Okechukwu, Souza, Davis, & de Castro, 2014; Priest et al., 2013; Schmitt, Branscombe, Postmes, & Barcia, 2014).

1. "The most robust etiologic findings pertain to positive associations between discrimination and psychological distress;
2. Growing evidence links exposure to discrimination to increased likelihood of adverse health behaviors (e.g., adverse use of psychoactive substances such as tobacco, alcohol, and other drugs; unsafe sex);
3. Evidence for associations between discrimination and somatic health remains inconsistent and weak, whether for the still-dominant work focused on cardiovascular outcomes (for which the evidence is stronger for cardiovascular reactivity than it is for hypertension), for the smaller number of new studies analyzing immunological and hormonal biomarkers of stress response, or for the handful of studies focused on obesity and on other noncommunicable and infectious disease outcomes; and
4. Indirect and increasingly experimental evidence supports the hypothesis that decisions of health care providers can be adversely affected by bias (unconscious as well as conscious)." (Krieger, 2014, p. 687)

In addition, research in this area has begun to identify protective factors that are associated with increased resilience in the face of exposure to discrimination (e.g., older age, social advantage) and some of the potential biological pathways through which exposure may have an impact on health (Hatzenbuehler et al., 2013; Schmitt et al., 2014). However, there remains little evidence in relation to protective factors that is specifically drawn from research with people with intellectual disability.

4. INTELLECTUAL DISABILITY: EXPOSURE TO INTERPERSONAL DISCRIMINATION

4.1 Public Attitudes

While pejorative and discriminatory attitudes about intellectual disability may be less common than a century ago (Trent, 1994; Wolfensberger, 1975), it is clear that a significant minority of people in high-income countries continue to hold negative attitudes about people with intellectual disabilities (Scior, 2011). Three examples are given below:

1. In a telephone survey of 1605 randomly selected adults in the province of Québec, Canada, 30% of respondents reported that adults with intellectual disability should not have the right to have children, and 25%

reported that adults with intellectual disability should not have the right to walk about town unaccompanied (Morin, Rivard, Crocker, Boursier, & Caron, 2013).

2. 10% of a random sample of over 3000 British adults reported that they would not be comfortable interacting with a neighbor with intellectual disability, while 20% reported that they *would* feel comfortable with others saying negative things about people with intellectual disabilities (Stainland, 2011).
3. One in three of a random sample of 822 adults in Hong Kong reported in a telephone survey that people with intellectual disabilities should stay within their supported accommodation services, one in six reported that these services should be built "far away" from residential centers (Lau & Cheung, 1999).

These estimates of the prevalence of negative attitudes are likely to underestimate the actual prevalence given the operation of social desirability effects in answering such types of survey questions (Stainland, 2011).

The importance of these depreciatory beliefs is threefold. First, to the extent that they are embedded in our social institutions they restrict the access of people with intellectual disability to living conditions that are associated with better health (e.g., better education, wealth, autonomy and power, better quality housing, secure and rewarding employment, access to timely and effective health care). Second, members of the public that hold strong negative beliefs may be more likely to avoid, ridicule, harass, abuse, bully or in extreme cases perpetrate violent crimes against people with intellectual disabilities. Finally, people with intellectual disabilities may become aware of the pejorative beliefs of others with negative consequences for their self-concept, self-esteem, health and well-being.

4.2 The Prevalence of Exposure to Interpersonal Discrimination

Surprisingly little robust research has been undertaken on the extent to which people with intellectual disability are exposed to acts of interpersonal discrimination. The available evidence, however, suggests that this is not an infrequent event. Four examples drawn from population-based studies undertaken since 2000 are presented below.

1. The risk of British children being bullied at school at age 11 is over four times greater for those with intellectual disability than other children, a finding that is consistent across child self-report, parental report, and teacher-report measures (Public Health England, 2015).

2. 27% of 13–14 year-old English adolescents with mild to moderate intellectual disabilities attending mainstream school reported being bullied at least weekly (compared to 13% of children without intellectual disabilities) (Emerson, Baines, Allerton, & Welch, 2011; Naylor, Dawson, Emerson, & Tantam, 2011).
3. In a nationally representative survey of UK adults, 11% of adults with intellectual or cognitive impairments reported having been the victim of violent crime and 9% the victim of hate crime in the previous 12 months (compared to rates of 4% and 2% among adults with no impairments) (Emerson & Roulstone, 2014).
4. In a nationally representative survey of English adults with intellectual disabilities, 50% of respondents reported being bullied at school, and 34% reported that someone had been unpleasant to them in the last 12 months due to their intellectual disability (Emerson, 2010; Emerson, Malam, Davies, & Spencer, 2005).

The results of these studies are consistent with the results of: (1) other studies addressing peer victimization among children with intellectual disability (e.g., Carter & Spencer, 2006; Christensen, Fraynt, Neece, & Baker, 2012; Cooney, Jahoda, Gumley, & Knott, 2006; Didden et al., 2009; Forte, Jahoda, & Dagnan, 2011; Larkin, Jahoda, MacMahon, & Pert, 2012; Norwich & Kelly, 2004); (2) the results of studies addressing peer victimization of children with disabilities more generally (Carter & Spencer, 2006; Jones et al., 2012; Rose, Forber-Pratt, Espelage, & Aragon, 2013; Sentenac et al., 2013); and (3) the results of population-based studies investigating exposure to violence among adults with disabilities (Emerson & Roulstone, 2014; Hahn, McCormick, Silverman, Robinson, & Koenen, 2014; Hughes et al., 2012; Khalifeh, Howard, Osborn, Moran, & Johnson, 2013; Mitra & Mouradian, 2014; Olofsson, Lindqvist, & Danielsson, 2014). The existing literature on stigma and intellectual disability also indicates that people with less severe intellectual disabilities are aware of the devalued social status associated with intellectual disability, although many do not see this identity as being applicable to themselves (Beart, Hardy, & Buchan, 2005; Finlay & Lyons, 2000; Jahoda et al., 2010).

4.3 The Experience of Interpersonal Discrimination

The full spectrum of interpersonal discrimination against people with disabilities is yet to be understood, with potentially many discriminatory acts being largely invisible, underreported and hidden particularly in the absence of safeguards including public scrutiny of the treatment of people with disabilities.

Gaining the perspective of people with disabilities who have experienced interpersonal discrimination is fundamental to understanding the nature and extent of discriminatory acts, which they encounter in their daily lives. An area which has attracted considerable attention is the bullying and victimization of children and young people with disabilities at school. There is an expanding knowledge base in this area derived from qualitative studies aiming to capture the perspective of children and young people with disabilities on bullying in classrooms and the playground by their peers, older children, and school personnel (Bourke & Burgman, 2010; Briggs & Hawkins, 2005; Lindsay & McPherson, 2012; McMaugh, 2011). The strengths of the qualitative designs of these studies include exploration of what children and young people with disabilities identify as discriminatory (in contrast to adult conceptualizations of discrimination) and the nature and extent of what happens, for whom, under what circumstances, and in what ways as well as the depth and breadth of the responses of these children and young people to interpersonal discriminatory acts and behaviors. These qualitative approaches permit understanding of whether discriminatory actions and behaviors vary according to personal (e.g., gender, age, sexual orientation), locational (e.g., public or private spaces such as the classroom, playground, or bathroom), and social factors including for example ethnicity, family relationships, and parental educational background. Although this literature exploring children and young people's perspectives is still in its infancy, especially for children with intellectual disabilities, it has the potential to broaden the scope of interpersonal discriminatory acts to include for example theft, threat of physical attack, being forced to do something against one's will, refusal of something essential for one's well-being, humiliation, and social rejection as suggested by Reiter, Bryen, and Shachar (2007). Similarly, qualitative research designs are being utilized to explore the meaning of well-being for children and youth with disabilities (e.g., Foley et al., 2012), a fundamental step to underpin research into the association between discrimination and well-being.

There are various research designs (and methods) well utilized in anthropology and sociology that have attracted attention for exploring the life circumstances and perspectives of people with intellectual disabilities. Of particular interest is life history research which now utilizes stand-alone visual and graphic methods (such as photovoice) or combines these methods with life narratives including those captured by visual social media such as Instagram or Facebook, or through professional photography, an early example of the latter being the work of Burton Blatt and Fred Kaplan on institutional life in the United States and more recently that of Belinda Mason in Australia about the lives of Aboriginal and Torres Strait Islander people with disabilities (Blatt & Kaplan, 1974; Mason, 2014). A seminal work from the 1980s by Levine and Langness (1986) illustrated the potential of life history research to bring together individual specificity situated within a particular time of life and grounded in geographical and societal contexts. More recent work moves beyond understanding of individual stories to that of social mechanisms, patterns, and conditions that facilitate (or hinder) interpersonal disability-based discriminatory acts and the impact thereof on individual's participation and well-being (e.g., Llewellyn & McConnell, 2010; Wedgwood et al., 2013). The focus on the contextual particularities of individual biographies has been found to be especially important when studying marginal groups, both as a tool for empowerment and as a way of revealing contradictions and exceptions unexpected by the research agenda (Plummer, 2001).

Life histories have been embraced by disability researchers, with the dynamics of creating these histories often more complex than conventional understandings of the method. Life history work in disability in the US (Bogdan & Taylor, 1994; Taylor, 1995), the UK (Atkinson, McCarthy, & Walmsley, 2000), and our work in Australia (Llewellyn & McConnell, 2005) provides clear guidance for using life history approaches with people with disabilities including those with complex communication needs (Dew, Balandin, & Llewellyn, 2011).

5. INTELLECTUAL DISABILITY: THE ASSOCIATION BETWEEN DISCRIMINATION AND HEALTH

Given that little robust research has been undertaken on the extent to which people with intellectual disability are exposed to acts of interpersonal discrimination, it is hardly surprising that very few studies indeed have investigated the association between exposure and health among people with intellectual disabilities. As noted above, the majority of studies undertaken on the association between discrimination and health have used indirect methods. That is, if the extent to which health outcomes of dominant and oppressed groups can be accounted for by differences in exposure to environmental risk factors associated with poorer health (e.g., unemployment, low education, low income, unsafe neighborhoods) *which can plausibly be attributed to the impact of discrimination* (rather than defining between-group characteristics, e.g., skin color or other factors), then discrimination is *assumed* to play an important role. The key assumption underlying indirect studies is that differences in exposure to environmental risk factors associated with poorer health (e.g., low educational attainment) are primarily the result of *structural* discrimination.

However, the use of evidence from indirect studies involving people with intellectual disabilities is problematic. The key assumption that differences in exposure to environmental risk factors associated with poorer health (e.g., low educational attainment) are primarily the result of structural discrimination is much less tenable for people with intellectual disabilities given that: (1) people with intellectual disabilities by definition have intellectual impairments, which will have a significant impact on their capacity to attain the types of higher educational qualifications, which are a prerequisite for employment in most higher paid and professional jobs; and (2) intellectual disability is associated from birth onward with environmental risk factors associated with poorer health (e.g., poverty, cf. Emerson, 2007, 2013; Emerson & Brigham, 2015a; Gore, Emerson, & Brady, 2015), a form of association which is difficult to attribute to discrimination at such an early age. Given these concerns, the growing body of evidence that the health inequities experienced by children and adults with intellectual disability can, in part, be potentially attributed to their poorer living conditions (i.e., studies that adopt the logic of indirect studies, e.g., Emerson, 2013; Emerson, Blacher, et al., 2014; Emerson & Brigham, 2015b; Emerson & Hatton, 2007a, 2007b, 2007c, 2014; Emerson, Hatton, Robertson, & Baines, 2014; Emerson, Robertson, et al., 2014; Robertson, Emerson, Baines, & Hatton, 2014) cannot be accepted as evidence of the impact of discrimination (either structural or interpersonal).

We could only identify three published population-based studies that have directly investigated the association between exposure to interpersonal discrimination and the well-being of people with intellectual disabilities.

1. Emerson (2010) undertook secondary analysis of deidentified cross-sectional data extracted from the survey of *Adults with Learning Difficulties in England 2003/4*, a nationally representative sample of over 1273 British adults with intellectual disability who were capable of self-reporting on their general health status (Emerson et al., 2005). 50% of respondents reported that they had been bullied at school, and 34% reported exposure to overt acts of interpersonal discrimination ("have people been rude or nasty to you because of your learning difficulty?") in the last year. Both self-reported exposure to bullying while at school and self-reported exposure to overt acts of disablism over the previous 12 months were associated with poorer health on all six measured outcomes ("fair" or

"poor" self-reported health, "sometimes/not" happy, "never" confident, sad "a lot," helpless "a lot," left out "a lot") when controlling for variables associated with both exposure and health status (gender, age, poverty status, area deprivation, level of support needs, marital status, employment status). The effect sizes of the associations were small in 50% of instances and moderate in 50%. In the vast majority of instances, these associations were stronger for people with lower levels of material or social resources.

2. Emerson, Robertson, et al. (2014) undertook secondary analysis of deidentified cross-sectional data extracted from the first waves of the *Life Opportunities Survey* (Office for Disability Issues, 2011). Adults who had self-reported difficulties in learning or understanding coexisting with very low self-reported educational attainment aged 16–49 ($n = 316$, 1.7% of the unweighted age-restricted sample) had poorer self-rated health than their peers ($n > 18{,}000$) and were also more likely within the last 12 months to have been treated unfairly due to a personal characteristic (36% vs 12%; OR = 4.06, 95% CI 2.83–5.82). This same group were also more likely to have been a victim of or exposed to "violence or force used or threatened against you" (13% vs 6%; OR = 2.47, 95% CI 1.58–3.87) and to have been a victim of "hate" crime (8% vs 2%; OR = 3.71, 95% CI 1.97–6.99). Controlling for between-group differences in exposure to these indicators of interpersonal discrimination significantly reduced the magnitude of between-group differences in self-rated health even when simultaneously also controlling for between-group differences in socioeconomic position.

3. A report by Public Health England (2015) reported the results of secondary analysis of deidentified longitudinal data extracted from the first five waves of the UK's Millennium Cohort Study (Gallop et al., 2013; Hansen, 2014). Results indicated that higher risk of emotional difficulties of children with intellectual disability at age 11 ($n = 647$) was uniquely associated with them having been bullied at school (OR = 2.24, 95% CI 1.36–4.04). Recent research on peer victimization of disabled children more generally has also reported that bullying was associated with poor self-rated health, low life satisfaction, and multiple health complaints (Sentenac et al., 2013).

These results are broadly consistent with those of nonpopulation-based studies that have investigated the association between perceived stigma and psychological well-being among adults with mild intellectual disability

(Dagnan & Sandhu, 1999; Dagnan & Waring, 2004; Forte et al., 2011; Jahoda et al., 2010; Larkin et al., 2012; Szivos-Bach, 1993).

6. INTERVENTIONS TO REDUCE THE EXPOSURE TO OR IMPACT OF INTERPERSONAL DISCRIMINATION

Two recent systematic reviews have summarized current knowledge regarding the efficacy of interventions that have the potential to reduce the exposure of people with intellectual disabilities to acts of interpersonal discrimination. Seewooruttun and Scior (2014) reviewed English language studies published between 1990 and early 2014 that evaluated the impact of interventions to either increase knowledge about intellectual disability, or to reduce negative attitudes toward people with intellectual disabilities among lay people of working age. They identified 22 studies, the majority of which "reported promising outcomes, particularly those aimed at increasing knowledge of intellectual disability through education." They concluded that "support for the positive influence of contact with people with intellectual disabilities was demonstrated across several interventions [and that] interventions delivered at least partly by individuals with intellectual disabilities, and educational interventions appear to hold the most promise" (Seewooruttun & Scior, 2014, p. 3482). They also noted, however, that the evidence base is limited by the weaknesses of the measurement tools employed.

A systematic review undertaken by the World Health Organization identified 10 studies, which evaluated the effectiveness of interventions to prevent and mitigate the consequences of interpersonal violence against people with disabilities (Mikton, Maguire, & Shakespeare, 2014). Eight of these focused on people with intellectual disabilities or developmental disabilities. They concluded that "all studies received a weak rating on the quality assessment tool and none could be considered effective after taking risk of bias into account. In sum, the current evidence base offers little guidance to policy makers, program commissioners, and persons with disabilities for selecting interventions" (Mikton et al., 2014, pp. 3207–3208).

7. PRIORITIES FOR FUTURE RESEARCH

We do not yet have the knowledge to be able to answer key questions about the nature and impact of interpersonal discriminatory acts directed toward people with intellectual disabilities:

7.1 What Is the Nature and Extent of Interpersonal Discrimination Experienced by People with Intellectual Disabilities?

Research efforts on discrimination in the field of intellectual disabilities have primarily focused on institutional, systemic, or structural discrimination resulting in a large body of evidence on institutional discrimination such as segregation and abuse of adults and children with intellectual disabilities; on systemic discrimination which involves rejection and exclusion from mainstream social systems such as schooling and health care; and on structural discrimination in which practices such as involuntary sterilization and determination of legal capacity are "reserved" only for those with "diminished intellectual capacity." This research while critically important, we contend, overlooks the overt (and covert) embedded and potentially more pernicious discrimination that the research reviewed in this chapter suggests may be a common experience for people with intellectual disabilities in their everyday lives. A first priority in research directions is to investigate the nature and extent of interpersonal discrimination experienced by people with intellectual disabilities.

7.2 Who Is Most at Risk of Experiencing Different Forms of Interpersonal Discrimination?

Current research on interpersonal discrimination for people with intellectual disabilities does not permit answers to this question. For example, are men or women most at risk and if so, to which particular forms of interpersonal discrimination? Is age a determining factor in being at risk? Are particular communities more at risk than others and if so, what factors influence a heightened community interpersonal discrimination risk profile? Are those individuals with more resources—either personal (such as educational achievement) or economic, for example—less likely to be "targeted" and/or more able to resist interpersonal discrimination? For example, the very limited evidence in this area suggests that discrimination involving violence is more commonly enacted toward people living in more socially deprived communities (Emerson & Roulstone, 2014). As in other areas of health and well-being research for people with intellectual disabilities, intersectionality (the intersections between different forms or systems of discrimination based on ethnicity, age, gender, geographic location, socioeconomic resources, and so on) is likely to play a part in determining those most and those least at risk for adverse discrimination experiences and associated health outcomes. Krieger (2014), citing her work on the ecosocial inverse hazard law (Krieger et al., 2008), notes that an integrated approach is needed to study discrimination exposure and health outcomes in the population more generally. Her law which posits that "the accumulation of health hazards tends to vary inversely with the power and resources of the populations affected," (Krieger et al., 2008, p. 1971) appears particularly apt to the historically and socioculturally determined lack of power and resources afforded to people with intellectual disabilities. Qualitative studies may have particular value here in allowing researchers to examine the perspectives of people with intellectual disability in a way that does not reduce the intersectionality of discriminatory experiences to simply the sum of discrete variables associated with disadvantage.

7.3 How Does This Vary across Time and Place?

The dearth of literature about the experience of people with intellectual disability living in low- and middle-income countries makes it impossible to assess variation in the extent and nature of discrimination faced by people with intellectual disabilities across different cultures and countries that vary with regard to such factors as wealth, equality, political ideology, major faiths, and political commitment to promoting human rights (Lewis-Gargett et al., in press). Further longitudinal work, using both quantitative and qualitative methods, is needed to assess variance in experiences of interpersonal discrimination for individuals and groups of people with intellectual disability over time. It is unclear whether interpersonal discrimination is more likely in specific contexts or at different times—for example at night time, on public transport, when a person with intellectual disability is alone, in disability service settings—and how these experiences might be mediated by other factors, including changing social, political, and media environments.

7.4 In What Ways Do People with Intellectual Disabilities Change Their Lives in Response to Interpersonal Discrimination?

Little is understood about whether and how people with intellectual disabilities respond to and manage exposure to interpersonal discrimination. It is unclear whether interpersonal discrimination causes people with intellectual disabilities to not get out and about on their own in public, or to disengage with particular institutions (such as schools). There is, for example, limited evidence from the UK to suggest that peer victimization is associated with higher rates of children with disabilities leaving school at the earliest possible age (Naylor et al., 2011).The changes that people may make to their lives—including withdrawal from social situations and reduced participation (including economic participation)—may have a protective function for persons experiencing interpersonal discrimination, but may also have potentially harmful secondary impacts on a range of measures of health and well-being. Discrimination has also been identified as a direct barrier to health care services for people with intellectual disability (Ali et al., 2013), but less is known about how people with intellectual disability subsequently negotiate (or not) their access to care following experiences of interpersonal discrimination.

7.5 What Is the Impact of Interpersonal Discrimination on the Health and Well-being of People with Intellectual Disabilities?

As noted above, there is a dearth of information on this issue. Notwithstanding the challenges associated with the measurement of exposure to interpersonal discrimination discussed above, there is a clear need for more qualitative and/or well-constructed longitudinal quantitative studies that can begin to identify possible causal pathways from exposure to interpersonal discrimination and subsequent changes in health.

7.6 Why Are Some People with Intellectual Disabilities More Resilient and Others More Vulnerable to the Negative Outcomes Associated with Interpersonal Discrimination in Public?

Historically, resilience has often been used to refer to the attributes and characteristics of individuals (e.g., temperament) that may make them more or less susceptible to the impact of exposure to adversities. A more contemporary approach, however, also includes consideration of a wide range of environmental protective factors that make people more or less resilient or vulnerable when exposed to adversity (Buck & Gregory, 2013; Davydov, Stewart, Ritchie, & Chaudieu, 2010; Friedli, 2009; Goldstein & Brooks, 2006; Jenkins, 2008; Luthar, 2003; Masten, 2001; Sapienza & Masten, 2011; Seccombe, 2002; Ungar, 2008). These include: individual capabilities such as intelligence, self-regulation, and problem-solving skills; individual characteristics such as faith, hope, spirituality (with associated beliefs that life has meaning), perceived efficacy, having a sense of control, having a sense of belonging; positive relationships with caring adults, acquaintances, friends, and romantic partners; and access to resources such as effective caregiving and parenting, teachers and schools, health and welfare services, social capital, wealth and power.

Little research has been undertaken on the resilience of people, and especially children, with intellectual disabilities (Broberg, Blacher, & Emerson, 2009; Gilmore, Campbell, Shochet, & Roberts, 2013; Murray & Doren, 2013; see also Emerson and Spencer, in this volume). However, the available evidence does suggest that when compared with their nondisabled peers, people (primarily adults) with intellectual disabilities: (1) tend to have fewer friends, smaller social networks, and receive less social support; (2) show patterns of association between having friends, more extensive social networks and social support, and more positive indicators of well-being that are similar to their nondisabled peers (Gilmore et al., 2013; Jahoda & Pownall, 2014; Kersh, Corona, & Siperstein, 2013; Public Health England, 2015; Tipton, Christensen, & Blacher, 2013). As discussed above, families supporting children with intellectual disabilities are significantly less likely than other families to have access to such resources as wealth and power. In addition, a number of reports have highlighted the disadvantages faced by people with intellectual disabilities in accessing timely, effective, and appropriate health care (Department of Health, 2001, 2009; Disability Rights Commission, 2006; Mencap, 2007, 2012; Michael, 2008; US Department of Health & Human Services, 2002a, 2002b).

Further work is warranted on resilience among people with intellectual disabilities generally, and also on the predictors of resilience when faced with interpersonal discrimination.

7.7 What Works to Reduce Exposure to Interpersonal Discrimination and to Help People Be More Resilient?

Not enough is known about the "perpetrators" of interpersonal discrimination against people with intellectual disabilities, and how to best intervene to shift deeply held stigmatizing attitudes (Mikton et al., 2014; Scior, 2011; Seewooruttun & Scior, 2014). In general, people with higher levels of education, people with higher incomes, women and public sector employees express more positive attitudes toward people with disabilities. However, these demographic characteristics interact with both the situation in which a person with disabilities would be encountered and the impairment that they have in influencing the attitudes people hold (Stainland, 2011). There exists a more extensive, though itself limited and often flawed, literature on the use of mass media campaigns, targeted training, and interpersonal contact approaches to reduce the stigma associated with mental health problems (Clement et al., 2013; Collins, Wong, Cerully, Schultz, & Eberhart, 2012; Pettigrew & Tropp, 2006). While evidence suggests all three types of approaches may have benefits, the effect sizes are often small.

In order to reduce the degree to which people with intellectual disability are exposed to interpersonal discrimination, it is necessary to use evidence generated in response to the questions above to develop, trial, and evaluate interventions. An action research approach, where research teams work with people with intellectual disability (and their carers and supporters), would enable assessment of "what works" to include the perspectives of people with intellectual disability themselves.

Future research aiming to generate knowledge about these questions will benefit from including people with disabilities as part of the research team. Arguments in support of an inclusive approach to disability research include that (1) the quality of the evidence generated will be strengthened by an insider perspective, (2) people with disability have the right to participate in research that is about them, and (3) that an inclusive approach is more effective in translating to policy, practice, and social change (Garcia Iriarte, O'Brien, & Chadwick, 2014). In addition to meeting obligations enshrined in the UN Convention on the Rights of Persons with Disabilities, research teams that are disability inclusive may be best placed to generate evidence about interpersonal discrimination and its impact on health that is genuinely informed by the lived expertise of people with intellectual disabilities.

REFERENCES

Ali, A., Scior, K., Ratti, V., Strydom, A., King, M., & Hassiotis, A. (2013). Discrimination and other barriers to accessing health care: perspectives of patient with mild and moderate intellectual disability and their carers. *PLoS One, 8*, e70855. 70810.71371/journal.pone.0070855.

Angermeyer, M., Buyantugs, L., Kenzine, D., & Matschinger, H. (2004). Effects of labelling on public attitudes towards people with schizophrenia: are there cultural differences? *Acta Psychiatrica Scandinavica, 109*, 420–425.

Atkinson, D., McCarthy, M., & Walmsley, J. (Eds.). (2000). *Good times, bad times: Women with learning difficulties telling their stories*. Kidderminster: BILD.

Atkinson, J. P., & Ward, K. M. (2012). The development of an assessment of interpersonal violence for individuals with intellectual and developmental disabilities. *Sexuality and Disability, 30*, 301–309.

Beail, N., & Williams, K. (2014). Using qualitative methods in research with people who have intellectual disabilities. *Journal of Applied Research in Intellectual Disabilities, 27*, 85–96.

Beart, S., Hardy, G., & Buchan, L. (2005). How people with intellectual disabilities view their social identity: a review of the literature. *Journal of Applied Research in Intellectual Disabilities, 18*, 47–56.

Berkman, L. F., Kawachi, I., & Glymour, M. M. (Eds.). (2014). *Social epidemiology* (2nd ed.). Oxford: Oxford University Press.

Blatt, B., & Kaplan, F. (1974). *Christmas in purgatory. A photographic essay on mental retardation.* Syracuse, NY: Human Policy Press.

Bogdan, R., & Taylor, S. J. (1994). *The social meaning of mental retardation: Two life stories: A reissued edition of "inside out" with a new postscript.* New York, NY: Teachers College Press.
Booth, T., & Booth, W. (1995). Unto us a child is born: the trials and rewards of parenthood for people with learning difficulties. *Australia and New Zealand Journal of Developmental Disabilities, 20*, 25–39.
Booth, T., & Booth, W. (2003). In the frame: photovoice and mothers with learning difficulties. *Disability & Society, 18*, 431–442.
Bourke, S., & Burgman, I. (2010). Coping with bullying in Australian schools: how children with disabilities experience support from friends, parents and teachers. *Disability & Society, 25*, 359–371.
van Brakel, W., Anderson, A. M., Mutatkar, R. K., Bakirtzief, Z., Nicholls, P. G., & Raju, M. S. (2006). The participation scale: measuring a key concept in public health. *Disability and Rehabilitation, 28*, 193–203.
Braveman, P., Egerter, S., & Williams, D. R. (2011). The social determinants of health: coming of age. *Annual Review of Public Health, 32*, 381–398.
Briggs, F., & Hawkins, R. (2005). Personal safety issues in the lives of children with learning disabilities. *Children Australia, 30*, 19–27.
Broberg, M., Blacher, J., & Emerson, E. (2009). Editorial: resilience. *Journal of Intellectual Disability Research, 53*, 955–956.
Buck, D., & Gregory, S. (2013). *Improving the public's health. A resource for local authorities.* London: The King's Fund.
Burns, J. K. (2009). Mental health and inequity: a human rights approach to inequality, discrimination, and mental disability. *Health and Human Rights, 11*, 19–31.
Carter, B. B., & Spencer, V. G. (2006). The fear factor: bullying and students with disabilities. *International Journal of Special Education, 21*, 11–23.
Christensen, L. L., Fraynt, R. J., Neece, C. L., & Baker, B. L. (2012). Bullying adolescents with intellectual disability. *Journal of Mental Health Research in Intellectual Disabilities, 5*, 49–65.
Clement, S., Lassman, F., Barley, E., Evans-Lacko, S., Williams, P., & Yamaguchi, S. (2013). Mass media interventions for reducing mental health-related stigma (review). *The Cochrane Library*, 7. http://onlinelibrary.wiley.com/doi/10.1002/14651858.CD14009453.pub14651852/pdf.
Collins, R. L., Wong, E. C., Cerully, J. L., Schultz, D., & Eberhart, N. K. (2012). *Interventions to reduce mental health stigma and discrimination: A literature review to guide evaluation of California's mental health prevention and early intervention initiative.* Santa Monica, CA: RAND Corporation.
Cooney, G., Jahoda, A., Gumley, A., & Knott, F. (2006). Young people with learning disabilities attending mainstream and segregated schooling: perceived stigma, social comparisons and future aspirations. *Journal of Intellectual Disability Research, 50*, 432–445.
Dagnan, D., & Sandhu, S. (1999). Social comparison, self-esteem and depression in people with learning disabilities. *Journal of Intellectual Disability Research, 43*, 372–379.
Dagnan, D., & Waring, M. (2004). Linking stigma to psychological distress: a social-cognitive model of the experience of people with learning disabilities. *Clinical Psychology & Psychotherapy, 11*, 247–254.
Davydov, D., Stewart, R., Ritchie, K., & Chaudieu, I. (2010). Resilience and mental health. *Clinical Psychology Review, 30*, 479–495.
Department of Health. (2001). *Valuing people: A new strategy for learning disability for the 21st century.*
Department of Health. (2009). *Valuing people now: A new three-year strategy for people with learning disabilities.* London: Department of Health.
Dew, A., Balandin, S., & Llewellyn, G. (2011). Using a life course approach to explore how the use of AAC impacts on adult sibling relationships. *Augmentative and Alternative Communication, 27*(4), 245–255.

Didden, R., Scholte, R. H. J., Korzilius, H., de Moor, J. H. M., Vermeulen, A., & O'Reilly, M. (2009). Cyberbullying among students with intellectual and developmental disability in special education settings. *Developmental Neurorehabilitation, 12*, 146–151.

Diderichsen, F., Evans, T., & Whitehead, M. (2001). The social basis of disparities in health. In T. Evans, M. Whitehead, F. Diderichsen, A. Bhuiya, & M. Wirth (Eds.), *Challenging inequities in health: From ethics to action*. Oxford: Oxford University Press.

Disability Rights Commission. (2006). *Equal treatment: Closing the gap*. London Disability Rights Commission.

Dolezsar, C. M., McGrath, J. J., Herzig, A. J. M., & Miller, S. B. (2014). Perceived racial discrimination and hypertension: a comprehensive systematic review. *Health Psychology, 33*, 20–34.

Emerson, E. (2007). Poverty and people with intellectual disability. *Mental Retardation and Developmental Disabilities Research Reviews, 13*, 107–113.

Emerson, E. (2010). Self-reported exposure to disablism is associated with poorer self-reported health and well-being among adults with intellectual disabilities in England: cross sectional survey. *Public Health, 124*, 682–689.

Emerson, E. (2013). Commentary: childhood exposure to environmental adversity and the well-being of people with intellectual disabilities. *Journal of Intellectual Disabilities Research, 57*, 589–600. http://dx.doi.org/10.1111/j.1365-2788.2012.01577.x.

Emerson, E., Baines, S., Allerton, L., & Welch, V. (2011). *Health inequalities and people with learning disabilities in the UK: 2011*. Durham: Improving Health and Lives: Learning Disabilities Observatory.

Emerson, E., Blacher, J., Einfeld, S., Hatton, C., Robertson, J., & Stancliffe, R. (2014). Environmental risk factors associated with the persistence of conduct difficulties in children with and without intellectual disabilities or autistic spectrum disorders. *Research in Developmental Disabilities, 35*, 3508–3517.

Emerson, E., & Brigham, P. (2015a). Exposure of children with developmental delay to social determinants of poor health: cross sectional study. *Child: Care Health Development, 41*, 249–257. http://dx.doi.org/10.1111/cch.12144.

Emerson, E., & Brigham, P. (2015b). Exposure of children with developmental delay to social determinants of poor health: cross sectional study. *Child: Care Health Development, 41*, 249–257. http://dx.doi.org/10.1111/cch.12144.

Emerson, E., & Hatton, C. (2007a). The contribution of socio-economic position to the health inequalities faced by children and adolescents with intellectual disabilities in Britain. *American Journal on Mental Retardation, 112*, 140–150.

Emerson, E., & Hatton, C. (2007b). The mental health of children and adolescents with intellectual disabilities in Britain. *British Journal of Psychiatry, 191*, 493–499.

Emerson, E., & Hatton, C. (2007c). Poverty, socio-economic position, social capital and the health of children and adolescents with intellectual disabilities in Britain: a replication. *Journal of Intellectual Disability Research, 51*, 866–874.

Emerson, E., & Hatton, C. (2014). *Health inequalities and people with intellectual disabilities*. Cambridge: Cambridge University Press.

Emerson, E., Hatton, C., Robertson, J., & Baines, S. (2014). Perceptions of neighbourhood quality, social and civic participation and the self rated health of British adults with intellectual disability: cross sectional study. *BMC Public Health, 14*, 1252. 1210.1186/1471-2458-1214-1252.

Emerson, E., Malam, S., Davies, I., & Spencer, K. (2005). *Adults with learning difficulties in England 2003/4*. Leeds: Health & Social Care Information Centre.

Emerson, E., Robertson, J., Baines, S., & Hatton, C. (2014). The self-rated health of British adults with intellectual disability. *Research in Developmental Disabilities, 35*, 591–596.

Emerson, E., & Roulstone, A. (2014). Developing an evidence base for violent and disablist hate crime in the Britain: findings from the life opportunities survey. *Journal of Interpersonal Violence, 29*, 3086–3104.

Emerson, E., Vick, B., Graham, H., Hatton, C., Llewellyn, G., & Madden, R. (2012). Disablement and health. In N. Watson, C. Thomas, & A. Roulstone (Eds.), *Routledge Companion to disability studies*. London: Routledge.
Finlay, W. M., & Lyons, E. (2000). Social categorisations, social comparisons and stigma: presentations of self in people with learning difficulties. *British Journal of Social Psychology, 39*, 129–146.
Foley, K. R., Blackmore, A. M., Girdler, S., O'Donnell, M., Glauert, R., & Llewellyn, G. (2012). To feel belonged: the voices of children and youth with disabilities on the meaning of wellbeing. *Child Indicators Research, 5*, 375–391.
Forte, M., Jahoda, A., & Dagnan, D. (2011). An anxious time? Exploring the nature of worries experienced by young people with a mild to moderate intellectual disability as they make the transition to adulthood. *British Journal of Clinical Psychology, 50*, 398–411.
Friedli, L. (2009). *Mental health, resilience and inequalities*. Copenhagen: World Health Organization, Europe.
Gallop, K., Rose, N., Wallace, E., Williams, R., Cleary, A., & Thompson, A. (2013). *Millennium cohort study fifth sweep (MCS5): Technical report*. London: Ipsos Mori.
Garcia Iriarte, E., O'Brien, P., & Chadwick, D. (2014). Involving people with intellectual disabilities within research teams: lessons learned from an Irish experience. *Journal of Policy and Practice in Intellectual Disabilities, 11*, 149–157.
Garland-Thomson, R. (2009). *Staring: How we look*. Oxford University Press.
Gibbs, S., Brown, M., & Muir, W. (2008). The experiences of adults with intellectual disabilities and their carers in general hospitals: a focus group study. *Journal of Intellectual Disability Research, 52*, 1061–1077.
Gilmore, L., Campbell, M., Shochet, I., & Roberts, C. (2013). Resiliency profiles of children with intellectual disability and their typically developing peers. *Psychology in the Schools, 50*, 1032–1043.
Goldstein, S., & Brooks, R. B. (Eds.). (2006). *Handbook of resilience in children*. New York: Springer.
Gore, N., Emerson, E., & Brady, S. (2015). Rates of breastfeeding and exposure to socioeconomic adversity amongst children with intellectual disability. *Research in Developmental Disabilities, 39*, 12–19.
Hahn, J. W., McCormick, M. C., Silverman, J. G., Robinson, E. B., & Koenen, K. C. (2014). Examining the impact of disability status on intimate partner violence victimization in a population sample. *Journal of Interpersonal Violence, 29*(17), 3063–3085.
Hansen, K. (Ed.). (2014). *Millennium cohort study: A guide to the datasets* (8th ed.). London: Centre for Longitudinal Studies, Institute of Education, University of London. First, Second, Third, Fourth and Fifth Surveys.
Hatzenbuehler, M. L., Phelan, J. C., & Link, B. G. (2013). Stigma as a fundamental cause of population health inequalities. *American Journal of Public Health, 103*, 813–821.
Herek, G. M. (2014). HIV-related stigma. In P. W. Corrigan (Ed.), *The stigma of disease and disability* (pp. 121–138). Washington, DC: American Psychological Association.
Hoglund, B., & Larsson, M. (2013). Struggling for motherhood with an intellectual disability—a qualitative study of women's experiences in Sweden. *Midwifery, 29*, 698–704.
Hughes, K., Bellis, M. A., Jones, L., Wood, S., Bates, G., & Eckley, L. (2012). Prevalence and risk of violence against adults with disabilities: a systematic review and meta-analysis of observational studies. *Lancet, 379*(9826), 1621–1629.
Imrie, R. (2000). Disability and discourses of mobility and movement. *Environment and Planning A, 32*(9), 1641–1656.
Institute of Medicine, & National Research Council. (2014). *Investing in the health and well-being of young adults*. Washington, DC: The National Academies Press.

Jahoda, A., & Markova, I. (2004). Coping with social stigma: people with intellectual disabilities moving from institutions and family home. *Journal of Intellectual Disability Research, 48*, 719–729.

Jahoda, A., & Pownall, J. (2014). Sexual understanding, sources of information and social networks; the reports of young people with intellectual disabilities and their non-disabled peers. *Journal of Intellectual Disabilities Research, 58*, 430–441.

Jahoda, A., Wilson, A., Stalker, K., & Cairney, A. (2010). Living with stigma and the self-perceptions of people with mild intellectual disabilities. *Journal of Social Issues, 66*, 521–534.

Jenkins, J. (2008). Psychosocial adversity and resilience. In M. Rutter, D. Bishop, D. Pine, S. Scott, J. Stevenson, E. Taylor, et al. (Eds.), *Rutter's child and adolescent psychiatry* (5th ed.). (pp. 377–391). Oxford: Blackwell.

Jones, L., Bellis, M. A., Wood, S., Hughes, K., McCoy, E., & Eckley, L. (2012). Prevalence and risk of violence against children with disabilities: a systematic review and meta-analysis of observational studies. *Lancet, 380*(9845), 899–907.

Jones, N., & Corrigan, P. W. (2014). Understanding stigma. In P. W. Corrigan (Ed.), *The stigma of disease and disability* (pp. 9–34). Washington, DC: Americal Psychological Association.

Kelders, R., Van Brakel, W., Beise, K., & Irwanto. (2012). Testing and validating a simplified scale to measure social participation of people with disabilities in Indonesia. *Disability and Rehabilitation, 34*, 638–646.

Kersh, J., Corona, L., & Siperstein, G. (2013). Social wellbeing and friendship of people with intellectual disability. In M. L. Wehmeyer (Ed.), *The Oxford handbook of positive psychology and disability* (pp. 60–81). Oxford: Oxford University Press.

Khalifeh, H., Howard, L., Osborn, D., Moran, P., & Johnson, S. (2013). Violence against people with disability in England and Wales: findings from a national cross-sectional survey. *PLoS One, 8*(2), e55952.

Kingori, C., Reece, M., Obeng, S., Murray, M., Shacham, E., & Dodge, B. (2013). Psychometric evaluation of a cross-culturally adapted felt stigma questionnaire among people living with HIV in Kenya. *AIDS Patient Care and STDs, 27*, 418–488.

Krahn, G., & Fox, M. H. (2014). Health disparities of adults with intellectual disabilities: what do we know? what do we do? *Journal of Applied Research in Intellectual Disability, 27*, 431–446. http://dx.doi.org/10.1111/jar.12067.

Krahn, G., Hammond, L., & Turner, A. (2006). A cascade of disparities: health and health care access for people with intellectual disabilities. *Mental Retardation and Developmental Disabilities Research Reviews, 12*, 70–82.

Krieger, N. (1999). Embodying inequality: a review of concepts, measures, and methods for studying health consequences of discrimination. *International Journal of Health Services, 29*, 295–352.

Krieger, N. (2014). Discrimination and health inequities. *International Journal of Health Services, 44*, 643–710.

Krieger, N., Chen, J. T., Waterman, P. D., Hartman, C., Stoddard, A. M., & Quinn, M. M. (2008). The inverse hazard law: blood pressure, sexual harassment, racial discrimination, workplace abuse and occupational exposures to US low-income black, white and Latino workers. *Social Science and Medicine, 67*, 1970–1981.

Krieger, N., Smith, K., Naishadham, D., Hartman, C., & Barbeau, E. M. (2005). Experiences of discrimination: validity and reliability of a self-report measure for population health research on racism and health. *Social Science & Medicine, 61*, 1576–1596.

Larkin, P., Jahoda, A., MacMahon, K., & Pert, C. (2012). Interpersonal sources of conflict in young people with and without mild to moderate intellectual disabilities at transition from adolescence to adulthood. *Journal of Applied Research in Intellectual Disabilities, 25*, 29–38.

Lau, J. T.-F., & Cheung, C.-K. (1999). Discriminatory attitudes to people with intellectual disability or mental health difficulty. *International Social Work, 42*, 431–444.
Levine, H. G., & Langness, L. L. (1986). *Culture and mental retardation: Life histories of mildly mentally retarded persons in American society*. Boston: D. Reidel Publishing Co.
Lewis-Gargett, A., Barton, R., Llewellyn, G., Tsaputra, A., Soe, K. Z. S., & Tawake, S. Global cultures and understandings of disability. In R. McConkey, E. García Iriarte, & R. Gilligan (Eds.), *Disability in a Global age: A human rights-based approach*. Melbourne: Palgrave Macmillan, in press.
Li, L., & Moore, D. (1998). Acceptance of disability and its barriers. *Journal of Social Psychology, 138*, 13–25.
Lindsay, S., & McPherson, A. C. (2012). Experiences of social exclusion and bullying at school among children and youth with cerebral palsy. *Disability & Rehabilitation, 34*, 101–109.
Link, B. G., & Phelan, J. C. (2001). Conceptualising stigma. *Annual Review of Sociology, 27*, 363–385.
Livingston, J., & Boyd, J. (2010). Correlates and consequences of internalized stigma for people living with mental illness: a systematic review and meta-analysis. *Social Sciences and Medicine, 71*, 2150–2161.
Llewellyn, G., & McConnell, D. (2005). You have to prove yourself all the time. *Learning Disability, 441*.
Llewellyn, G., & McConnell, D. (2010). You have to prove yourself all the time: people with learning disabilities as parents. In G. Grant, P. Ramcharan, M. Flynn, & M. Richardson (Eds.), *Learning disability: A life cycle approach* (pp. 311–328). Berkshire: Open University Press.
Luthar, S. S. (Ed.). (2003). *Resilience and vulnerability: Adaptation in the context of childhood adversities*. Cambridge: Cambridge University Press.
Marmot, M., & Wilkinson, R. G. (Eds.). (1999). *Social determinants of health*. Oxford Oxford University Press.
Marmot, M., & Wilkinson, R. G. (Eds.). (2006). *Social determinants of health* (2nd ed.). Oxford: Oxford University Press.
Mason, B. (2014). *Unexpected business. Stories from Australian and Torres Strait Islander people with disabilities*. http://unfinishedbusiness.net.au/.
Masten, A. S. (2001). Ordinary magic: resilience processes in development. *American Psychologist, 56*, 227–238.
Mayes, R., & Llewellyn, G. (2012). Mothering differently: narratives of mothers with intellectual disability whose children have been compulsorily removed. *Journal of Intellectual & Developmental Disability, 37*, 121–130.
Mayes, R., Llewellyn, G., & McConnell, D. (2006). Misconception: the experience of pregnancy for women with intellectual disabilities. *Scandinavian Journal of Disability Research, 8*, 120–133.
Mayes, R., Llewellyn, G., & McConnell, D. (2011). "That's who I choose to be": the mother identity for women with intellectual disabilities. *Women's Studies International Forum, 34*, 112–120.
McMaugh, A. (2011). En/countering disablement in school life in Australia: children talk about peer relations and living with illness and disability. *Disability & Society, 26*, 853–866.
Mencap. (2007). *Death by indifference*. London: Mencap.
Mencap. (2012). *Death by indifference: 74 deaths and counting. A progress report 5 years on*. London: Mencap.
Michael, J. (2008). *Healthcare for all: Report of the independent inquiry into access to healthcare for people with learning disabilities*. London: Independent Inquiry into Access to Healthcare for People with Learning Disabilities.

Mikton, C., Maguire, H., & Shakespeare, T. (2014). A systematic review of the effectiveness of interventions to prevent and respond to violence against persons with disabilities. *Journal of Interpersonal Violence, 29*, 3207–3226.

Mitra, M., & Mouradian, V. E. (2014). Intimate partner violence in the relationships of men with disabilities in the United States: relative prevalence and health correlates. *Journal of Interpersonal Violence, 29*(17), 3150–3166.

Morin, D., Rivard, M., Crocker, A. G., Boursier, C. P., & Caron, J. (2013). Public attitudes towards intellectual disability: a multidimensional perspective. *Journal of Intellectual Disabilities Research, 57*, 279–292.

Murray, C. J. L., & Doren, B. (2013). Resilience and disability: concepts, examples, cautions and prospects. In M. L. Wehmeyer (Ed.), *The Oxford handbook of positive psychology and disability* (pp. 182–197). Oxford: Oxford University Press.

Naylor, P., Dawson, J., Emerson, E., & Tantam, D. (2011). Prevalence of bullying in secondary school by SEN type: analysis of combined NPD and LSYPE data files. In *End of award report to ESRC*. Swindon: ESRC.

Norwich, B., & Kelly, N. (2004). Pupils' views on inclusion: moderate learning difficulties and bullying in mainstream and special schools. *British Educational Research Journal, 30*, 43–65.

Office for Disability Issues. (2011). *Life opportunities survey: Wave one results, 2009/11*. London: Office for Disability Issues.

Okechukwu, C. A., Souza, K., Davis, K. D., & de Castro, A. B. (2014). Discrimination, harassment, abuse, and bullying in the workplace: contribution of workplace injustice to occupational health disparities. *American Journal of Iindustrial Medicine, 57*, 573–586.

Olofsson, N., Lindqvist, K., & Danielsson, I. (2014). Higher risk of violence exposure in men and women with physical or sensory disabilities: results from a public health survey. *Journal of Interpersonal Violence*. pii: 0886260514548585. [Epub ahead of print].

Parker, R., & Aggleton, P. (2003). HIV and AIDS -related stigma and discrimination: a conceptual framework and implications for action. *Social Science and Medicine, 57*, 13–24.

Peters, R. M. H., Dadun, Van Brakel, W. H., Zweekhorst, M. B. M., Damayanti, R., & Bunders, J. F. G. (2014). The cultural validation of two scales to assess social stigma in leprosy. *PLoS Neglected Tropic Diseases, 8*, e3274.

Pettigrew, T. F., & Tropp, L. R. (2006). A meta-analytic test of intergroup contact theory. *Journal of Personality & Social Psychology, 90*, 751–783.

Plummer, K. (2001). *Documents of life 2: An invitation to a critical humanism*. London: Sage.

Priest, N., Paradies, Y., Trenerry, B., Truong, M., Karlsen, S., & Kelly, Y. (2013). A systematic review of studies examining the relationship between reported racism and health and wellbeing for children and young people. *Social Science & Medicine, 95*, 115–127.

Public Health England. (2015). *The determinants of health inequalities experienced by children with learning disabilities*. London: Public Health England.

Reiter, S., Bryen, D. N., & Shachar, I. (2007). Adolescents with intellectual disabilities as victims of abuse. *Journal of Intellectual Disabilities, 11*, 371–387.

Robertson, J., Emerson, E., Baines, S., & Hatton, C. (2014). Obesity and health behaviours of British adults with self-reported intellectual impairments: cross sectional survey. *BMC Public Health, 14*, 219.

Rose, C. A., Forber-Pratt, A. J., Espelage, D. L., & Aragon, S. R. (2013). The influence of psychosocial factors on bullying involvement of students with disabilities. *Theory Into Practice, 52*, 272–279.

Roulstone, A., & Mason-Bish, H. (2012). *Disability, hate crime and violence*. Routledge.

Sapienza, J. K., & Masten, A. S. (2011). Understanding and promoting resilience in children and youth. *Current Opinion in Psychiatry, 24*, 267–273.

Scambler, S. (2012). Disabling conditions and disability theory. In N. Watson, A. Roulstone, & C. Thomas (Eds.), *Routledge handbook of disability studies* (pp. 136–150). London: Routledge.

Schmitt, M. S., Branscombe, N. R., Postmes, T., & Barcia, A. (2014). The consequences of perceived discrimination for psychological well-being: a meta-analytic review. *Psychological Bulletin, 140*, 921–948.

Scior, K. (2011). Public awareness, attitudes and beliefs regarding intellectual disability: a systematic review. *Research in Developmental Disabilities, 32*, 2164–2182.

Seccombe, K. (2002). "Beating the odds" versus "changing the odds": poverty, resilience, and family policy. *Journal of Marriage and Family, 64*, 384–394.

Seewooruttun, L., & Scior, K. (2014). Interventions aimed at increasing knowledge and improving attitudes towards people with intellectual disabilities among lay people. *Research in Developmental Disabilities, 35*, 3482–3495.

Sen, A. (2001). *Development as freedom*. Oxford: Oxford University Press.

Sentenac, M., Gavin, A., Gabhainn, S. N., Molcho, M., Due, P., & Ravens-Sieberer, U. (2013). Peer victimization and subjective health among students reporting disability or chronic illness in 11 western countries. *European Journal of Public Health, 23*, 421–426.

Sermrittirong, S., & van Brakel, W. H. (2014). Stigma in leprosy: concepts, causes and determinants. *Leprosy Review, 85*, 36–47.

Shakespeare, T. (2006). *Disability rights and wrongs*. Routledge.

Shakespeare, T. (2013). *Disability rights and wrongs revisited*. London: Routledge.

Sherry, M. (2010). *Disability hate crimes: Does anyone really hate disabled people?* Burlington: Ashgate.

Stainland, L. (2011). *Public perceptions of disabled people: Evidence from the British social attitudes survey 2009*. Sheffield: Office for Disability Issues.

Szivos-Bach, S. E. (1993). Social comparisons, stigma and mainstreaming: the self esteem of young adults with a mild mental handicap. *Mental Handicap Research, 6*, 217–236.

Taylor, S. J. (1995). Children's division is coming to take pictures: family life and parenting in a family with disabilities. In *The variety of community experience: Qualitative studies of family and community life* (pp. 23–46).

Thomas, C. (2007). *Sociologies of disability and illness. Contested ideas in disability studies and medical sociology*. Basingstoke: Palgrave Macmillan.

Thornicroft, G., Rose, D., & Kassam, A. (2007). Discrimination in health care against people with mental illness. *International Review of Psychiatry, 19*, 113–122.

Tipton, L. A., Christensen, L., & Blacher, J. (2013). Friendship quality in adolescents with and without an intellectual disability. *Journal of Applied Research in Intellectual Disabilities, 26*, 522–532.

Trent, J. W. (1994). *Inventing the feeble mind: A history of mental retardation in the United States*. Berkeley, CA: University of Calfornia Press.

Ungar, M. (2008). Resilience across cultures. *British Journal of Social Work, 38*, 218–235.

US Department of Health & Human Services. (2002a). *Closing the gap: A national blueprint to improve the health of persons with mental retardation*. Rockville, MD: US Department of Health and Human Services.

US Department of Health & Human Services. (2002b). *Report of the surgeon general's conference on health disparities and mental retardation*. Rockville: Closing the gap.

Watson, N., Thomas, C., & Roulstone, A. (2012). *The Routledge Companion to disability studies*. London: Routledge.

Wedgwood, N., Smith, L., Shuttleworth, R., & Llewellyn, G. (2013). An eye opening experience: a critical turning point in the life of a young woman with a severe visual impairment. *Journal of Social Inclusion, 4*(1), 5–23.

Weiss, M. G., Ramakrishna, J., & Somma, D. (2006). Health-related stigma: rethinking concepts and interventions. *Psychology, Health & Medicine, 11*, 277–287.

Wilkinson, R. G., & Pickett, K. E. (2009). *The spirit level: Why more equal societies almost always do better*. London: Penguin.
Williams, D. R., Yu, Y., Jackson, J. S., & Anderson, N. B. (1997). Racial differences in physical and mental health: socioeconomic status, stress, and discrimination. *Journal of Health Psychology, 2*, 335–351.
Wolfensberger, W. (1975). *The origin and nature of our institutional models*. Syracuse: Human Policy Press.
World Health Organization. (2008). *Closing the gap in a generation: Health equity through action on the social determinants of health*. Final report of the Commission on the Social Determinants of Health. Geneva: World Health Organization.
World Health Organization. (2011). *Rio political declaration on social determinants of health*. Geneva: World Health Organization. http://www.who.int/sdhconference/declaration/en/.
World Health Organization Regional Office for Europe. (2013). *Report on social determinants and the health divide in the WHO European Region: Final Report*. Copenhagen: World Health Organization Regional Office for Europe.
World Health Organization and World Bank. (2011). *World report on disability*. Malta: World Health Organization.

CHAPTER FOUR

Health Surveillance and People with Intellectual Disabilities

Chris Hatton[*,1], **Alexandra Bonardi**[§,¶], **Eric Emerson**[*,||], **Michael H. Fox**[#], **Gyles Glover**[**], **Gloria L. Krahn**[§§], **Hélène Ouellette-Kuntz**[¶¶,||||], **Sue Turner**[##]
[*]Centre for Disability Research, Lancaster University, Lancaster, Lancashire, UK
[§]Center for Developmental Disabilities Evaluation and Research (CDDER), E.K. Shriver Center, University of Massachusetts Medical School, Boston, MA, USA
[¶]Human Services Research Institute (HSRI), Cambridge, MA, USA
[||]Centre for Disability Research and Policy, University of Sydney, NSW, Australia
[#]National Center for Birth Defects and Developmental Disabilities, Centers for Disease Control and Prevention, Atlanta, GA, USA
[**]Learning Disabilities Team, Public Health England, UK
[§§]College of Public Health and Human Sciences, Oregon State University, Corvallis, OR, USA
[¶¶]Department of Public Health Sciences, Queen's University, Kingston, ON, Canada
[||||]Ongwanada, Kingston, ON, Canada
[##]National Development Team for Inclusion, Bath, UK
[1]Corresponding author: e-mail address: chris.hatton@lancaster.ac.uk

Contents

International Review of Research in Developmental Disabilities, Volume 48
ISSN 2211-6095
http://dx.doi.org/10.1016/bs.irrdd.2015.04.002

Abstract

In this chapter we use three case studies (from the USA, Canada, and England) to frame a discussion of key conceptual and methodological issues associated with health-surveillance programs for people with intellectual disabilities. These include the challenges associated with (1) identifying people with intellectual disabilities in administrative databases; (2) identifying people with intellectual disabilities in population-based surveys through data linkage and cognitive testing and self- or informant report; (3) sampling issues; (4) the use of specific intellectual disability surveys; and (5) challenges in measuring health. We conclude with a discussion of the relationship between health surveillance and health policy.

1. INTRODUCTION

The final report of the World Health Organization's Commission on the Social Determinants of Health made three overarching recommendations for achieving health equity (World Health Organization, 2008): (1) improve daily living conditions; (2) tackle the inequitable distribution of power, money, and resources; and (3) measure and understand the problem and assess the impact of action (World Health Organization, 2008). The third recommendation highlighted the critical importance of effective health surveillance systems for identifying the level and distribution of need, monitoring progress, and evaluating the impact of interventions.

More recently, there has been a growing awareness within the international public health community that achieving health equity will, in part, be dependent on addressing the inequities experienced by particular marginalized or vulnerable groups (World Health Organization, 2011; World Health Organization Regional Office for Europe, 2013). For example, Recommendation 2(c) of the World Health Organization's recent review of the health divide in Europe calls on countries to "take action to develop systems and processes within societies that are more sustainable, cohesive and inclusive, *focusing particularly on groups most severely affected by exclusionary processes*" (World Health Organization Regional Office for Europe, 2013). People with disabilities constitute one such group (World Health Organization and the World Bank, 2011), and within that wider group people with intellectual disabilities appear particularly vulnerable to both marginalization and poor health (Emerson & Hatton, 2014; Krahn & Fox, 2014; O'Hara, McCarthy, & Bouras, 2010; Taggart & Cousins, 2014).

Health surveillance systems typically utilize two forms of data: administrative data collected by health-care systems (e.g., records of hospital admissions) and surveys of the health of populations of interest. Unfortunately, people with intellectual disabilities are largely invisible within many existing health surveillance systems. For example, a review of 123 European health surveys reported that only 7 (8%) contained items that had the potential to identify respondents with intellectual disability (Linehan et al., 2009). Similarly, administrative data collected by health-care systems often fails to record that patients have intellectual disabilities. For example, in only 0.05% of hospital admissions in England are patients identified as having intellectual disability using the relevant ICD-10 codes (Glover & Emerson, 2012).

The importance of addressing the invisibility of people with intellectual disabilities in existing health surveillance systems is being increasingly recognized with a number of specific initiatives being undertaken in the UK, North America, and elsewhere (e.g., Centers for Disease Control and Prevention (CDC), 2011; Centers for Disease Control and Prevention (CDC) & National Center on Birth Defects and Developmental Disabilities (NCBDDD) Health Surveillance Work Group, 2009; Glover, Emerson, & Baines, 2011; Krahn, Fox, Campbell, Ramon, & Jesien, 2010; Lunsky, Klein-Geltink, & Yates, 2013). The aim of this chapter is to briefly review the nature of three of these initiatives and discuss some of the key methodological issues involved in developing health surveillance systems for people with intellectual disabilities.

2. CASE STUDIES

2.1 Improving Health and Lives: England's Specialist Public Health Observatory on Intellectual Disabilities for England

2.1.1 Background

The health inequities experienced by people with intellectual disabilities were established as a significant policy concern in England following the publication of two highly critical reports in 2006 and 2007. First, the UK's Disability Rights Commission undertook a formal investigation of the health inequalities experienced by people with intellectual disabilities and people with mental health problems (Disability Rights Commission, 2006). Its report, *Equal Treatment: Closing the Gap*, revealed "an inadequate response from the health services and governments ... to the major physical health inequalities experienced by some of the most socially excluded citizens: those with [intellectual] disabilities and/or mental health problems" (Disability Rights Commission, 2006, p. 3). The following year Mencap, a major charity supporting people with intellectual disabilities and their families in the UK, published *Death by Indifference*, a report that documented the untimely deaths of six people with intellectual disabilities while in NHS care (Mencap, 2007). Following this, the English government established an independent enquiry into the health of people with intellectual disabilities. One of the 10 recommendations in its final report *Healthcare for All* was that the English Department of Health should establish a national specialist Public Health Observatory on intellectual disability in order to "raise awareness in the health service of the risk of premature avoidable death, and to promote sustainable good practice in local assessment, management and evaluation of services" (Michael, 2008).

2.1.2 Description

The English Specialist Public Health Observatory on intellectual disabilities (given the name *Improving Health and Lives* [IHaL] by people with intellectual disabilities at Mencap; www.ihal.org.uk) was established in April 2010. It was formed of a consortium of three separate organizations: the North East Public Health Observatory (one of the 10 regional Public Health Observatories operating in England at the time), the Centre for Disability Research at Lancaster University (www.lancaster.ac.uk/cedr/index.php), and the National Development Team for Inclusion (NDTi, www.ndti.org.uk), a nongovernmental service development agency. In April 2013, IHaL was incorporated into the newly formed Public Health England (www.gov.uk/government/organisations/public-health-england), the agency responsible for national health promotion and protection activities.

IHaL has three main aims. First, to add to collective public health *knowledge and intelligence* through the analysis, collation, and dissemination of information that is relevant and important to the process of commissioning services that may have an impact on the health of people with intellectual disabilities. Second, to identify significant *gaps in information* and knowledge that could be addressed through viable changes to existing national and local data collection systems, and to work with relevant agencies to support the implementation of these changes. Third, to provide *advice and support* to enable people involved in commissioning at local and national level, service providers, and people who use services and their families to make better use of the information that is available. Examples of activities in each of these three areas are provided in the following subsections.

2.1.2.1 Public Health Knowledge and Intelligence

A number of specific projects have been undertaken to make better use of available data and knowledge and to disseminate this information through an open access web-based centralized information resource (www.ihal.org.uk), including the routine production of easy read summaries and factsheets. All reports cited in the following paragraphs are freely available at www.improvinghealthandlives.org.uk/publications. These projects include:

- The publication of an annual report that provides an overview of information collected across government departments, which is relevant to commissioning services for people with intellectual disabilities (Hatton et al., 2014).
- The development of *Local Health Profiles* for each Local Authority in England based on 23 indicators relating to the health and health care of people with intellectual disabilities (www.improvinghealthandlives.org.uk/profiles/).
- Monitoring progress and local variations in reducing health inequities (Christie, Baines, Hatton, Glover, & Turner, 2014), including by regularly monitoring the uptake of health checks by adults with intellectual disabilities (Glover, 2014).
- The publication of thematic reports on specific topics, such as the extent and causes of the health inequities experienced by people with intellectual disabilities (Emerson, Baines, Allerton, & Welch, 2012; Emerson, Hatton, Robertson, & Baines, 2015), the causes of death among people with intellectual disabilities (Glover & Ayub, 2010), the prevalence of intellectual disabilities and autism (Emerson & Baines, 2010), ways of collating and using data from local primary health-care information systems (Glover, Emerson, & Eccles, 2012), the regulation and inspection of services (Baines & Hatton, 2015), local strategic planning systems (Baines & Hatton, 2014), emergency hospital admissions for ambulatory

care sensitive conditions (Glover & Evison, 2013), and the nature of reasonable adjustments made by health services to take account of the specific needs of people with intellectual disabilities (Hatton, Roberts, & Baines, 2011).
- Undertaking systematic reviews of topics particularly relevant to reducing the health inequalities experienced by people with intellectual disabilities (Robertson, Hatton, Emerson, & Baines, 2014; Robertson, Hatton, Emerson, & Baines, 2015; Robertson, Roberts, Emerson, Turner, & Greig, 2011).
- Undertaking secondary analysis of data collected in existing health and social surveys to increase our understanding of the health inequities experienced by people with intellectual disabilities and the socioeconomic factors associated with these inequities (Emerson, Hatton, Robertson, & Baines, 2014; Emerson, Robertson, Baines, & Hatton, 2014; Robertson, Emerson, Baines, & Hatton, 2014).

2.1.2.2 Identifying and Addressing Gaps in Information and Knowledge

Soon after the establishment of IHaL, a review was undertaken of the extent to which existing health information systems could provide credible information on the health and health care of people with intellectual disabilities, and recommendations were made for strengthening the capacity of systems in this area (Glover et al., 2011). Following this, work commenced with the Health and Social Care Information Centre (www.hscic.gov.uk) to provide a new annual statistical extract from primary care information systems, which will describe at a local level, the demography (including mortality) of people with intellectual disabilities, the prevalence of important long-term illnesses, the management and outcomes of those illnesses, relevant aspects of health-related lifestyles and the advice provided for them, and the preventive health interventions people receive. In addition, new questions to better identify respondents with intellectual disabilities have been piloted in the annual Health Survey for England (www.hscic.gov.uk/healthsurveyengland) and the latest English Adult Psychiatric Morbidity Survey (www.natcen.ac.uk/our-research/research/adult-psychiatric-morbidity-survey/).

2.1.2.3 Advice and Support

Practical guidance has been provided on a number of high-priority issues to help local agencies make reasonable accommodations to their services to ensure equality of access and outcomes for people with intellectual disabilities. These reports have covered such areas as the provision of health checks and the development of health action plans in primary care services (Giraud-Saunders, Marriott, & Turner, 2015; Kenney, Turner, Glover, & Hatton, 2014), cancer screening (Turner, Emerson, Glover, & the Cornwall Cancer Screening Team, 2012), epilepsy services (Marriott & Robertson, 2014), dementia services (Kenney, 2013), diabetes services (Turner & Emerson, 2013; Turner, Kill, & Emerson, 2013), dentistry (Turner, Emerson, & Glover, 2012), end of life care (Giraud-Saunders, Marriott, Hatton, Turner, & Kenney, 2014), social care services (Turner & Robinson, 2014), and commissioning health services (Hoghton, Turner, & Hall, 2013). Specific guidance has been typically associated with free to attend learning events held around England and supported by a searchable database of examples of good practice in making reasonable accommodations in a range of health service settings (www.improvinghealthandlives.org.uk/adjustments/).

2.1.3 Barriers to/Facilitators of Impact

As a public health observatory, IHaL does not have the power to change policies or to direct changes in practice. Instead IHaL attempts to provide the best available evidence to inform changes to policies and practices that will improve the health of and reduce the health inequities experienced by people with intellectual disabilities. This inevitably involves working with others, within a much broader context of health and social policy and practice.

Unusually for a public health observatory in England, IHaL was set up as a consortium involving public health expertise, academic expertise in research with people with intellectual disabilities, and third sector expertise in policy analysis and practice implementation. This wide range of skills has been essential in producing credible products that combine public health data, research evidence, and policy/practice advice, with IHaL becoming a trusted source of information recognized by government (Department of Health, 2013). The consortium approach has also brought with it diverse networks that have improved the quality of intelligence gained by IHaL as well as providing multiple routes for sharing IHaL information and guidance. These networks (including public health specialists, policy makers across government, health and social care, academics, practitioners and service providers, nongovernmental organizations (NGOs), and self-advocacy and family groups) have been consistently supportive of the work of IHaL.

Although initially set up as a project largely independent of mainstream public health infrastructure, IHaL is now embedded within Public

Health England, a national executive agency of the health ministry (www.gov.uk/government/organisations/public-health-england). This signals the importance of the health inequities experienced by people with intellectual disabilities as a public health issue, brings extra credibility to the work of IHaL, and provides opportunities for IHaL's work to influence other parts of Public Health England, such as cancer screening programs and healthy living programs.

A major part of the work of IHaL has been simply to try and establish the health inequities experienced by people with intellectual disabilities as a public health issue, rather than an inevitable consequence of disability or an issue for which specialist intellectual disability services are wholly responsible. Due to a highly public scandal involving the mistreatment of people with intellectual disabilities in a specialist inpatient service, a continuing policy focus in England on the number and situation of people with intellectual disabilities in specialist inpatient services has been helpful in keeping people with intellectual disabilities high on the health policy agenda (Department of Health, 2012; NHS England, 2015). However, it has been important for IHaL to ensure that providing evidence to inform this agenda has not been at the expense of activities relating to a broader public health perspective.

The first 5 years of IHaL have also occurred within a time of radical changes to health-care commissioning structures/functions and the structure of health-care provision, with further changes toward the integration of health and social care likely (King's Fund, 2015). For IHaL, this has hindered activities designed to engage and establish ongoing productive working relationships with various aspects of health systems. Resource constraints on funding for health and social care in England have also created a difficult environment for encouraging innovation and the improved treatment of poorly served groups (Demos, 2013; Hastings, Bailey, Bramley, Gannon, & Watkins, 2015).

2.2 Expanding Public Health Surveillance for People with Intellectual and Developmental Disabilities in the USA

2.2.1 Background

Surveillance, as used in public health, refers to tracking incidence and prevalence of target populations as well as identifying characteristics that can influence or contribute to their health. A frequently cited figure for intellectual disabilities and developmental disabilities prevalence in the USA suggests about 4.6 million Americans live with these conditions, or about 1.5% of the population (Fujiura & Taylor, 2003; Larson et al., 2000, 2001). There are two primary reasons why this figure continues to be cited about 15 years after its initial publication. The first is that it uses data from a supplement to a well-respected, national health survey of people in the American population conducted in two phases during 1994–1995, but not administered since. Absent a more recent update, the Disability Supplement to the National Health Interview Survey (Centers for Disease Control and Prevention (CDC), 2015) continues to be used in spite of health and demographic changes in our general population since then that may call into question the accuracy of these prevalence numbers today. The second reason relates to the structural difficulties inherent in population-based surveillance for people with intellectual disabilities and developmental disabilities using other approaches. These include a lack of a widely agreed upon operational definition, and challenges in administering surveys for intellectual disabilities and developmental disabilities populations relating to communication, overcoming stigmatization, maintaining confidentiality, and assuring accurate proxy reporting.

In spite of these structural difficulties that may have prevented broad surveillance of intellectual disabilities and developmental disabilities, smaller studies have documented the health status and health needs of people with intellectual disabilities and developmental disabilities. As a group, adults with an intellectual disability experience substantially poorer health outcomes than adults without an intellectual disability (Anderson et al., 2013; Krahn & Fox, 2014; Krahn et al., 2010). Compared with peers of a similar age, they are more likely to live with complex health conditions (Krahn, Hammond, & Turner, 2006), have poorly managed chronic conditions such as epilepsy, hypertension, and obesity (e.g., Balogh, Brownell, Ouellette-Kuntz, & Colantonio, 2010; Bowley & Kerr, 2000; Janicki et al., 2002; McDermott et al., 2005), have limited access to appropriate health-care and health promotion programs (Hayden, Kim, & DePaepe, 2005), receive breast cancer and other health screenings at lower rates than those among the general population (Parish & Saville, 2006), have undetected vision and hearing loss (Woodhouse, Adler, & Duignan, 2004), and have mental health problems and potential overuse of psychotropic medications (Bartlo & Klein, 2011; Emerson, 2011; Holden & Gitlesen, 2004; Lewis, Lewis, Leake, King, & Lindemann, 2002).

With this expanding body of evidence pointing to health disparities, the need for ongoing and more sustainable health surveillance for intellectual disabilities and developmental disabilities populations in the USA has become clearer. But even as the need for this surveillance has become apparent, so have its technical challenges. Three primary issues on data collection efforts for intellectual disabilities and developmental disabilities populations are:

1. *Representativeness*: the difficulty of surveillance approaches to include a representative sample of adults with intellectual disabilities and developmental disabilities.
2. *Validity*: the lack of appropriate validated measures to identify people with intellectual disabilities and developmental disabilities.
3. *Methodology*: methodologies that prevent people with intellectual disabilities and developmental disabilities from participating.

Each of these issues can be found when examining more closely two current health assessment tools that capture data for intellectual disabilities and developmental disabilities.

2.2.2 Extant Health Assessment Tools

National Core Indicators (NCI: HSRI & NASDDDS, 2015). Begun as a state-level quality assurance tool, National Core Indicators collects indicator information from a sample of people receiving developmental disabilities services from state agencies. From an initial 13 participating states in 1997, the project has grown to include 42 US states (including DC) and 22 substate regions. It serves as a multistate database on outcomes for people who are receiving long-term services and has been used to explore programmatic and demographic issues affecting people with intellectual disabilities and their families. Reports examine the use of psychotropic medications, health behaviors, access to primary health care, and document significant disparities in health and health-care utilization compared to the general population (Havercamp & Scott, 2015). Its primary limitations are that its sample is limited to people receiving services, and questions persist about true randomization of sample and adequate standardization in data collection. Proxy reporting is allowed for a portion of the data collection to ensure people who are not able to self-report are included in the data set, but these proxy responses are not collected for subjective measures of quality of life as these have not been shown to be valid or reliable (Andresen, Vahle, & Lollar, 2001).

Special Olympics Healthy Athletes (Special Olympics International). Special Olympics has been collecting health screening data on its participating athletes for more than two decades, and its findings were the impetus for the 2002 Surgeon General's report on health needs of people with intellectual disability (US Department of Health & Human Services, 2002a, 2002b). Numerous studies have reported on Healthy Athletes screening data for oral health, obesity, vision, hearing, nutrition, and general fitness (Foley, Lloyd, & Temple, 2014; Horowitz, Kerker, Ownes, & Zigler, 2000; Lloyd, Foley, & Temple, 2014; Special Olympics, 2009). Limitations of this data set for population health surveillance are its limitation to Special Olympics athletes who volunteer to participate, and the lack of an individual identifier to reduce redundancies and allow longitudinal monitoring over successive screenings.

2.2.3 CDC Activities Associated with Expanding Surveillance for Intellectual Disabilities and Developmental Disabilities

The Centers for Disease Control and Prevention's (CDC) National Center on Birth Defects and Developmental Disabilities has played a major role in helping to expand understanding of health disparities associated with people with intellectual disabilities and developmental disabilities. Three meetings held between 2009 and 2011 attended by researchers, self-advocates, and policy experts became the springboard for a series of activities to promote intellectual disability surveillance (Figure 1). The term "intellectual disability" rather than "intellectual disabilities and developmental disabilities" was used throughout these meetings, but the discussions were generalizable to intellectual disabilities and developmental disabilities. The activities followed an action plan drafted at the second meeting and summarized in Krahn, Fox, Campbell, Ramon, and Jesien (2010). This plan included five steps, summarized as follows.

First was to define intellectual disabilities in ways that are clinically, functionally, and operationally valid, as well as determining the feasibility of incorporating this definition into activities identifying people across the full range of intellectual disabilities at the population level.

Second was to compile and synthesize a knowledge base of research, practices, policies, and procedures, including data sources and surveillance techniques that summarize our understanding of intellectual disabilities and the relationship of intellectual disabilities to health, community participation, and public health practice.

Third was to extend previous analyses of existing data sources to provide a more complete delineation of what is known about the health status of people with intellectual disabilities and identify gaps for enhanced surveillance. This meant using available data that might not be population based or standardized in terms of how intellectual disabilities is defined, but still

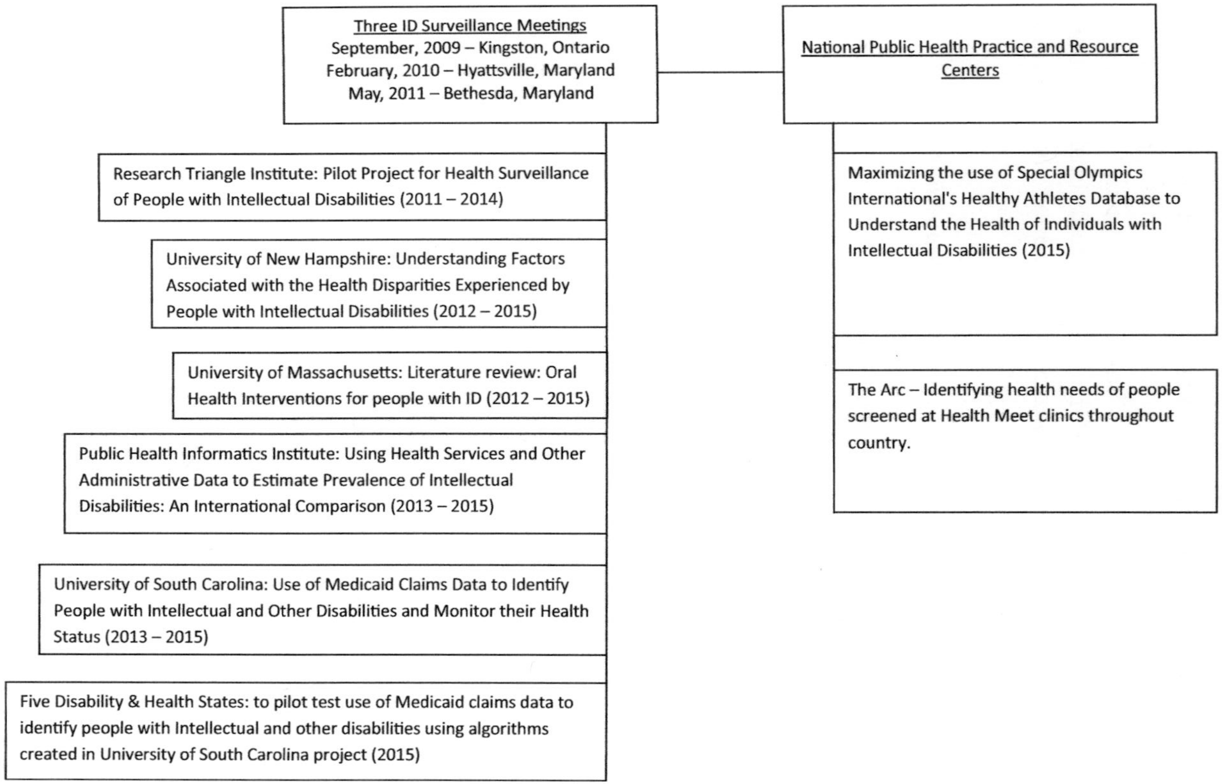

Figure 1 CDC activities to expand surveillance and reduce health disparities related to intellectual disabilities.

accounted for valid group comparisons (Courtney-Long, Stevens, Caraballo, Ramon, & Armour, 2014; Lloyd et al., 2014; Stevens, Courtney-Long, Gillespie, & Armour, 2014) and supplements other recent work that demonstrated disparities (Havercamp, Scandlin, & Roth, 2004; Havercamp & Scott, 2015; Krahn & Fox, 2014).

Fourth was to pilot state or regional demonstrations or to expand existing approaches to explore more comprehensive efforts on effective surveillance methodologies. Implicit was the need to link data from disparate sources to allow for improved understanding of the population with intellectual disabilities.

Finally, the intent was to develop sustainable approaches to expand surveillance. These might include conducting a national survey or using new surveillance tools applied to existing data that could provide reliable and valid surveillance in an ongoing and systematic manner in the USA. The promise of using administrative data sources such as Medicaid, Special Olympics, or National Core Indicators data makes this action step increasingly feasible.

CDC's efforts with partners since the three meetings have begun to address needs identified in each of the steps. Examples of completed and ongoing work are described in the following paragraphs.

A proposed definition of intellectual disabilities that can be operationalized for health surveillance resulted from a CDC partnership with the Association of University Centers on Disabilities (AUCD). CDC partnered with AUCD to develop *A Compendium of Health Data Sources for ID Surveillance* (CDDER—Center for Developmental Disabilities Evaluation and Research, 2011). It includes a review of national data sources that hold the potential for health surveillance in the adult population with intellectual disabilities, including the extent to which the population with intellectual disabilities can be identified. Data sources were identified and systematically reviewed to develop a ranking of data sources with high, moderate, and low potential to inform US surveillance of the health of the population with intellectual disabilities. Those data sources with a "high" potential have adequate capture of the population with intellectual disabilities and could be used for surveillance if the data collection methodology was modified, if sampling were adjusted, or if the data were linked to another administrative data set (CDDER—Center for Developmental Disabilities Evaluation and Research, 2011).

CDC is partnering with the Public Health Informatics Institute (PHII) to conduct a comparison of international studies that have used administrative data to study the prevalence of intellectual disabilities and associated health issues.

Studies linking national-level data sources and claims data to better understand the health and health needs of people with intellectual disabilities are currently underway in collaboration with the University of South Carolina.

CDC work with the Universities of South Carolina and New Hampshire is being conducted to develop algorithms to identify people with intellectual disabilities and developmental disabilities using administrative claims data (e.g., Medicaid). CDC is now partnering with AUCD to work with five States to pilot test use of the USC algorithms for Medicaid claims data to identify people with intellectual disabilities and developmental disabilities and to study the health of these populations. These efforts could have widespread application to improved surveillance.

CDC has also partnered with Research Triangle Institute (RTI) to identify the feasibility of developing pilot state intellectual disabilities and developmental disabilities surveillance systems.

CDC is partnering with the University of Massachusetts Medical School's Shriver Center to conduct a systematic review of oral health interventions that reduce oral health disparity in the population with intellectual disabilities, with the intent to inform future clinical and policy guidance.

Findings identified through improved and expanded surveillance of people with intellectual disabilities can be used to inform CDC's programmatic partnerships designed to improve the health of people with intellectual disabilities (e.g., Special Olympics and The Arc). Likewise, the work of these organizations provides critical insight into the health needs of this population that can help inform future surveillance efforts.

Table 1 summarizes works in progress from this stepwise approach to enhancing surveillance of the population with intellectual disabilities in the USA.

2.2.4 Summary

From the initial meeting in 2011 when 24 stakeholders grappled with the conundrum of *how* to conduct health surveillance on *what topics* for *which people* with intellectual disabilities to the present, substantial progress has been made in identifying the most difficult issues and working to identify potential solutions. Perhaps the greatest impact of this ongoing dialogue has been to better understand the problems so that achievable solutions are identified. Work to date has shown that no one data source effectively

Table 1 CDC Activities Associated with Efforts to Enhance Surveillance of Intellectual Disability: Action Steps and Expected Products

Steps/Plan	Selected Action Steps	Expected Products
1. Define ID ("who are we talking about?" "how do we identify them?")	Feasibility studies using different data sources	Proposed operational definition of ID
2. Compile and synthesize a knowledge base ("what do we know and what are the gaps?")	Systematic reviews of literature; international comparison of ID identification	Compendium of health data sources related to intellectual disability
3. Extend Past analyses of existing data sources that capture health information for people with an ID	Pilot study of administrative data analyses in South Carolina Pilot study of state-level data use for surveillance (RTI, 2013) Understanding factors associated with the health disparities experienced by people with intellectual disabilities using administrative data	Analysis of Medicaid data; systematic review of oral health interventions
4. Pilot state or regional demonstrations to expand surveillance	AUCD—pilot with five states (2015)	Proof of concept to determine if states can obtain and analyze Medicaid data
5. Develop sustainable approaches to expand surveillance	Build upon uses of administrative data to develop ongoing monitoring and tracking	Expanded health surveillance capacity for ID populations in the USA

AUCD, Association for University Centers; RTI, Research Triangle Institute, Inc.

captures both a representative sample of the population and health data for this population, so multiple data sources need to be utilized, including administrative data and national and state survey data. Data linkages hold promise as a powerful tool to maximize the coverage of any health surveillance system designed for this population.

The standard phrasing of questions and optional responses in most existing surveys can create a barrier for accurate responses from people with intellectual disabilities. Potential accommodations to enable people with intellectual disabilities to self-respond still need to be investigated (Chang & Krosnick, 2009), including interviews split into multiple, short sessions; alternative wording or communication strategies; and additional time to respond. Mixed-mode approaches may be useful for increasing response rates for people with disabilities while controlling costs. For example, interview protocols could include face-to-face meeting with the person with a disability and allows for telephonic follow-up with a proxy for a portion of the questions.

While self-response is always desirable and should be used as much as possible (Kaye, 2007; Stancliffe, 1999), assisted or proxy responses can facilitate the inclusion of a more representative sample of people with intellectual disabilities by including people who are not able to respond for themselves (Kaye, 2007).

In order to fully understand the health of people with intellectual disabilities, ongoing, improved surveillance is necessary. Ideally, it would include multiple approaches that identify and track children and adults across the life span, inclusive of both varying levels of disability and all types of living arrangements. These could include persons living with their families, independently, in community-based settings, and those living in nursing or facility-based settings, and be independent of where intellectual disabilities and developmental disabilities services occur. This surveillance system should provide a benchmark for assessing overall shifts in the number, demographics, and indicators of health of people with intellectual disabilities, accounting for this population's heterogeneity of conditions, experience of disability, and participation in public programs.

In the near term, expanded use of administrative data appears to offer the greatest promise for improving our understanding of the health of people with intellectual disabilities and developmental disabilities in the USA in ways that may be sustainable under general principles of uniformity, simplicity, and brevity that characterize successful surveillance systems (Wharton, Chorba, Vogt, Morse, & Buhler, 1990). The primary advantages of moving forward is building on existing systems in ways that align with many existing resources supporting service delivery, while being able to operationally define intellectual disabilities and developmental disabilities in ways that many people understand. The primary disadvantages include the limited information available from these resources (e.g., health behaviors, living arrangements, severity of symptoms over different life stages, and participation in or access to public programs). Working toward overcoming these remaining obstacles while expanding and refining the use of administrative data can continue to inform improvements in surveillance efforts for intellectual disabilities and developmental disabilities. With improved surveillance, the health needs of people with intellectual disabilities and developmental disabilities can be better identified and addressed.

2.3 Health-Care Access and Developmental Disabilities Research Program in Ontario, Canada

2.3.1 Background

In 2000, researchers in the field of intellectual and developmental disabilities in Canada recognizing the urgent need to develop training programs for health professionals who care for people with intellectual and developmental disabilities began meeting to formulate plans for action. Educators, practitioners, service providers, and researchers convened a national symposium in order to strategically address gaps in education on intellectual and developmental disabilities in the country. Among the priorities identified was the desirability of epidemiological data regarding intellectual and developmental disabilities collected consistently across all provinces and territories. It was felt that such data could help make the case for improved training and enhanced health-care provision.

Researchers undertook to address this need for evidence to influence policy development. The work resulted in a paper commissioned by the Canadian Institutes of Health Research (CIHR) for the International Think Tank on Reducing Health Disparities and Promoting Equity for Vulnerable Populations held in Ottawa, Canada (2003) and the recognition of individuals with intellectual and developmental disabilities as one of several key groups of Canadians experiencing health disparities (Ouellette-Kuntz et al., 2005). An International Association for the Scientific Study of Intellectual and Developmental Disabilities Health Special Interest Research Group roundtable subsequently held in Kingston, Ontario (2009) highlighted the importance of stakeholder engagement in knowledge creation and exchange to facilitate impact (Ouellette-Kuntz et al., 2010).

Coincidentally, the new millennium also prompted a series of consultations to identify research themes for future applied health services and policy research in Canada, generally. The process culminated with the publication of *Listening for Directions III* (Law, Flood, Gagnon, & on behalf of the Listening for Direction III partners, 2008). Eleven themes emerged as priorities. Theme 3 emphasized the need to better manage and integrate data sets across silos, and theme 11 recognized the intersectoral challenges inherent in identifying and addressing the health needs of vulnerable populations.

In Canada, supports for persons with intellectual and developmental disabilities fall under a myriad of government programs housed in diverse departments depending on the province since health, education, and social care are largely under provincial jurisdiction. Data required for conducting population-based health research on intellectual and developmental disabilities are housed within multiple government sectors and typically not shared. This "silo-ing" of health information impedes policy development for this vulnerable group. The way forward to health surveillance among persons with intellectual and developmental disabilities in Canada requires first developing the capacity for the collection, analysis, and use of population-based data within provinces.

Prior to 2010, only the province of Manitoba had used population-based administrative data to report on the health and health-care utilization of persons with intellectual and developmental disabilities (Balogh et al., 2010; Shooshtari et al., in press) and to describe the prevalence of intellectual and developmental disabilities (Ouellette-Kuntz et al., 2009). This capacity in Manitoba related to the well-established population health research repository in that province (Roos, Roos, Brownell, & Fuller, 2010).

Recognizing that understanding the health needs of this vulnerable population in Ontario (the most populous province of the country) was hampered by a lack of access to population-based health data, a group of researchers responded to a call for proposals from the CIHR to establish a partnership for health system improvement (http://webapps.cihr-irsc.gc.ca/cfdd/db_results_submit) with a focus on the primary care of adults with intellectual and developmental disabilities in the province. In 2010, the group was successful and a partnership was established among researchers, clinicians, service providers, and policy makers in both health and social services as a means of better understanding the health care provided to adults with intellectual and developmental disabilities in Ontario. The first goal was to create and evaluate population-based data sets containing health information about the population. Partners agreed that the priority was to describe primary-care-related health-care utilization patterns of adults with intellectual and developmental disabilities in the province compared to other adults in Ontario and to evaluate the extent to which the Ontario health system is providing guideline-recommended primary care to adults with intellectual and developmental disabilities.

The proposed research was timely, as it coincided with a period of significant system change across two critical government ministries responsible for the delivery of health services to adults with intellectual and developmental disabilities in Ontario: the Ministry of Health and Long-term Care (MOHLTC) and the Ministry of Community and Social Services (MCSS). The MOHLTC had launched primary care renewal in the province which included coordinated high-quality health care available around the clock that focuses on prevention, health promotion, and chronic disease management, guided by local population health indicators. At MCSS, a transformation of services governed by new legislation was guiding ways of delivering care to adults with intellectual and developmental disabilities. The vision was to create a fair, accessible, and sustainable community-based service system that would promote independence, dignity, and self-reliance for people with intellectual and developmental disabilities and their families. March 2009 marked the closure of the three remaining institutions for persons with intellectual and developmental disabilities in Ontario, with the understanding that, moving forward, all individuals with intellectual and developmental disabilities would access health services in their local communities, like everyone else. Given the increased risk of health problems faced by individuals with intellectual and developmental disabilities, there was an urgent need to make information related to their health care available to researchers and government decision makers to monitor changes in this evolving policy context.

Envisioning a broader scope than simply primary care, the partnership chose to name the program "Health Care Access Research and Developmental Disabilities (H-CARDD)".

2.3.2 Description

The overall goal of the H-CARDD program is to monitor and improve the health and health care of Ontarians with intellectual and developmental disabilities through engagement with researchers, policy makers, health-care planners, clinicians, adults with intellectual and developmental disabilities, and caregivers.

The partnership was initially a 3-year initiative funded through a CIHR Partnerships for Health System Improvement (PHSI) grant (2010–2013) with contributions from the Ontario Ministry of Community and Social Services, Surrey Place Centre (an agency supporting persons with intellectual and developmental disabilities), and the Ontario MOHLTC. The program has since received funding from the Ontario MOHLTC's Health Systems Research Fund (2013–2016) and a second CHIR PHSI grant (2013–2016). Both of these funding streams require contributions from partners, which the program has secured. H-CARDD's current partners include four government ministries, six hospitals, six universities, and several community organizations.

In its first phase (2010–2013), the program focused its efforts on primary health care. The first task was to link information from across government sectors in order to study as representative a group of adults with intellectual and developmental disabilities as possible from across Ontario. Through linking information across different government sectors it is now possible to study how over 66,000 adults with intellectual and developmental disabilities use health care (Lin et al., 2014). Since creating this cohort, H-CARDD has explored the quality of primary care for adults with intellectual and developmental disabilities in Ontario, based on Canadian guidelines related to this population. With its partners and knowledge users H-CARDD has identified some critical gaps in health-care services and some priority groups to study further.

The findings of this first research phase have been shared in a comprehensive report (Lunsky et al., 2013), presented through easy to understand summaries and a video available online (https://www.porticonetwork.ca/web/hcardd/program/atlas-on-primary-care), and published in peer-reviewed journals. Under the broad heading of primary care, this work has included examination of uptake of the periodic health examination (Lunsky, Balogh, Sullivan, & Jaakkimainen, 2014; Ouellette-Kuntz, Cobigo, Balogh, Wilton, & Lunsky, 2015 online), diabetes prevalence and preventable hospital admissions (Balogh, Lake, Lin, Wilton, & Lunsky, 2015), cancer screening (Cobigo et al., 2013; Ouellette-Kuntz et al., 2015 online; Ouellette-Kuntz, Coo, Cobigo, & Wilton, 2015), and polypharmacy (Stortz, Lake, Cobigo, Ouellette-Kuntz, & Lunsky, 2014).

The ongoing work of H-CARDD is aligned with recent provincial policy including the Ontario Women's Health Framework (2011), Open Minds, Healthy Minds: Ontario's Comprehensive Mental Health and Addictions Strategy (Ministry of Health and Long-Term Care and Ministry of Community and Social Services, 2011), the Aging at Home Strategy (Government of Ontario, 2012), and the Joint Policy Guideline for the

Provision of Community Mental Health and Developmental Services for Adults with a Dual Diagnosis (Ministry of Health and Long-Term Care and Ministry of Community and Social Services, 2008).

Topics examined in the second phase include women's health (Brown, Cobigo, Lunsky, Wilton, & Vigod, in press), addiction and mental health problems, aging (Ouellette-Kuntz, Martin, & McKenzie, 2015), and the transition to adulthood.

In addition, H-CARDD is conducting research relevant to program and policy questions that matter to those seeking knowledge about health-care planning. Under the current funding model, H-CARDD devotes a significant proportion of resources to responding to research questions posed by knowledge users (policy makers or program administrators). To date, these have included questions related to use of health care and medication use among adults living in group homes, quality care in the emergency department, substance use, aging profiles, cerebral palsy, complex needs, and young adults with autism spectrum disorder. Summaries of these reports are available at https://www.porticonetwork.ca/web/hcardd/kte/applied-health-research-questions/reports.

2.3.3 Barriers to/Facilitators of Impact

While H-CARDD is not a public health authority, it makes a unique contribution to health surveillance among adults with intellectual and developmental disabilities by providing the expertise (through university-appointed faculty members) for data linkage and analysis. Many of these academics are experts in the field of intellectual and developmental disabilities with strong collaborations with local stakeholders across four regions of the province. They facilitate the involvement of trainees in the program thereby enhancing capacity for health research, and surveillance specifically, in the field of intellectual and developmental disabilities. Of note, the academics leading the research are paid by their respective academic institutions/universities and not the H-CARDD program's grants.

H-CARDD started out with the goal of linking data, but it has done much more. It has resulted in meaningful links among sectors essential to advancing the health and well-being of persons with intellectual and developmental disabilities in Ontario. Not only have researchers partnered with knowledge users (policy makers, program managers, and clinicians), but also H-CARDD has linked health and social services sectors enhancing understanding of their respective and dependent roles like never before. This collaboration offers promise for the future.

Additional data linkages would further enhance the program's impact. In particular, data about children with intellectual and developmental disabilities are needed to better project needs and understand the impact of health promotion and prevention in intellectual and developmental disabilities. Since the Ministry of Children and Youth Services and the Ministry of Education have joined the H-CARDD for the second phase of the partnership, the dialogue necessary for enhanced data linkage has begun.

As H-CARDD is funded through research grants and contributions from partners, researchers must continually apply for funds in a very competitive environment to continue the work. As such, the program's future is unknown. After only 5 years, much has been achieved but much more is yet to be done. Furthermore, H-CARDD offers a model for other provinces and territories in Canada to emulate.

3. METHODOLOGICAL CHALLENGES

3.1 Identifying People with Intellectual Disabilities in Administrative Databases

Data extracted from a range of administrative systems associated with health and health care can provide important information on population health. These include data from such diverse sources as certification of causes of death, registration, and use of primary care services, hospital admissions, and health-care insurance-based funding systems.

A critical determinant of the validity of such data for health surveillance of people with intellectual disabilities is the accuracy of with which people with intellectual disabilities are identified in health-related administrative data sets. Unfortunately, this can often be problematic. For example, the presence of intellectual disability is supposed to be recorded (using ICD-10 codes) for all hospital episodes in England. However, only 0.05% of hospital episodes use the appropriate ICD-10 codes (F70—F799), although the code "F819" ("Developmental disorder of scholastic skills, unspecified") is used much more frequently (0.23% of episodes), apparently as an alternative given the pejorative terminology used in ICD-10 to describe intellectual disability ("mental retardation") (Glover & Emerson, 2012). Tracking individuals over time in such systems can increase the identification rate by identifying people who have ever been identified as having intellectual disability. However, in English Hospital Episode Statistics this information is only recorded in 27% of their hospital admissions (Glover & Emerson, 2012).

Coding accuracy is likely to vary as a function of a number of factors (Glover & Emerson, 2012; Iezzoni, 2002; Lin et al., 2014). These include the ease of identification of intellectual disability or particular conditions associated with intellectual disability (e.g., Down syndrome); professional awareness of these conditions; the nature and duration of the health-care contact; and the extent to which the identification of intellectual disability is considered to result in practical benefits to either the health-care system or the individual. All of these factors are likely to change over time and vary across jurisdictions, leading at times to substantial difficulty in untangling the underlying causes of changes in administrative prevalence rates (e.g., Elsabbagh et al., 2012).

Issues of coding accuracy are likely to be particularly problematic in identifying people with less severe intellectual disability in generic administrative data sets (i.e., those not collected by developmental disability agencies). For example, the administrative age-specific prevalence of intellectual disability in England drops from about 40–50 per 1000 (based on educational records of children) to 6–7 per 1000 (based on primary care health records of younger adults) (Emerson & Glover, 2012). What is particularly notable in these data is that the administrative age-specific prevalence for younger adults is very similar to the administrative age-specific prevalence of severe intellectual disability among children. It is inconceivable that the marked drop in prevalence in early adulthood reflects a change in true prevalence. More likely, this "transition cliff" in administrative prevalence reflects the marked under-identification of adults with less severe intellectual disabilities in primary care health records (Kiely, 1987; National Center on Birth Defects and Developmental Disabilities, 2010). Given that adults with less severe intellectual disabilities may be ineligible for disability services or may not wish to be identified as being disabled, the under-identification of adults with less severe intellectual disabilities is also likely in administrative data sets collected by developmental disability agencies. As such, they become part of the "hidden majority" of adults with mild intellectual disability who are largely invisible in administrative data systems (Emerson, 2011; Tymchuk, Lakin, & Luckasson, 2001).

One partial solution to the problems associated with identification is the use of data linkage to extract a composite data set from multiple administrative information systems (e.g., Leonard et al., 2013; Lin et al., 2014). Given that educational records of intellectual disability are generally considered the most comprehensive, the linkage to educational records over a sufficient period of time (e.g., Leonard et al., 2013) has the potential for addressing the under-identification of people with mild intellectual disabilities, at least in the younger adult age range. While data linkage is not without its difficulties (cf., Lin et al., 2013, 2014), it clearly has the potential to address some of the biases in identification evident in particular data systems.

3.2 Identifying People with Intellectual Disabilities in Population-Based Surveys

Repeated cross-sectional surveys of the health of populations and exposure to health risks among populations provide one of the main foundations of many health surveillance systems. However, as noted in the introduction, people with intellectual disabilities are rarely identifiable in existing health surveys (Fujiura, Rutkowski-Kmitta, & Owen, 2010; Linehan et al., 2009). Three approaches for improving the identification of respondents with intellectual disabilities are considered in the following subsections: (1) data linkage to administrative data sets, (2) classification based on cognitive and/or psychological testing, and (3) self- or informant report.

3.2.1 Data Linkage

While a rarity at present, there is a growing trend to link (with consent) survey data to administrative data held by public agencies. In the UK, for example, three longitudinal surveys (the Longitudinal Study of Young People in England, the Millennium Cohort Study, and child data from Understanding Society) have been linked to information held by the English Department for Education on whether the child has been identified through educational systems as having a special educational need associated with intellectual or developmental disability. This facility has enabled researchers to investigate the association between intellectual disability and antisocial behavior (Emerson & Halpin, 2013) and peer victimization (Naylor, Dawson, Emerson, & Tantam, 2011). While we are not aware of examples of data linkage being used to identify participants with intellectual disability in recurring cross-sectional health surveys, such a facility is likely to become more viable in the future given the increasing focus in many countries of the possible benefits arising from data linkage (Hodapp, Goldman, & Urbano, 2013).

3.2.2 Cognitive Testing

Child cognitive development is a key outcome of interest in most large-scale birth-cohort and child-development studies. As such, they typically involve repeated cognitive testing of child participants. Most studies include sample weights to ensure that data can be analyzed in a manner that is representative of the population under study. As such, it is possible to identify children with intellectual disability as those scoring two standard deviations below the weighted sample mean on test results. This approach has been used by researchers to investigate the association between intellectual disability and obesity, child health behaviors and child physical, mental and behavioral health (Emerson et al., 2015). While such an approach is sufficiently robust to identify children with intellectual disability according to ICD-10 criteria, it is insufficient by itself to identify children with intellectual disability by DSM-IV or American Association on Intellectual and Developmental Disabilities criteria (Einfeld & Emerson, 2008). However, it may be possible to combine the results of cognitive testing with survey items indicative of deficits in adaptive behaviors in order to approximate meeting the latter criteria.

More recently, major household panel studies in the UK and Australia have undertaken cognitive testing of all adult respondents. As above, this opens up the opportunity for identifying adult respondents who are performing in the intellectually disabled range of intellectual functioning. Such surveys do not contain direct information on whether any evidence of impaired intellectual functioning originated in childhood. They do, however, usually contain relevant (if indirect) information on educational attainment during childhood. Combining low assessed cognitive performance with evidence of very low educational attainment in childhood has been used to identify adult respondents who may have intellectual disability and examine the association between intellectual disability and self-rated health (Emerson, Hatton et al., 2014).

A critical consideration in the use of cognitive test results to identify respondents with potential intellectual disability is the likely association between the tests employed and validated measures of general intelligence. This is particularly relevant as, due to time constraints, both child and adult surveys typically use either selected subtests of validated measures of general intelligence or brief measures developed specifically for survey use whose association with validated measures of general intelligence is unknown. One approach used in such instances is to use principal components analysis to extract the first component from the tests used as an estimate of general intelligence (Emerson, Hatton et al., 2014; Jones & Schoon, 2008).

3.2.3 Self- or Informant Report

Child-focused surveys that do not involve either data linkage or cognitive testing will often collect parental reports of the presence of child impairments or disabilities or receipt of professional diagnosis or classification associated with intellectual or developmental disabilities. Relatively little is currently known about the validity of informant responses to these types of questions and about the extent to which accuracy of informant reports may be moderated by potentially important contextual factors. The available evidence suggests, however, that parental report about developmental concerns should be treated with considerable caution, given its low sensitivity and the strong association between increased false-negative reporting and higher socioeconomic position (Emerson, Felce, & Stancliffe, 2013).

The identification of adults with intellectual disability through self-report in large-scale surveys is problematic, although not impossible (see, e.g., Larson et al., 2001). An increasing number of surveys collect information on whether adult respondents have a disability and, if so, on the type(s) of impairment(s) associated with the disability. For example, the legislatively mandated development of standard disability identifier questions for use in public health surveys in the USA includes the question: "Because of a physical, mental or emotional condition, do you have serious difficulty concentrating, remembering or making decisions?" (Madans, Loeb, & Altman, 2011). The harmonized question set on impairments developed in the UK contains in response to the question "Do any of these conditions or illnesses affect you in any of the following areas?" the option "Learning or understanding or concentrating" (Office for National Statistics, 2011). While such questions may capture persons with intellectual disabilities, they will not distinguish intellectual disabilities from other conditions such as dementia, traumatic brain injury, or mental health problems.

It is, however, sometimes possible to combine responses to such items with other information contained within the survey (e.g., very low educational attainment and difficulties with literacy and numeracy) within restricted age ranges (e.g., 18—49) to operationally identify a subgroup of people who may have intellectual disabilities (e.g., Hindmarsh, Llewellyn, & Emerson, 2014; Robertson, Emerson et al., 2014). It is important, however, to test the face validity of such approaches by examining the extent to which the observed prevalence of intellectual disability varies in the expected manner in relation to gender (higher among men), age (steady decline with age), and socioeconomic position (higher among participants with lower socioeconomic position).

3.2.4 Sampling Issues

Even where identification is possible, the resulting data may be of questionable value on two counts. First, the sampling frame for most surveys used for health surveillance is based on general households. While this ensures coverage of the vast majority of the population, it excludes people who are either homeless or living in some form of institutional arrangement. While there is no reliable information on the extent of homelessness among people with intellectual disabilities, it is clear that a significant proportion of adults with intellectual disabilities who are known to services live in supported accommodation arrangements, some of which are likely to be excluded from samples of general households (Emerson et al., 2013; Krahn & Fox, 2014).

Second, we are not aware of any surveys used for health surveillance that make any reasonable accommodations to either the consent or interview procedure for participants with cognitive impairments, thus depriving many people with intellectual disabilities of the opportunity to participate. For example, while the English Health Survey for England does contain an item to identify respondents with intellectual disabilities the ascertained prevalence rate is less than 0.3% (Glover et al., 2011), much lower than expected rates (Maulik, Mascarenhas, Mathers, Dua, & Saxena, 2011).

3.3 Specific Intellectual Disability Surveys

Given the challenges involved in recruiting people with intellectual disability to and identifying them in population-based health surveys and identifying them in administrative data systems, consideration may be given to supplementing the information from these sources with data from intellectual-disability-specific surveys. Such an approach is often used within public health surveillance to better understand the health needs and status of hard to survey populations or low-prevalence populations (e.g., Jackson et al., 2004; Nazroo, 1998; Wilper et al., 2009). The majority of surveys undertaken on the health of people with intellectual disabilities use small underpowered samples with a very high risk of bias (Emerson & Hatton, 2014), as such the information generated is of little value in the context of health surveillance. There are, however, a small number of intellectual-disability-specific surveys that have employed more robust sampling strategies and have generated information on the health of people with intellectual disabilities that could potentially be used in health surveillance systems (Burke, McCallion, & McCarron, 2014; Emerson, Malam, Davies, & Spencer, 2005; Malam, Emerson, & Davies, 2014; National Core Indicators, 2014; Stancliffe et al., 2011, 2012). Typically, these have used sampling frames based on administrative databases of known users of intellectual disability services and have the potential to collect information comparable to that collected in population-based surveys. As such, they can help to redress some of the problems associated with a reliance on information generated through the use of general household sampling frames. Occasionally, they have also been supplemented by general household sampling methods (e.g., Emerson et al., 2005; Malam et al., 2014).

The main drawback associated with utilizing intellectual-disability-specific surveys in health surveillance is the high cost involved in commissioning and undertaking new data collections, a particular problem in times of fiscal restraint. As a result, the frequency of data collection is likely to be low and the surveys highly vulnerable to being terminated. One notable exception is the US's National Core Indicators project, an annual system of data collection that currently involves the participation of 42 states (http://www.nationalcoreindicators.org/). While the health data collected in the National Core Indicators project are limited, it has proven of value in monitoring such issues as obesity (Stancliffe et al., 2011) and the health-care needs and experiences of specific subpopulations of people with intellectual disabilities (Stancliffe et al., 2012).

3.4 Challenges in Measuring Health

An individual's capacity to monitor, reflect on, and report on aspects of their health plays a crucial role in many approaches to health measurement. Many diagnoses (especially of mental health disorders) require self-report information. Some aspects of health (e.g., pain) are only accessible through self-report, and many health measurement scales and questionnaires are dependent on self-report (McDowell, 2006). This gives rise to some challenges and dilemmas in assessing the health of people with intellectual disabilities (Fujiura, 2012), especially if we wish to make comparisons between the health of people with intellectual disabilities and their nondisabled peers. Emerson and Hatton (2014) identify four questions that need to be kept in mind when evaluating how trustworthy information based on self-report measures for people with intellectual disabilities:

1. "To what extent can people with intellectual disabilities use self-report measures that have been developed for the general population?
2. What impact does making 'reasonable adjustments' (e.g., simplified wording) to standard self-report measures or diagnostic systems to maximise the participation of people with intellectual disabilities have on the validity of the information collected?
3. If a person cannot self-report, does proxy reporting (e.g., carer report) represent a valid alternative?
4. If a person cannot self-report, do we need to change diagnostic criteria?" (Emerson & Hatton, 2014, p. 47)

There exists an extensive literature on the difficulties people with intellectual disabilities may have in self-reporting on aspects of their experience, including their health, and of the specific risks for acquiescent responding (agreeing with the question) and response bias (e.g., using just the extreme points of response scales) (e.g., Finlay & Lyons, 2001; Fujiura, 2012; Hartley & MacLean, 2006; Prosser & Bromley, 2012). What remains unclear, however, is how common these difficulties are in representative population-based samples of people with intellectual disabilities. Emerson and Hatton (2014), for example, report that while the majority of adults with intellectual disabilities not in contact with intellectual disability services were considered to reliably self-report on their general health status, only a minority of those in contact with intellectual disability services were able to do so (apart from the 5% of those in contact with intellectual disability services who were living independently) (data extracted from Emerson et al., 2005). Similarly, high rates of ability to self-report have been observed in population-based samples of adolescents with intellectual disability (Emerson, 2005).

One response to the low rates of self-report among people with more severe intellectual disability has been to make "reasonable accommodations" to the self-report process (e.g., simplified wording, use of pictorial cues, and personal support in reading and answering the question) (e.g., Finlay & Lyons, 2001; Fujiura, 2012; Hartley & MacLean, 2006; Hatton & Taylor, 2013; Malam et al., 2014; Prosser & Bromley, 2012). While such adjustments are typically successful in increasing response rates, it is unclear how comparable the resulting information may be with that produced by the unaltered standardized scale.

An enduring concern with assessing the health and well-being of people with intellectual disabilities is the validity and acceptability of collecting information from proxy respondents (typically paid or unpaid carers) when the person himself/herself does not have the capacity to answer. The research that has been undertaken in this area has primarily focused on two areas: (1) evaluating the degree of agreement between people with intellectual disabilities and carers and (2) evaluating the degree of agreement between carer report and professional evaluation of health status (Emerson et al., 2013).

For obvious reasons it is only possible to evaluate the degree of agreement between people with intellectual disabilities and carers if both parties are capable of self-reporting and as Stancliffe has commented, "it remains an open question as to whether findings of agreement between proxies and self-reports from verbal individuals can be generalized to non-verbal people with more profound intellectual disability who cannot respond for themselves" (Stancliffe, 2000). Nevertheless, this body of research has highlighted the variable and at times very poor degree of agreement between people with intellectual disabilities and carers, especially for reports of internal states and feelings (Cummins, 2002; Perry, 2004; Stancliffe, 2000). For example, Turk and colleagues compared self-report and carers' responses to a simple health checklist for 59 adults with intellectual disabilities (Turk, Khattran, Kerry, Corney, & Painter, 2012). They reported good agreement for two items (epilepsy and asthma), moderate agreement for five items (ear problems, eye problems, weight problems, skin problems, and allergies) and poor agreement for the remaining nine items (including depression, anxiety, headache/migraine, dental problems). There is also a small body of evidence that suggests that carers of people with intellectual disabilities may perceive the person they care for to be healthier than suggested by the results of medical examinations (Beange, McElduff, & Baker, 1995; Wilson & Haire, 1990). Clearly, proxy responses are imperfect substitutes for self-report and should be used with considerable caution.

4. CONCLUSIONS: FROM HEALTH SURVEILLANCE TO POLICY IMPACT?

Clearly, health surveillance programs have been designed to improve the evidence base concerning the health of people with intellectual and developmental disabilities. How might this evidence have an impact on policy, practice, and ultimately the health of people with intellectual and developmental disabilities? Perhaps implicitly, health surveillance programs have aimed to provide the essentials of "evidence-based public health," outlined by Killoran and Kelly (2010) as comprising:

1. *Conceptual plausibility*, that is, is there a clear understanding of the causal pathways defining which factors are important causally and what the potential is for interventions.
2. Using different types of evidence to determine what works for whom in what circumstances.
3. Using the evidence to produce practical guidance for policy and practice, taking into account any likely ethical issues and social values, and understanding what factors will be necessary for local implementation.
4. Making this guidance relevant to governance mechanisms, and engaging with these mechanisms to integrate evidence-based guidance within policy.

5. Advancing policies and interventions that are (cost-) effective, and directing research and evaluation resources to gaps in the evidence base.

However, the path from evidence to policy is likely to be more complex than this rational, linear approach would suggest. In an analysis of the relationship between public health evidence and the formation of public health policy across the four parts of the United Kingdom (England, Northern Ireland, Scotland, and Wales), Smith (2013) suggests that "robust" evidence alone (on any criteria) does not guarantee passage into policy. Instead, evidence firstly needs to become an "idea" that can fit within prevalent "institutional ideas," the fundamental and largely unquestioned assumptions made by politicians and policy makers. Regarding health, within the UK for at least the past 35 years Smith (2013) suggests two major "institutional ideas" with which public health evidence/ideas would need to be consistent to have any chance of becoming policy:

1. A medical model of health, where good health is assumed to be the norm from which ill health deviates, health is the responsibility of individuals and medical/health interventions are the solution.
2. Economic growth being the primary objective of all policy (not just policies that are clearly "economic" in focus).

Furthermore, even if the public health idea is consistent with these broad institutional ideas, Smith (2013) suggests that there are three major "policy facilitators" that increase the chances of an idea being taken up and implemented:

1. Presenting a positive policy alternative, rather than just a critique of current arrangements.
2. Building a broad coalition (e.g., academics, politicians, policy champions, NGOs, journalists, and think tanks) with an agreed idea and a specific program to support the implementation of that idea.
3. Having an idea that can be implemented within an existing institutional structure (such as a health service), rather than an idea that requires cutting across or changing existing institutional structures for it to be implemented.

In Smith's (2013) analysis, tobacco control is a case study of public health evidence making a "successful" transition into policy and practice, with fairly recent measures in the UK including increased investment in smoking cessation interventions, increases in taxes on tobacco, and a smoking ban in public places. Backed by strong evidence of clear "medical" causal links from smoking to poor health and early death, an economic case was made for the impact of smoking (including passive smoking) on economic productivity and increased usage of health services. This was promoted by a broad coalition with a clear and limited set of agreed goals, a clear set of proposed policy alternatives, and clear institutional "homes" to implement/enforce these measures (the health service for smoking cessation interventions, the treasury for increasing taxes, and local government for enforcing the smoking ban). However, even in this "successful" case study, Smith (2013) notes that elements of the tobacco control evidence fitting less easily within these institutional ideas (e.g., the socioeconomic determinants of taking up smoking in the first place) have not been implemented—Smith calls this, "flexing" the idea to fit institutional ideas and structures.

In contrast, Smith (2013) discusses the program of research on health inequalities, which despite a robust and consistent evidence base and some mention in government documents has led (in the UK, at least) to remarkably little policy change and implementation. Smith (2013) suggests that, to date, the health inequalities evidence is a direct challenge to the medical model of health, is only beginning to construct an economic case, has largely not moved beyond a critique of existing arrangements to presenting positive policy alternatives, has not constructed a united coalition with a small number of agreed goals, and requires large-scale and coordinated changes to a wide range of institutional structures—Smith (2013) calls this a "critical" idea that is unlikely to translate into major policy changes.

This framework could be useful in understanding health surveillance programs concerning people with intellectual and developmental disabilities, particularly in asking questions about the possibilities, limitations, strategies, and tactics involved in moving the evidence generated by health surveillance programs into policy and practice implementation.

Fundamentally, health surveillance programs concerning people with intellectual and developmental disabilities have to address not only a medical model of health, but also a medical model of disability. Perhaps paradoxically, a major role of health surveillance programs is to remove intellectual or developmental disability itself from the shadow of being a medical "disorder," so that the physical and mental health inequities experienced by people with intellectual and developmental disabilities can be more clearly seen as inequitable and requiring action rather than an inevitable consequence of a disability. In these circumstances, where even the medical resources of health systems are less often offered to people with intellectual and developmental disabilities, there is a strong pull for the (very important) issues of inequity in access to health services and medical interventions to be prioritized, with social determinants of health left off the agenda.

Similarly, economic cases for public health policy changes typically assume a default position of economic productivity which is threatened by poor health and will be enhanced by the policy change. However, at least in England there are extremely low employment rates for adults with intellectual disabilities; 7% of working-age adults with intellectual disabilities known to specialist services are in any form of paid or self-employment, with 70% of this 7% working less than 16 hours per week (Hatton et al., 2014); and 15% of adults with intellectual disabilities likely to be part of the "hidden majority" are employed 16 or more hours per week (Emerson, Hatton et al., 2014). In one sense, this suggests that a public health economic case based on radically improving employment rates could be an opportunity, although again assumptions about the unemployability of people with intellectual disabilities rather than a default assumption of economic productivity are extra obstacles to surmount.

Many of the social determinants of the health inequities experienced by people with intellectual and developmental disabilities, such as poverty, adversity, unemployment, poor education, and poor housing, are obviously shared with other people in the general population. However, again there are additional issues of discrimination faced by people with intellectual and developmental disabilities, which are crucial to address but are less frequently the focus of attention within public health. The complexity and range of policy change required is both a profound challenge to existing institutional structures and also a profound challenge to the development of the clear policy alternatives required to influence institutional structures. Given these complexities, again there is a strong pull toward clearly identifiable "health" interventions (such as annual health checks for adults with intellectual disabilities in England) that can be clearly located within existing institutional structures rather than more broad-ranging activities to address social determinants of health inequities. Finally, participating in broad coalitions, whether formal or looser and informal, will be crucial but can be difficult for health surveillance programs with certain obligations to government, and the divergent positions of different actors in these coalitions can make agreed ideas difficult to develop and sustain.

The framework outlined by Smith (2013) suggests some fundamental questions for health surveillance programs:

1. Is the aim to work and make compelling cases for change within existing institutional ideas, or to challenge or hold out for radical changes to these institutional ideas (what Smith (2013) calls "charismatic" ideas, which overturn existing institutional ideas but are extremely rare)?

2. Depending on the answer to the first question, what are the clear policy alternatives to focus on and make the case for?
3. What coalitions need to be brought together, and can they agree on these policy alternatives?
4. What evidence exists in relation to these policy alternatives, and what further evidence (of what types) is needed?

The fundamental project that seems to be shared by health surveillance programs concerning people with intellectual and developmental disabilities is encapsulated by this quote from Vickers (1958): "The landmarks of political, economic and social history are the moments when some condition passed from the category of the given into the category of the intolerable. I believe that the history of public health might well be written as a record of successive re-definings of the unacceptable."

5. DISCLAIMER

The findings and conclusions in this manuscript are those of the author(s) and do not necessarily represent the official position of the Centers for Disease Control and Prevention or Public Health England. The opinions, results, and conclusions in the H-CARDD case study are those of the author (H. Ouellette-Kuntz) and are not necessarily those of the funding sources or partners. No endorsement by the Ontario Ministry of Health and Long-Term Care, the Ministry of Community and Social Services, or the Institute for Clinical Evaluative Sciences is intended or should be inferred.

REFERENCES

Anderson, L. L., Humphries, K., McDermott, S., Marks, B., Sisarak, J., & Larson, S. (2013). The state of the science of health and wellness for adults with intellectual and developmental disabilities. *Intellectual & Developmental Disabilities, 51*, 385–398.

Andresen, E. M., Vahle, V. J., & Lollar, D. (2001). Proxy reliability: health-related quality of life (HRQoL) measures for people with disability. *Quality of Life Research, 10*, 609–619.

Baines, S., & Hatton, C. (2014). *Joint strategic needs assessments 2014: How well do they address the needs of people with learning disabilities?* London: Public Health England.

Baines, S., & Hatton, C. (2015). *CQC inspection reports of NHS trusts: How do they address the needs of people with learning disabilities? An interim analysis*. London: Public Health England.

Balogh, R., Brownell, M., Ouellette-Kuntz, H., & Colantonio, A. (2010). Hospitalisation rates for ambulatory care sensitive conditions for persons with and without an intellectual disability—a population perspective. *Journal of Intellectual Disability Research, 54*, 820–832.

Balogh, R., Lake, J., Lin, E., Wilton, A., & Lunsky, Y. (2015). Disparities in diabetes prevalence and preventable hospitalizations in persons with intellectual disabilities in Ontario. *Diabetic Medicine, 32*, 235–242. http://dx.doi.org/10.1111/dme.12573.

Bartlo, P., & Klein, P. J. (2011). Physical activity benefits and needs in adults with intellectual disabilities: systematic review of the literature. *American Journal of Intellectual and Developmental Disabilities, 116*, 220–232.

Beange, H., McElduff, A., & Baker, W. (1995). Medical disorders of adults with mental retardation: a population study. *American Journal on Mental Retardation, 99*, 595–604.

Bowley, C., & Kerr, M. (2000). Epilepsy and intellectual disability. *Journal of Intellectual Disability Research, 44*, 529–543.

Brown, H.K., Cobigo, V., Lunsky, Y., Wilton, D., & Vigod, S. Pregnancy in women with intellectual and developmental disabilities. *Journal of Obstetrics and Gynaecology Canada*, in press.

Burke, E., McCallion, P., & McCarron, M. (2014). *Advancing years, different challenges: Wave 2 IDS-TILDA*. Dublin: Trinity College, The University of Dublin.

CDDER—Center for Developmental Disabilities Evaluation and Research. (2011). *Compendium of health data sources for adults with intellectual disabilities*. Boston, MA: CDDER—Center for Developmental Disabilities Evaluation and Research. Available at http://shriver.umassmed.edu/sites/shriver.umassmed.edu/files/documents/Compendium%20of%20Health%20Data%20Sources%20for%20Adults%20with%20Intellectual%20Disabilities%20(PDF).pdf.

Centers for Disease Control and Prevention (CDC). (2011). *CDC health disparities and inequalities report—United States, 2011*. Atlanta: Centers for Disease Control and Prevention.

Centers for Disease Control and Prevention (CDC). (2015). *National health interview survey on disability*. Altanta, GA: Centers for Disease Control and Prevention (CDC). Available at http://www.cdc.gov/nchs/nhis/nhis_disability.htm.

Centers for Disease Control and Prevention (CDC), & National Center on Birth Defects and Developmental Disabilities (NCBDDD) Health Surveillance Work Group. (2009). *U.S. surveillance of health of people with intellectual disabilities*. Atlanta: CDC/NCBDDD.

Chang, L., & Krosnick, J. (2009). National surveys via RDD telephone interviewing versus the internet: comparing sample representativeness and response quality. *Public Opinion Quarterly, 73*, 641–678.

Christie, A., Baines, S., Hatton, C., Glover, G., & Turner, S. (2014). *Joint health and social care self-assessment framework 2013: Detailed report and thematic analyses*. London: Public Health England.

Cobigo, V., Ouellette-Kuntz, H., Balogh, R., Leung, F., Lin, E., & Lunsky, Y. (2013). Are cervical and breast cancer screening programs equitable? The case of women with developmental disabilities. *Journal of Intellectual Disability Research, 57*, 478–488.

Courtney-Long, E., Stevens, A., Caraballo, R., Ramon, I., & Armour, B. S. (2014). Disparities in current cigarette smoking prevalence by type of disability, 2009-2011. *Public Health Reports, 129*, 252–260.

Cummins, R. (2002). Proxy responding for subjective well-being: a review. In L. M. Glidden (Ed.), *International review of research in mental retardation* (Vol. 25, pp. 183–207). San Diego, CA: Academic Press.

Demos. (2013). *Health in austerity*. London: Demos.

Department of Health. (2012). *Transforming care: A national response to Winterbourne View hospital*. Final Report. London: Department of Health.

Department of Health. (2013). *Six lives: Progress report on healthcare for people with learning disabilities*. London: Department of Health.

Disability Rights Commission. (2006). *Equal treatment: Closing the gap*. London Disability Rights Commission.

Einfeld, S., & Emerson, E. (2008). Intellectual disability. In M. Rutter, D. Bishop, D. Pine, S. Scott, J. Stevenson, E. Taylor, et al. (Eds.), *Rutter's child and adolescent psychiatry* (5th ed.). Oxford: Blackwell.

Elsabbagh, M., Divan, G., Koh, Y., Kim, Y. S., Kauchali, S., & Marcín, C. (2012). Global prevalence of autism and other pervasive developmental disorders. *Autism Research, 5*, 160–179.

Emerson, E. (2005). Use of the strengths and difficulties questionnaire to assess the mental health needs of children and adolescents with intellectual disabilities. *Journal of Intellectual & Developmental Disability, 30*, 14–23.

Emerson, E. (2011). Health status and health risks of the 'hidden majority' of adults with intellectual disability. *Intellectual & Developmental Disabilities, 49*, 155–165.

Emerson, E., & Baines, S. (2010). *The estimated prevalence of autism among adults with learning disabilities in England*. Durham: Improving Health & Lives: Learning Disabilities Observatory.

Emerson, E., Baines, S., Allerton, L., & Welch, V. (2012). *Health inequalities & people with learning disabilities in the UK: 2012*. Durham: Improving Health & Lives: Learning Disabilities Observatory.

Emerson, E., Felce, D., & Stancliffe, R. (2013). Issues concerning self-report data and population-based data sets involving people with intellectual disabilities. *Intellectual and Developmental Disabilities, 51*, 333–348.

Emerson, E., & Glover, G. (2012). The 'transition cliff' in the administrative prevalence of learning disabilities in England. *Tizard Learning Disability Review, 17*, 139–143.

Emerson, E., & Halpin, S. (2013). Anti-social behaviour and police contact among 13–15 year-old English adolescents with and without mild/moderate intellectual disability. *Journal of Applied Research in Intellectual Disabilities, 26*(5), 362–369.

Emerson, E., & Hatton, C. (2014). *Health inequalities and people with intellectual disabilities*. Cambridge: Cambridge University Press.

Emerson, E., Hatton, C., Robertson, J., & Baines, S. (2014). Perceptions of neighbourhood quality, social and civic participation and the self rated health of British adults with intellectual disability: cross sectional study. *BMC Public Health, 14*, 1252, 1210.1186/1471-2458-1214-1252.

Emerson, E., Hatton, C., Robertson, J., & Baines, S. (2015). *The determinants of health inequalities experienced by children with learning disabilities*. London: Public Health England.

Emerson, E., Malam, S., Davies, I., & Spencer, K. (2005). *Adults with learning difficulties in England 2003/4*. Leeds: Health & Social Care Information Centre.

Emerson, E., Robertson, J., Baines, S., & Hatton, C. (2014). The self-rated health of British adults with intellectual disability. *Research in Developmental Disabilities, 35*, 591–596.

Finlay, W. M. L., & Lyons, E. (2001). Methodological issues in interviewing and using self-report questionnaires with people with mental retardation. *Psychological Assessment, 13*, 319–335.

Foley, J. T., Lloyd, M., & Temple, V. A. (2014). Obesity trends of 8–18 year old Special Olympians: 2005–2010. *Research in Developmental Disabilities, 35*, 705–710.

Fujiura, G. T. (2012). Self-reported health of people with intellectual disability. *Intellectual and Developmental Disabilities, 50*, 352–369.

Fujiura, G. T., Rutkowski-Kmitta, V., & Owen, R. (2010). Make measurable what is not so: national monitoring of the status of persons with intellectual disability. *American Journal of Intellectual and Developmental Disabilities, 35*, 244–258.

Fujiura, G. T., & Taylor, S. J. (2003). Continuum of intellectual disability: demographic evidence for the "forgotten generation". *Mental Retardation, 41*, 420–429.

Giraud-Saunders, A., Marriott, A., Hatton, C., Turner, S., & Kenney, A. (2014). *Making reasonable adjustments to end of life care for people with learning disabilities*. London: Public Health England.

Giraud-Saunders, A., Marriott, A., & Turner, S. (2015). *Health checks for people with learning disabilities: Including young people aged 14 and over, and producing health action plans*. London: Public Health England.

Glover, G. (2014). *The uptake of learning disability health checks 2013 to 2014*. London: Public Health England.

Glover, G., & Ayub, M. (2010). *How people with learning disabilities die*. Durham: Improving Health & Lives: Learning Disabilities Observatory.

Glover, G., & Emerson, E. (2012). *Have you got a learning disability? Asking the question and recording the answer for NHS healthcare providers*. Durham: Improving Health & Lives: Learning Disabilities Public Health Observatory.

Glover, G., Emerson, E., & Baines, S. (2011). *NHS data gaps for learning disabilities: The information we need to monitor the health and healthcare of people with learning disabilities*. Durham: Improving Health & Lives: Learning Disabilities Observatory.

Glover, G., Emerson, E., & Eccles, R. (2012). *Using local data to monitor the health needs of people with learning disabilities*. Durham: Improving Health & Lives: Learning Disabilities Public Health Observatory.

Glover, G., & Evison, F. (2013). *Hospital admissions that should not happen: Admissions for ambulatory care sensitive conditions for people with learning disabilities in England*. Stoickton-on-Tees: Leraning Disabilities Public Health Observatory.

Government of Ontario. (2012). *News: Aging at home strategy retrieved November 2012*. From http://news.ontario.ca/mohltc/en/2010/08/aging-at-home-strategy.html.

Hartley, S., & MacLean, W. (2006). A review of the reliability and validity of Likert-type scales for people with intellectual disabilities. *Journal of Intellectual Disabilities Research, 50*, 813–827.

Hastings, A., Bailey, N., Bramley, G., Gannon, M., & Watkins, D. (2015). *The cost of the cuts: The impact of local government and poorer communities*. York: Joseph Rowntree Foundation.

Hatton, C., Emerson, E., Glover, G., Robertson, J., Baines, S., & Christie, A. (2014). *People with learning disabilities in England 2013*. London: Public Health England.

Hatton, C., Roberts, H., & Baines, S. (2011). *Reasonable adjustments for people with learning disabilities in England: A national survey of NHS trusts*. Durham: North East Public Health Observatory.

Hatton, C., & Taylor, J. L. (2013). The assessment of mental health problems in adults with intellectual disabilities. In J. L. Taylor, W. R. Lindsay, R. P. Hastings, & C. Hatto (Eds.), *Psychological therapies for adults with intellectual disabilities* (pp. 31–54). Cichester: Wiley-Blackwell.

Havercamp, S., Scandlin, D., & Roth, M. (2004). Health disparities among adults with developmental disabilities, adults with other disabilities, and adults not reporting disability in North Carolina. *Public Health Reports, 119*, 418–426.

Havercamp, S. M., & Scott, H. M. (2015). National health surveillance of adults with disabilities, adults with intellectual and developmental disabilities, and adults with no disabilities. *Disability and Health Journal, 8*, 165–172.

Hayden, M. F., Kim, S., & DePaepe, P. (2005). Health status, utilization patterns, and outcomes of persons with intellectual disabilities: review of the literature. *Mental Retardation, 43*, 175–195.

Hindmarsh, G., Llewellyn, G., & Emerson, E. (2014). Mothers with intellectual impairment and their 9-month-old infants. *Journal of Intellectual Disabilities Research, 6*, 541–550. http://dx.doi.org/10.1111/jir.12159.

Hodapp, R. M., Goldman, S. E., & Urbano, R. C. (2013). Using secondary datasets in disability research: special issues, special promise. *International Review of Research in Developmental Disabilities, 45*, 1–34.

Hoghton, M., Turner, S., & Hall, I. (2013). *Improving the health and wellbeing of people with learning disabilities: An evidence-based commissioning guide for clinical commissioning groups (CCGs)*. London: Public Health England.

Holden, B., & Gitlesen, J. P. (2004). Psychotropic medication in adults with mental retardation: prevalence, and prescription practices. *Research in Developmental Disabilities, 25*(6), 509–521.

Horowitz, S. M., Kerker, B. D., Ownes, P. L., & Zigler, E. (2000). *The health status and needs of individuals with mental retardation*. Washington, DC: Special Olympics, Inc.

HSRI & NASDDDS. (2015). *National core indicators project*. From: http://www.nationalcoreindicators.org/.

Iezzoni, L. I. (2002). Using administrative data to study persons with disabilities. *The Milbank Quarterly, 80*, 347–379.

Jackson, J. S., Torres, M., Caldwell, C. H., Neighbors, H. W., Nesse, R. M., & Taylor, R. J. (2004). The National Survey of American Life: a study of racial, ethnic and cultural influences on mental disorders and mental health. *International Journal of Methods in Psychiatric Research, 13*, 196–207.

Janicki, M. P., Davidson, P. W., Henderson, C. M., McCallion, P., Taets, J. D., & Force, L. T. (2002). Health characteristics and health services utilization in older adults with intellectual disability living in community residences. *Journal of Intellectual Disability Research, 46*, 287–298.

Jones, E. M., & Schoon, I. (2008). Child cognition and behaviour. In K. Hansen, & H. Joshi (Eds.), *Millennium cohort study third survey: A user's guide to initial findings* (pp. 118–144). London: Centre for Longitudinal Studies, Institute of Education, University of London.

Kaye, H. S. (2007). Inclusion of people with disabilities in the NHIS and NHIS-D: non-response, proxy response, and assisted response. In T. Kroll, D. Keer, P. Placedk, J. Cyril, & G. E. Hendershot (Eds.), *Towards best practices for surveying people with disabilities* (Vol. 1, pp. 105–125). Nova Science Publishers.

Kenney, A. (2013). *Making reasonable adjustments to dementia services for people with for people with learning disabilities*. London: Public Health England.

Kenney, A., Turner, S., Glover, G., & Hatton, C. (2014). *Making reasonable adjustments to primary care services: Supporting the implementation of annual health checks for people with learning disabilities*. London: Public Health England.

Kiely, M. (1987). The prevalence of mental retardation. *Epidemiologic Reviews, 9*, 194–218.

Killoran, A., & Kelly, M. P. (2010). Introduction: effectiveness and efficiency in public health. In A. Killoran, & M. P. Kelly (Eds.), *Evidence-based public health: Effectiveness and efficiency*. Oxford, UK: Oxford University Press.

King's Fund. (2015). *The NHS under the coalition government – Part one: NHS reform*. London: King's Fund.

Krahn, G., & Fox, M. H. (2014). Health disparities of adults with intellectual disabilities: what do we know? What do we do? *Journal of Applied Research in Intellectual Disability, 27*, 431–446. http://dx.doi.org/10.1111/jar.12067.

Krahn, G., Fox, M. H., Campbell, V. A., Ramon, I., & Jesien, G. (2010). Developing a health surveillance system for people with intellectual disabilities in the United States. *Journal of Policy & Practice in Intellectual Disabilities, 7*, 155–166.

Krahn, G. L., Hammond, L., & Turner, A. (2006). A cascade of disparities: health and health care access for people with intellectual disabilities. *Mental Retardation and Developmental Disabilities Research Reviews, 12*, 70–82.

Larson, S. A., Lakin, K. C., Anderson, L., Kwak, N., Lee, J. H., & Anderson, D. (2000). *Prevalence of mental retardation and/or developmental disabilities: Analysis of the 1994/1995 NHIS-D. MR/DD data brief, 1(2)*. Minnesota, MN: University of Minnesota.

Larson, S., Lakin, K. C., Anderson, L., Kwak, N., Lee, J. H., & Anderson, D. (2001). Prevalence of mental retardation and developmental disabilities: estimates from the 1994/1995 National Health Interview Survey Disability Supplements. *American Journal on Mental Retardation, 106*, 231–252.

Law, S., Flood, C., Gagnon, D., &, on behalf of the Listening for Direction III partners. (2008). *Listening for direction III: National consultation on health services and policy issues 2007–2010*. Available on CHSRF and Health Canada web sites www.chsrf.ca http://hc-sc.gc.ca/sr-sr/part/ngo-ong/index_e.htm.

Robertson, J., Hatton, C., Emerson, E., & Baines, S. (2014). Health checks for people with intellectual disabilities: an updated systematic review of evidence. *Research in Developmental Disabilities, 35*, 2450–2462.

Robertson, J., Hatton, C., Emerson, E., & Baines, S. (2015 early online) Systematic reviews of the health or healthcare of people with intellectual disabilities: a systematic review to identify gaps in the evidence base. *Journal of Applied Research in Intellectual Disabilities*, http://dx.doi.org/10.1111/jar.12149.

Robertson, J., Roberts, H., Emerson, E., Turner, S., & Greig, R. (2011). The impact of health checks for people with intellectual disabilities: a systematic review of evidence. *Journal of Intellectual Disabilities Research, 55*, 1009–1019.

Roos, N. P., Roos, L. L., Brownell, M., & Fuller, E. L. (2010). Enhancing policymakers' understanding of disparities: relevant data from an information-rich environment. *Milbank Quarterly, 88*, 382–403.

RTI (2013). Health surveillance in the population with intellectual disability: Case definition in state level data. Conference presentation, 141st APHA Annual Meeting and Exposition, Nov 2013.

Shooshtari, S., Brownell, M., Ouellette-Kuntz, H., Yu, C.T., Naghipur, S., & Hennen, B. Comparing hospitalized dental care between individuals with and without developmental disabilities in Manitoba: a population-based study. *Journal on Developmental Disabilities*, in press.

Smith, K. (2013). *Beyond evidence-based policy in public health: The interplay of ideas.* Basingstoke, UK: Palgrave.

Special Olympics. (2009). *Health, well-being and opportunity for people with intellectual disability – a global imperative. Status and prospects of persons with intellectual disability.* Washington, DC: Special Olympics, Inc.

Stancliffe, R. J. (1999). Proxy respondents and the reliability of the Quality of Life Questionnaire Empowerment factor. *Journal of Intellectual Disability Research, 43*, 185–193.

Stancliffe, R. (2000). Proxy respondents and quality of life. *Evaluation and Programme Planning, 23*, 89–93.

Stancliffe, R. J., Lakin, K. C., Larson, S., Engler, J., Bershadsky, J., & Taub, S. (2011). Overweight and obesity among adults with intellectual disabilities who use intellectual disability/developmental disability services in 20 U.S. states. *American Journal on Intellectual and Developmental Disabilities, 116*, 401–418.

Stancliffe, R. J., Lakin, K. C., Larson, S. A., Engler, J., Taub, S., & Fortune, J. (2012). Demographic characteristics, health conditions, and residential service use in adults with down syndrome in 25 U.S. states. *Intellectual and Developmental Disabilities, 50*, 92–108.

Stevens, A., Courtney-Long, E., Gillespie, C., & Armour, B. S. (2014). Hypertension among US adults by disability status and type, National Health and Nutrition Examination Survey, 2001–2010. *Preventing Chronic Disease, 11*, E139.

Stortz, J., Lake, J. K., Cobigo, V., Ouellette-Kuntz, H., & Lunsky, Y. (2014). Lessons learned from our elders: how to study polypharmacy in populations with intellectual and developmental disabilities. *Intellectual and Developmental Disabilities, 52*, 60–77.

Taggart, L., & Cousins, W. (Eds.). (2014). *Health promotion for people with intellectual and developmental disabilities.* Maidenhead, UK: McGraw Hill.

Turk, V., Khattran, S., Kerry, S., Corney, R., & Painter, K. (2012). Reporting of health problems and pain by adults with an intellectual disability and by their carers. *Journal of Applied Research in Intellectual Disability, 25*, 155–165.

Turner, S., & Emerson, E. (2013). *Making reasonable adjustments to diabetes services for people with learning disabilities.* London: Public Health England.

Turner, S., Emerson, E., & Glover, G. (2012). *Making reasonable adjustments to dentistry services for people with learning disabilities.* Durham: North East Public Health Observatory.

Turner, S., Emerson, E., Glover, G., &, the Cornwall Cancer Screening Team. (2012). *Making reasonable adjustments to cancer screening for people with learning disabilities*. Durham: North East Public Health Observatory.

Turner, S., Kill, S., & Emerson, E. (2013). *Making reasonable adjustments to eye care services for people with learning disabilities*. London: Public Health England.

Turner, S., & Robinson, C. (2014). *Improving the health and wellbeing of people with learning disabilities: Guidance for social care providers and commissioners (to support implementation of the health charter)*. London: Public Health England.

Tymchuk, A. J., Lakin, K. C., & Luckasson, R. (Eds.). (2001). *The forgotten generation: The status and challenges of adults with mild cognitive limitations*. Baltimore: Brookes.

US Department of Health & Human Services. (2002a). *Closing the gap: A national blueprint to improve the health of persons with mental retardation*. Rockville, MD: US Department of Health and Human Services.

US Department of Health & Human Services. (2002b). *Report of the Surgeon General's conference on health disparities and mental retardation*. Rockville: Closing the gap.

Vickers, G. (1958). What sets the goals of public health? *Lancet, 1*, 599–604.

Wharton, M., Chorba, T., Vogt, R., Morse, D., & Buhler, J. (1990). Centers for disease control and prevention, case definitions for public health surveillance. *Morbidity and Mortality Weekly Review, 39*(RR13).

Wilper, A. P., Woolhandler, S., Boyd, J. W., Lasser, K. E., McCormick, D., & Bor, D. H. (2009). The health and health care of US prisoners: results of a nationwide survey. *American Journal of Public Health, 99*, 666–672.

Wilson, D., & Haire, A. (1990). Health care screening for people with mental handicap living in the community. *British Medical Journal, 301*, 1379–1381.

Woodhouse, J. M., Adler, P., & Duignan, A. (2004). Vision in athletes with intellectual disabilities: the need for improved eye care. *Journal of Intellectual Disability Research, 48*, 736–774.

World Health Organization. (2008). *Closing the gap in a generation: Health equity through action on the social determinants of health*. Geneva: World Health Organization. Final report of the Commission on the Social Determinants of Health.

World Health Organization. (2011). *Rio political declaration on social determinants of health*. Geneva: World Health Organization. http://www.who.int/sdhconference/declaration/en/.

World Health Organization Regional Office for Europe. (2013). *Report on social determinants and the health divide in the WHO European region: Final report*. Copenhagen: World Health Organization Regional Office for Europe.

World Health Organization and the World Bank. (2011). *World report on disability*. Geneva: World Health Organization.

CHAPTER FIVE

Adults with Cerebral Palsy: Physical and Mental Health Issues and Health Service Use Patterns

C. McMorris*,§, J.K. Lake*, Y. Lunsky*, K. Dobranowski¶, D. Fehlings||, M. Bayley#,**, C. McGarry*, R.S. Balogh¶,§§,1

*Centre for Addiction and Mental Health, Toronto, ON, Canada
§Psychology Department, York University, Toronto, ON, Canada
¶University of Ontario Institute of Technology, Oshawa, ON, Canada
||Holland Bloorview Kids Rehabilitation Hospital, Department of Paediatrics, University of Toronto, Toronto, ON, Canada
#Brain and Spinal Cord Rehabilitation Program – UHN Toronto Rehabilitation Institute, Toronto, ON, Canada
**Division of Physical Medicine and Rehabilitation, Faculty of Medicine, University of Toronto, Toronto, ON, Canada
§§Physical Therapy Department, University of Toronto, Toronto, ON, Canada
[1]Corresponding author: e-mail address: Robert.Balogh@uoit.ca

Contents

Abstract

Children with cerebral palsy (CP) experience high rates of comorbid physical and mental health issues. As individuals with CP age and become adults, the risk for physical and mental health issues persists, and the need for health care support also increases. Despite this, compared to children with CP, the health needs of adults with CP are

International Review of Research in Developmental Disabilities, Volume 48
ISSN 2211-6095
http://dx.doi.org/10.1016/bs.irrdd.2015.03.003

poorly understood. To better appreciate these issues, we conducted a comprehensive literature review of the physical and mental health issues, and health service use patterns among adults with CP, with and without an intellectual disability. In total, 18 articles were reviewed; seven related to physical health, three mental health, and eight health service use. Overall, our review showed that adults with CP frequently suffer from a variety of chronic physical and mental health issues, such as bladder issues, musculoskeletal problems, chronic pain, depression, and self-injurious behavior. Despite these chronic health problems, research to date fails to demonstrate a consistent pattern of health service use among adults with CP. These results highlight the significant physical and mental health issues experienced by this population, as well as considerable gaps in the literature. Our review also highlights disparities related to health and health service issues experienced by the following groups: (1) children compared to adults with CP; (2) individuals with CP compared to other clinical populations; and (3) adults with CP compared to the general population. Lastly, we discuss clinical implications of this review as it pertains to health care professionals supporting adults with CP.

1. INTRODUCTION

Cerebral palsy (CP) is the most common cause of complex, chronic physical disability in childhood (Young et al., 2011), occurring in 2–2.5 per 1000 live births (Vincer et al., 2006). CP is a set of nonprogressive and heterogeneous movement disorders resulting from injury to the central nervous system early in development, primarily impacting movement and posture (Henderson et al., 2009). Given the severe motor impairments inherent to those with CP, individuals tend to experience activity limitations and difficulties in daily functioning (Rosenbaum, Paneth, Leviton, Goldstein, & Bax, 2006).

There are three primary types of CP: (1) *spastic,* the most common type of CP (80% of cases), often leads to stiffness and movement difficulties; (2) *dyskinetic* which leads to uncontrolled and involuntary movements (10–20% of cases); and (3) *ataxic* in which fine motor skills, depth perception, balance, and walking are affected (5–10%) (Krigger, 2006). Individuals with CP can have varying degrees of motor impairment, which can effect activities of daily living (ADLs). The Gross Motor Function Classification System is used to determine the severity of these effects. Additionally, individuals with CP may also experience difficulties in cognition, communication, behavior, motor control, and perception (Bax et al., 2005). A large proportion of individuals with CP also have an intellectual disability (ID; Krigger, 2006; Mutch, Alberman, Hagberg, Kodama, & Perst, 1992), with some studies reporting that approximately two-thirds of CP patients have intellectual impairments (Krigger, 2006). Taken together, these difficulties can further complicate symptom presentation, assessment and diagnosis, and impact service provision.

In adulthood, many individuals with CP develop additional physical and mental health issues, which may increase in severity during this life stage, and thus often require added support (Young et al., 2007). For example, musculoskeletal issues increase with time, that is, the progression of contractures, congenital hip dysplasia, osteoporosis-associated fractures, or premature osteoarthritis due to abnormal alignment of joint and the associated pain, become more common and/or severe in adulthood. Common age-associated physical health issues in adults with CP, such as cardiovascular disease, can also limit physical activity. Although life expectancy is quite low for adults with CP compared to the general population (Hemming, Hutton, & Pharoah, 2006; Strauss, Cable, & Shavelle, 1999), it is improving. The main causes of death for individuals with CP are typically attributed to a variety of comorbid physical health issues, including respiratory disease, illness or infection, cancer, and cardiovascular disease (Strauss et al., 1999).

Physical and mental health issues affecting individuals with CP are well documented in the literature among children (Liptak et al., 2001); however, few studies have examined these issues among adults with CP. Specifically, it remains unknown what chronic physical and mental health issues identified in early childhood persist into adulthood, what symptoms change or present differently as individuals age, and whether new issues emerge in adulthood. All of these have major clinical implications for this population. Despite knowledge that adults with CP are at risk for experiencing multiple physical and mental health concerns, we also know little about the frequency and type of health services they use. This is particularly concerning in the context of adolescents with CP transitioning from the child to the adult health care system, where medical and mental health services may become scarce, and the criteria to access services are more stringent. As such, there is an imperative need to better understand the health service utilization patterns of adults with CP in order to help identify gaps in services and supports, and to guide funding and service provision.

Due to the unique, complex physical and mental health issues associated with CP, it is important to obtain a comprehensive understanding of the current literature related to the health and service needs of this population. Systematic reviews in CP exist; however, they largely focus on treatment effectiveness (e.g., Dodd, Taylor, & Damiano, 2002), etiological factors (e.g., Wu, 2002), or severity of functioning (e.g., Ketelaar, Vermeer, &

Helders, 1998). We address this gap by systematically reviewing the literature on the physical and mental health conditions, and health service use patterns experienced by adults with CP, with and without ID. In the concluding section of this review, we consider health disparities between those with CP and other clinical populations, as well as those without disabilities. This work has the potential to inform service delivery and provision for the aging CP population, and to ensure services adequately meet their needs. To our knowledge, this is the first systematic literature review that considers these factors, and their impact on services.

2. METHODS

A systematic search strategy was conducted to identify relevant literature from the following databases: Medline, EMBASE, and PsycINFO. Search terms were used that were specific to CP, mental health, chronic physical health conditions, and health service use. Terms were then combined using the following search engines: OVID and Web of Science. The full search strategy can be obtained from the authors.

The first author independently extracted all titles and abstracts, and relevant articles were selected and reviewed by two other authors. Only English articles published in peer-reviewed journals were considered. Inclusion and exclusion criteria for this review were:

1. Present findings specific to individuals with CP (not specific to type of CP);
2. Include a sample of adults who were 18 years or older; and
3. Relate to one of three subject areas—chronic physical disease, mental health, or health service use.

If articles met all three criteria, the full manuscript was obtained and reviewed. Figure 1 outlines the number of articles retained at each stage of the literature review process. Although we describe all physical conditions from studies, we specifically searched for chronic diseases, rather than specific physical conditions. Also, of note, we did not search specifically for mortality; however, our search related to physical health yielded papers related to mortality and cause of death. Lastly, we did not include studies that described specific injuries in adults with CP, nor those that described physical manifestations directly related to CP, such as spasticity.

If findings discussed more than one subject area, the article was included in the section that was *most consistent* with the article's findings. When

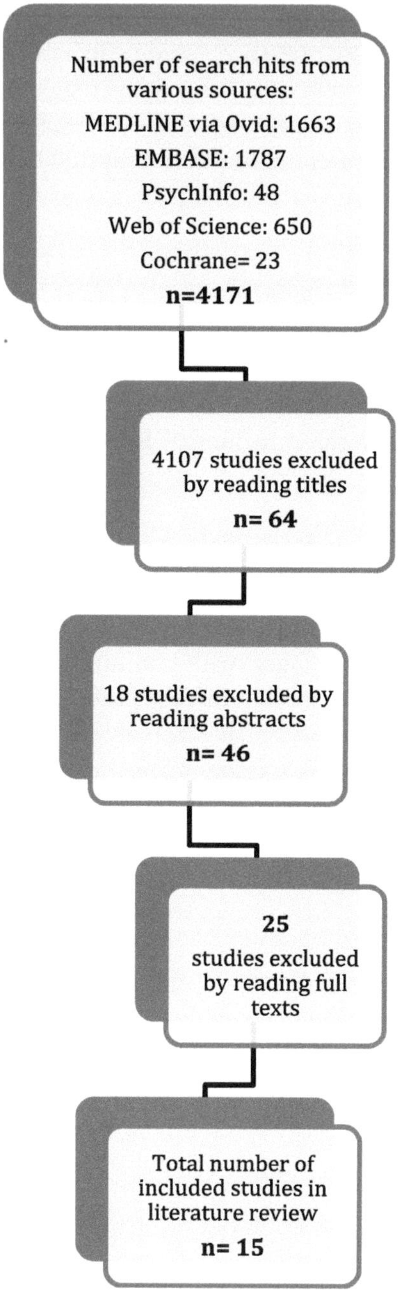

Figure 1 Flow diagram outlining included the studies for literature review.

presenting findings from the literature review, the term "CP (ID status unknown)" is used to describe those studies in which the presence of ID was not reported by the authors. For studies that did report the presence of ID, those that included a sample of adults with CP with a comorbid diagnosis of ID (CP with ID) were distinguished from those that included a sample of adults with CP without ID.

3. RESULTS

Eighteen articles met inclusion criteria for this review: seven articles, including two studies related to mortality and cause of death, were related to physical health issues; three to mental health issues; and eight to health service use.

3.1 Chronic Physical Health Issues in Adults with CP

Overall, results from our review showed that individuals with CP presented with a number of comorbid physical health issues in various systems (e.g., cardiovascular, respiratory, digestive). Common chronic physical health issues in adults with CP included bladder issues, musculoskeletal problems, and chronic pain. These issues substantially impeded their functioning and, in some cases, led to mortality. The health of adults with CP, as reported by caregivers, was fair to poor. Generally speaking, physical health issues appeared to be unrelated to the type of CP; however, difficulties in motor activity and ADLs may have contributed to some of these health concerns. In some studies, gender impacted the prevalence or risk for certain comorbid physical issues, such as fragility fractures from osteopenia in women (Henderson et al., 2009). Additionally, other social determinants of health, such as ethnicity or socioeconomic status (SES), may also impact the prevalence of comorbid physical issues in individuals with CP, although these were not specifically examined in the reviewed literature.

Only one of the studies reviewed (Henderson et al., 2009) investigated physical health issues in a sample of adults with CP and ID. Although Turk, Geremski, Rosenbaum, and Weber (1997) indicated that the sample included individuals with CP and ID; the authors failed to present findings specific to individuals with CP and ID. Further, the majority of studies reviewed failed to report on the type or severity of CP, and it was unclear how certain demographic (e.g., age, gender, and residency), clinical (e.g., level of ID, severity of CP, medication use), or service variables, impacted physical health issues. Although all studies reported the prevalence of specific physical conditions, only two studies (Koritsas & Iacono, 2009; Turk et al., 1997) identified which issues were secondary (i.e., associated, or comorbid) issues to CP. Thus, it remains unclear if having CP puts individuals at a higher risk for specific physical health issues, or whether physical health issues are inherent among those with CP. Additionally, it is also unknown whether social determinants of poor health (e.g., SES, education, ethnicity, and access to health services) are more likely amongst people with CP, or that people with CP have greater vulnerability when faced with adverse circumstances. Considering these limitations, the prevalence of comorbid physical health issues among adults with CP with and without ID compared to the general population remains unclear. Additionally, it is unknown whether rates of physical health issues differ when ID is or is not present.

The present literature search yielded two studies that examined mortality rates and cause of death among adults with CP. Both studies identified that compared to the general population, adults with CP die at a younger age. That is, over half of individuals with CP died between 35 and 64 years of age. When examining the most frequently cited cause of death, findings varied across studies, but included respiratory problems, circulation issues, tumors, infections, digestive issues, and cancer. Strauss et al. (1999) identified that cause of death also varied by age, with children with CP dying more often as a result of brain cancer compared to children in the general population. The authors also noted how findings highlighted problems with diagnosis/identification and treatment of these diseases in individuals with CP. One study examined the role that CP severity had on life expectancy and cause of death (Strauss et al., 1999); however, both studies failed to consider type of CP when examining mortality rates in this population (Durfule-tapin et al., 2014; Strauss et al., 1999). Further research is needed to ensure appropriate diagnosis and treatment of major diseases that occur in this population in order to avoid preventable deaths (Table 1).

3.2 Mental Health Issues in Adults with CP

Our search identified three studies focused on mental health issues in adults with CP. Two of the studies reviewed examined comorbid mental health disorders in adults with CP and ID, and the sample's ID status was unknown in the third study. Results demonstrated that depression or depressive symptoms were common among adults with CP, with and without ID. Depressive symptoms appeared to be related to the severity of CP; however, none of the studies reviewed examined how the type of CP might be associated

Table 1 Literature Review Findings: Physical Health Issues

Study Reference (Authors, Year)	CP Sample Size (*n*) and Study Design (Admin Data, Chart Review, Survey, etc.)	Demographic Information (Age, Gender, etc.)	CP Type, CP Severity, and Presence and Severity of ID	Study Objectives and Findings
Henderson et al. (2009) *Location*: USA	Adults with CP ($N = 177$) Survey completed by nursing staff or service coordinators of group homes for adults with ID	33–79 years ($M = 53.5$; $SD = 11.1$) Males: 53%	Two groups: (1) CP with ID and (2) ID only Severity of CP determined by a functional impairment index (construct created by authors) *Study did not report on CP type, and severity of ID of CP adults	**Study objective:** To examine the health status of adults with ID with or without a comorbid diagnosis of CP. **Findings:** • 55 individuals with CP with ID were obese, 6 reported bowel obstruction, 12 had gastroesophageal reflux, 6 had osteoarthritis; 6 had osteoporosis, 26 had an urinary tract infection (UTI), 19 had pneumonia/bronchitis; 6 had dysphagia; and 6 reported fractures. • Compared to individuals with ID only, CP adults with ID showed significantly higher prevalence for obesity, gastroesophageal reflux, UTIs, and dysphagia. • Gender was a significant predictor of certain physical health issues. Males: gastroesophageal reflux; females: osteoarthritis, UTI, fractures, and overweight status/obesity. • Predictors of physical conditions in those with CP with ID compared to those with ID only: impairment in activities of daily living (ADLs) and walking capabilities (not just CP alone), accounted for differences in the prevalence of these medical conditions, except dysphagia.

Koritsas and Iacono (2009) American Journal on Intellectual and Developmental Disabilities *Location*: Australia	($N = 113$; CP = 29) Caregiver survey Three groups (ASD, Down syndrome, and CP) Time 1 (2001–2002) and time 2 (2004–2005)	CP = 19–71 years ($M = 34.3$; $SD = 14.1$) Male: 11; Female: 18	CP (ID status unknown) *Study did not report on CP type, CP severity, or presence or severity of ID	**Study objectives:** (1) determine whether adults with Down syndrome, autism, and CP differed in the degree to which their life participation and independence was impacted by secondary conditions, as rated by their caregivers/parents and (2) examine whether the degree of limitation on life participation and independence in these three groups changed over a period of time (2–3 years). **Findings:** • At time 1, medication side effects, osteoporosis, arthritis, urinary tract infections, and injuries due to loss of sensation were the secondary health conditions that were rated by caregivers/parents as leading to the most limitations on activity and independence in adults with CP. • At time 2, medication side effects, gastrointestinal problems, arthritis, urinary tract infections, and injuries due to loss of sensation were the secondary conditions identified by caregivers as leading to the most limitations on activity and independence in adults with CP. • Diabetes, cardiovascular problems, and respiratory problems were other secondary health conditions noted to lead to limitations in adults with CP at time 1 and time 2; but were not ranked as high as the other conditions. • Overall, adults with CP had greater limitations due to secondary conditions than did the other groups in all areas, with the exception of medication side effects.

(*Continued*)

Table 1 Literature Review Findings: Physical Health Issues—cont'd

Study Reference (Authors, Year)	CP Sample Size (n) and Study Design (Admin Data, Chart Review, Survey, etc.)	Demographic Information (Age, Gender, etc.)	CP Type, CP Severity, and Presence and Severity of ID	Study Objectives and Findings
Murphy, Boutin, and Ide (2012) Developmental Medicine & Child Neurology *Location*: USA	($N = 214$) Adults with CP ($n = 46$) Review of medical records of individuals with CP	**Two adult age groups:** 21–30 years ($n = 16$) and 30 + years ($n = 30$) **21–30 years group:** 8 males; 8 females **30+ years group:** 14 females; 16 males	CP *Study did not report on CP type or severity by age group, or presence or severity of ID	**Study objective:** To examine the prevalence of symptomatic neurogenic bladder (SNB) in a sample of individuals with CP. **Findings:** • Four (25%) adults in the 21–30 year age group and nine (30%) adults in the 30+ years group suffered from SNB.
Turk et al. (1997) Archives of Physical Medicine and Rehabilitation *Location*: USA	Adults with CP ($N = 63$); Survey (telephone questionnaire)	20–74 years ($M = 37.7$ years) Community sample of women	Majority of sample had CP (34% of sample had CP with ID; however, study did not specify findings specific to those	**Study objective:** To examine the health status, comorbid conditions, and health behaviors of women with CP living in the community. **Findings:** • 40% reported a history of seizures, 34% had ID, and 26% had a learning disability.

		with CP with ID versus those with CP without ID. Spastic diplegia (29%); dyskinesia (25%); spastic hemiplegia (18%); other (ataxia, hypotonia, mixed; 16%); spastic quadriplegia (11%). Participants presented with mild or moderate CP as indicated by quality of muscle tone and limb involvement *Study did not report on severity of ID.	• 84% reported pain; 59% hip and back deformities; 56% bowel problems; 49% bladder problem; 43% poor dental health; and 28% gastroesophageal reflux (28%); 35% had increased spasticity during menstruation; and 24% increased incontinence during menstruation. • Associations were also found between adults with CP and ID and pain, as well as ID and gastroesophageal reflux.

(*Continued*)

Table 1 Literature Review Findings: Physical Health Issues—cont'd

Study Reference (Authors, Year)	CP Sample Size (*n*) and Study Design (Admin Data, Chart Review, Survey, etc.)	Demographic Information (Age, Gender, etc.)	CP Type, CP Severity, and Presence and Severity of ID	Study Objectives and Findings
van der Slot et al. (2013) Journal of Rehabilitation Medicine *Location*: The Netherlands	Adults with CP ($N = 43$); Cross-sectional study	25–45 years ($M = 36.6$; $SD = 6$) Males: 27; females: 16	CP (ID status unknown) Type of CP: spastic bilateral cerebral palsy (SBCP) ⋆Study did not report on CP severity or presence or severity of ID ⋆Exclusion criteria: severe cognitive impairment	**Study objectives:** (1) to investigate the risk factors for cardiovascular disease (CVD), including blood pressure, and the 10-year risk of a fatal cardiovascular event in adults with CP and (2) to determine the association between 10-year risk and aerobic fitness, physical activity, and body fat. **Findings:** • Sample had a *low* 10-year fatal cardiovascular risk *but* several biological and lifestyle-related factors were present. • 28% had hypertension and 44% had prehypertensive values. • Adults with CP only had higher blood pressure compared to the general population. • Obesity, as measured by BMI, was reported more often in men with SBCP than men in the general population. • Controlling for gender, those with a higher waist circumference or BMI had a *higher* risk of CVD.

Mortality and Causes of Death				
Duruflé-Tapin et al. (2014) Annals of Physical and Rehabilitation Medicine *Location*: France	Deaths in individuals with CP ($N = 3031$) Admin data (death records between 2000 and 2008)	Median age at death (45–54 years) 58.1% of individuals with CP were male	CP (ID status unknown) *Study did not report on CP type, CP severity, or presence or severity of ID	**Study objective:** To examine age of death and cause of death among individuals with CP compared to the general population **Findings:** • Individuals with CP died at a younger age compared to the general population. • Death occurred between 35 and 64 years of age in almost half of all individuals with CP. • 24% of deaths in individuals with CP (compared to 7% in general population) were caused by symptoms, signs, and abnormal clinical and laboratory findings, not classified elsewhere, with circulatory and respiratory problems coded as the most common in this category (66%). • 19% of individuals with CP (vs 6% in general population) died from diseases of the respiratory system, with pneumopathies the most frequent cause of death (24.5%), followed by acute respiratory failure (21%), and influenza (2.4%). • Diseases of the circulatory system were the third most common cause of death (15% of those with CP), with 52% of deaths due cardiopathy and 46% due to cardiac arrest. • 7% of deaths among those with CP were coded as deaths caused by tumors. • Deaths caused by infections and parasitic diseases were the fifth most common cause of death (5% of those with CP).

(*Continued*)

Table 1 Literature Review Findings: Physical Health Issues—cont'd

Study Reference (Authors, Year)	CP Sample Size (*n*) and Study Design (Admin Data, Chart Review, Survey, etc.)	Demographic Information (Age, Gender, etc.)	CP Type, CP Severity, and Presence and Severity of ID	Study Objectives and Findings
Strauss et al. (1999) Developmental Medicine and Child Neurology *Location*: USA	Adults with CP, ≤ 35 years or older ($N = 4087$) Administrative data (death records)	Two groups of adults with CP: 35 −54 years and ≥ 55 years Two groups based on the severity of individuals with CP's impairment: (1) not severe and (2) severe	CP (ID status unknown) Type of CP: Spastic, ataxic, dyskinetic, hypotonic, or other/unspecified *Study did not report on presence or severity of ID	**Study objective:** To identify diseases that may be associated with CP, in addition to those diseases whose diagnosis and/or treatment require improvement **Findings:** • Compared to the general population, the standardized mortality ratio (SMR) was higher in individuals with CP. • SMRs due to diseases of the respiratory, circulatory, and digestive systems were high for individuals with CP. • Breast cancer was three times more prevalent in adults with CP than in the general population.

Not severe CP group: 55.5% male **Severe CP group:** 54.1% male *Study did not report demographic information (e.g., mean age) for the overall sample of adults with CP	• Similarly, mortality due to brain cancer was also elevated, particularly in children with CP. • SMRs due to breast cancer were higher in the severe CP group than in the not severe CP group. • Rates of mortality due to certain diseases varied by age for adults with CP, such as SMRs due to brain cancer and circulatory diseases being higher in younger individuals with CP. • Found excess mortality in individuals with CP due to external causes, such as drowning and pedestrian accidents.

CP, cerebral palsy; ID, intellectual disability; SD, standard deviation; BMI, body mass index.

with rates of depression. According to one study, a large majority of adults with CP and ID also engaged in self-injurious behavior (Lundqvist, 2013). Stereotyped behavior and aggressive/destructive behavior was also present in individuals with CP and ID, although not as common as self-injurious behavior. In terms of level of ID, only one study (Lundqvist, 2013) examined how level of ID was related to mental health issues. As expected, high prevalence of self-injurious behavior and stereotyped behavior was associated with more severe levels of ID. Given that the majority of the studies reviewed examined mental health issues in adults with CP and ID, it is unknown how common mental health concerns are in those with CP and no ID. Furthermore, it is unclear if mental health issues can be attributed to the presence of an ID, to CP, to the co-occurrence of these two conditions (CP and ID), or to the same range of social determinants of mental health problems that apply to the general population.

Consistent with the literature on chronic physical issues and CP, research to date has failed to examine how specific demographic and clinical variables impact the prevalence of mental health issues among adults with CP. Additionally, the majority of studies focused on depression and depressive symptoms, and it will be important to understand if other mental health issues, such as anxiety or psychotic disorders, are also prevalent in this population. The studies reviewed did not consider whether mental health issues co-occurred with other physical health issues. Similarly, only one study (Lundqvist, 2013) reported on the number of individuals with CP and ID with mental health issues who were currently accessing services for such issues. As such, it is unknown how access to mental health services is related to prevalence of mental health issues in this population. Importantly, difficulties with cognitive functioning and communication in individuals with CP and ID may impact how mental health issues in this population are assessed, diagnosed, and understood. Thus, it is unclear if the research to date has considered if and how this complex symptom presentation has impacted research findings related to the prevalence of mental health issues in this population (Table 2).

3.3 Health Service Use in Adults with CP

Overall, research to date fails to demonstrate a consistent pattern of health service use among adults with CP. In terms of primary and preventative outpatient care, one Canadian study reported that compared to youth with CP, adults with CP received primary care consistent with clinical standards for the general population (Young et al., 2007). Specifically, over one

Table 2 Literature Review Findings: Mental Health Issues

Study Reference (Authors, Year)	CP Sample Size (*n*) and Study Design (Admin Data, Chart Review, Survey, etc.)	Demographic Information (Age, Gender, etc.)	CP Type, CP Severity, and Presence and Severity of ID	Study Objectives and Findings
Lundqvist (2013) Research in Developmental Disabilities *Location*: Sweden	Adults with CP and ID ($N = 41$) Cross-sectional study (Questionnaires completed by informant who knew adult with CP for more than 1 month)	≥18 years *Study did not report demographic information (e.g., age, gender, etc.) in adults with CP and ID	CP with ID *Study did not report on CP severity or CP type	**Study objective:** To explore the prevalence of behavior problems among adults with CP with ID, and to determine potential risk factors for these problems. **Findings:** • 46.3% of adults with CP with ID engaged in self-injurious behaviors (SIB); 22.0% of adults with CP with ID engaged in stereotyped behavior (SB); and 19.5% of adults with CP with ID engaged in aggressive/destructive behavior (ADB). • Adults with ID only, as well as those with epilepsy, cerebral palsy or general psychopathology were more likely to engage in SB. • Adults with CP with ID were less likely to engage in SB compared to individuals with visual impairment, epilepsy, and Fragile X syndrome. • Similarly, adults with CP with ID were less likely to engage in ADB compared to those with general psychopathology.

(*Continued*)

Table 2 Literature Review Findings: Mental Health Issues—cont'd

Study Reference (Authors, Year)	CP Sample Size (*n*) and Study Design (Admin Data, Chart Review, Survey, etc.)	Demographic Information (Age, Gender, etc.)	CP Type, CP Severity, and Presence and Severity of ID	Study Objectives and Findings
				• Prevalence of SB and SIB increased with the severity of ID, with those with severe ID having more SB and SIB. • 15% of individuals with CP and ID had contact with a psychiatric clinic.
McDermott et al. (2005) Disability and Rehabilitation *Location*: USA	Adults with CP and ID ($N = 154$) Adults with CP without ID ($N = 23$) Review of medical records (1990s –2003)	All participants were adults ($M = 45.9$); *Study did not report on gender in adults with CP	CP with ID; and CP without ID *Study did not report on CP severity or CP type **Severity of primary diagnosis:** **For CP with ID:** mild (25.3%); moderate (34.4%); severe (40.3%) **For CP without ID:** mild (47.8%); moderate (26.1%); severe (26.1%)	**Study objective:** To determine if the prevalence of depression differs between adults with and without a disability. • 12.3% ($n = 19$) of individuals with CP and ID were diagnosed with depression (e.g., had an ICD code for depression in their medical record). **Findings:** • 34.8% ($n = 8$) of individuals with CP without ID had a previous diagnosis of depression. • Prevalence of depression was significantly higher in the groups with CP without ID (34.8%) than the comparison sample (individuals without a disability). • Individuals with *mild* developmental disabilities (ID, autism, CP with/without ID) were more likely to be depressed than individuals with moderate or severe developmental disabilities.

van der Slot et al. (2012) Developmental Medicine and Child Neurology *Location*: The Netherlands	Adults with CP ($N = 56$) Cross-section study (face-to-face interviews and questionnaires)	25−45 years ($M = 36$ years, 5 months; $SD = 5$ years, 10 months) 35 males; 21 females	CP (ID status unknown) Type of CP: SBCP Measured severity of CP by GMFCS level; 23% level 1: 50% level II; 20% level III; and 7% level IV Exclusion criteria was severe intellectual impairment (needed to understand/follow instructions)	**Study objective:** To examine the prevalence of chronic pain, fatigue, and depressive symptoms co-occurring in adults with CP, and how these symptoms relate to daily functioning. **Findings:** **Depressive symptoms:** Adults with CP reported more depressive symptoms than the general population, with no differences between sexes. Adults with CP who had level III or level IV severity (as measured by the GMFCS) had higher depressive symptom scale scores compared to those with level I or level II GMFCS. • **Chronic pain:** Compared to the general population (39%), the majority (75%) of adults with CP reported chronic pain for more than 3 months. • **Fatigue:** 20% of the sample were fatigued (scores on FSS $\geq$4.0−<5.1); and 41% of the sample were severely fatigued (scores on FSS $\geq$5.1). • Chronic pain and depressive symptoms were not related; however, individuals who reported greater fatigue were more depressed.

CP, cerebral palsy; ID, intellectual disability; SD, standard deviation; GMFCS, Gross Motor Function Classification System; FSS, Fatigue Severity Scale.

quarter of adults with CP had a primary care provider and received comprehensive care, that is, two annual physicals, and one other physician visit over a 4-year period. In contrast, a second study suggested that adults with CP were less likely to receive routine preventative care compared to adults with multiple sclerosis and spinal cord injury (Kroll & Neri, 2004). This same study showed that preventive care among adults with CP varied by the degree to which an individual's ADLs were impacted, such that adults with CP who had more severe limitations in their ADLs received less preventive care than those with less severe limitations.

In terms of outpatient care generally, it is unclear whether youth or adults with CP receive more care. Some studies found that adults with CP used outpatient services (e.g., visits to physicians in emergency rooms and specialists) more frequently than youth (Goodman et al., 2011; Young et al., 2007), while other studies reported the opposite pattern (Mesterman et al., 2010; Stevenson, Pharoah, & Stevenson, 1997). In terms of satisfaction with health care services, results remain unknown. Although Young et al. (2006) reported on satisfaction with health care and transition services, findings were not presented according to age or diagnostic group.

Hospitalizations were quite common among adults with CP (approximately 20%), and the primary reason for admission was for physical conditions (e.g., respiratory issues and infections; Young et al., 2011). Hospitalizations as a result of mental illness were also common and contributed to longer hospital stays (Young et al., 2007). In this same study, gender did not impact service utilization patterns; however, it did impact length of stay, with women staying longer in hospital than men. Adults with CP used pediatric hospitals more frequently than adults in the general population, largely due to barriers encountered transitioning to the adult medical system (e.g., psychosocial and family needs, systemic issues of coordinating the transition, and patient maturity). Findings were less consistent in terms of hospital admissions and emergency room (ER) visits between age groups (youth versus adults) with some studies reporting increased use with age, and others reporting the opposite pattern. Differences across studies may in part be attributed to differences in the sample and methodologies employed, as well as health service systems.

Our review also identified several key gaps in our understanding of health service utilization patterns among adults with CP. For example, it is unknown what outpatient services individuals with CP receive, particularly older adults. One study identified mental health issues as the primary reason for hospital admission (Young et al., 2011), but the authors failed to specify what mental health issue(s) was the primary concern (e.g., behavior, psychosis, anxiety, depression, suicide). Studies on health services also tended to focus on adults with CP without ID. Thus, it is not known whether service use increases or decreases with cognitive limitations. Finally, health service research to date has been largely descriptive; only one study examined what factors predicted service use in adults with CP (Houtrow, Kang, & Newcomer, 2012). Findings from this review highlight the need for further research examining how individuals with CP use health services and what barriers they experience accessing specific types of health services, for both those with and without ID (Table 3).

4. DISCUSSION

This chapter outlines results of a comprehensive literature review examining physical and mental health issues among adults with CP, along with what is known about their health service use patterns. Findings suggest that adults with CP are at risk for developing a variety of physical health issues, and that for some adults with CP, both depression and self-injurious behavior are major concerns. Given the likelihood of physical and mental health issues in adulthood, it is essential that adults with CP have access to appropriate and specialized health services. Indeed research would suggest that they are frequently hospitalized, but it is not clear whether needed specialized services are accessible to them in adulthood. In many jurisdictions, the main specialized health services for CP reside in pediatric hospital settings. It is possible that with increased availability of specialized and proactive health care for adults with CP, their health service patterns in adulthood could be modified. More generally, our review identified a number of gaps in the literature requiring further attention:

1. *What proportion of chronic physical or mental health issues are comorbid versus secondary to CP?* This is an important question to address, because if these conditions are not due to CP, the steps to prevent and manage them will differ.
2. *What is the impact of coincidental ID on long-term functioning in individuals with CP?* It is imperative that we understand more about the role that ID plays. Studies must specify how many individuals have comorbid ID and the two groups need to be described separately. This is because both CP and ID are associated with health disparities. Otherwise, we can generalize and make assumptions about one group that does not

Table 3 Literature Review Findings: Health Service Use

Study Reference (Authors, Year)	CP Sample Size (*n*) and Study Design (Admin Data, Chart Review, Survey etc.)	Demographic Information (Age, Gender etc.)	CP Type, CP Severity, and Presence and Severity of ID	Study Objectives and Findings
Goodman et al. (2011) Pediatrics *Location*: USA	Adults with CP $N = 1947$ (unique patients) Transitional group $N = 1300$; Adult group $N = 647$ Data obtained from the Pediatric Health Information System from 41 free-standing, tertiary care children's hospital	Three groups: Pediatric (<18 years); Transitional (18–21 year); and Adults (>21 years) *Study did not report on gender in adults with CP	CP (ID status unknown) *Study did not report on CP type, CP severity, or presence or severity of ID	**Study objective:** To explore the number of adults seeking inpatient care in children's hospitals. **Findings:** • Pediatric hospital utilization patterns of individuals with CP were presented over a 10-year period. • There was a significant reduction in the service utilization patterns, in particular, discharges, patient days, and charges of pediatric patients with CP over the 10-year period. • In transitional and adult patients with CP, service utilization patterns increased.
Houtrow et al. (2012) Journal on Pediatric Rehabilitation and Medicine *Location*: USA	Adults with CP ($N = 1723$) Males: 883; females: 840 Admin data for 2005	18–64 years	CP (ID status unknown) *Study did not report on CP type or CP severity • ¼ of adults had a cognitive	**Study objectives:** (1) to describe the sample and demographic variables (age and health characteristics) of adults with CP receiving In-Home Support Services and (2) which factors were associated with health care utilization—specifically hospital and emergency room use.

limitations, with the majority of these individuals (75%) having limitations in all three areas (memory, judgment, and orientation)	**Findings:**
	• Variables that predicted ER and hospital use:
	  ◦ *Ethnicity*: Adults with CP of Asian descent were less likely to use the ER or hospital.
	  ◦ *Cognitive limitations*: The odds of ER use in adults with CP who had at least one cognitive limitation in memory, judgment, or orientation were lower than those who did not have cognitive impairments.
	• Odds of hospital use increased when *other health conditions* were present, as did ER use.
	• Gender, cognitive or activity limitations, In-Home Support Service Provider (e.g., spouse, partner, relative, etc.) were not associated with hospital use.
	• The odds of ER use were higher in adults with a number of difficulties related to activities of daily living.

(*Continued*)

Table 3 Literature Review Findings: Health Service Use—cont'd

Study Reference (Authors, Year)	CP Sample Size (*n*) and Study Design (Admin Data, Chart Review, Survey etc.)	Demographic Information (Age, Gender etc.)	CP Type, CP Severity, and Presence and Severity of ID	Study Objectives and Findings
Kroll and Neri (2004) Managed Care Quarterly *Location*: USA	$N = 53$ Longitudinal national survey of men with CP, multiple sclerosis, and spinal cord injury	**Overall sample:** Range (18–89) *Study did not report information on age in adults with CP	CP (ID status unknown) *Study did not report on CP type, CP severity or presence or severity of ID	**Study objective:** To examine the factors associated with the receipt of health service use, (e.g., prostate exams, medical exams, cholesterol checks) among adults with CP, multiple sclerosis (MS), and spinal cord injury. **Findings:** • Individuals with CP were significantly less likely to obtain general medical exams, cholesterol checks, and prostrate exams compared to individuals with MS. • Men with CP were less likely to obtain routine primary prevention services, especially prostate exams, compared to the other clinical populations.
Mesterman et al., (2010) Journal of Child Neurology *Location*: Israel	Adults with CP ($N = 95$) Retrospective survey of individuals who had assessed and received treatment at a	Older age group (>18 years) ($M = 22.8$ years; *Median* = 23 years) *Study did not report on gender in adults with CP	CP (ID status unknown) Spastic unilateral (23%); spastic bilateral (64%); dyskinetic (10%); and ataxic cerebral palsy (3%)	**Study objective:** To describe outcomes of adults with CP, as indicated by their health, functional, educational, and psychosocial status and quality of life. **Findings:** • Adults accessed outpatient services less frequently than their younger counterparts.

	child development center		*Study did not report on CP severity, or presence or severity of ID	• 34% accessed neurology services; 22% orthopedic; 3% ophthalmology; 9% psychiatry; and 3% neurosurgery. • ⅓ of the sample were not able to walk independently.
Stevenson et al. (1997) Developmental Medicine and Child Neurology *Location*: UK	$N = 45$ (CP adults) Cross-sectional study (questionnaires and interview of individuals with CP, caregivers, and an informant when necessary—social worker, care assistant, etc.)	Older group = 20–22 years *Study did not report on gender in adults with CP	CP (ID status unknown) *Study did not report on CP type, CP severity, or presence or severity of ID	**Study objective:** To examine the health and social service utilization patterns of individuals with CP. **Findings:** • General health of adults with CP (as reported by caregivers) was considered good in 13 participants and poor in 9 participants. • Epilepsy was the most common associated condition ($n = 12$). • 22 of 40 participants in the older group reported at least one hospital visit (compared to 26 of 28 younger participants). • 21 of 36 participants indicated that physiotherapy was the most commonly accessed service, with 10 out of 42 individuals reporting that they had accessed physiotherapy in the last 12 months.

(Continued)

Table 3 Literature Review Findings: Health Service Use—cont'd

Study Reference (Authors, Year)	CP Sample Size (*n*) and Study Design (Admin Data, Chart Review, Survey etc.)	Demographic Information (Age, Gender etc.)	CP Type, CP Severity, and Presence and Severity of ID	Study Objectives and Findings
Young et al. (2006) Physical and Occupational Therapy in Pediatrics *Location*: Canada	Adults with CP (*N* = 70) Three approaches: (1) health care analysis with admin data; (2) life and health outcomes survey; and (3) qualitative examination of the experience of transition to adult health care	Two age groups: Youth (13–17.9) and Adult (23–32.9) *Study did not report demographic information (e.g., age, gender, etc.) in adults with CP	CP (ID status unknown) Severity in CP sample was assessed using the GMFCS levels Ambulation status and severity of communications limitations were all discussed for overall sample *Study did not report on presence or severity of ID	**Study objective:** To describe the health and life outcomes of youth and young adults with CP. **Findings:** • 20% of adults with CP reported that their global health was fair or poor (compared to 5.1% of the general population, 38.5% of individuals with SB, and 11.8% with ABI). • 21.4% of adults with CP reported their health as excellent (compared to 32.7% of general population, 15.4% with SB, and 11.8% with ABI).
Young et al. (2007) Archives of Physical and Medical Rehabilitation *Location*: Canada	Adults with CP (*N* = 477) Sex: Females = 202; males = 275 Admin data between 1999 and 2002)	Mean age: males: 26.3; females: 26.4	CP (ID status unknown) Severity in CP groups was assessed using the GMFCS levels and only available for 18% of the total CP sample (adult and youth) Adult CP severity: 36% mild; 19%	**Study objective:** To investigate the health care utilization patterns of youth and young adults with CP. **Findings:** • Total visits to physician: 12,218 visits by adults with CP. Adults had 5.8% more visits than youth with CP, and 86.7% more visits than adults in the general population. • 52.8% of outpatient care for adults with CP was provided by primary care physicians

		moderate; 45% severe *Study did not report on CP type, CP severity, or presence or severity of ID in adults with CP	(PCP) in their office (51.4% from general practitioners and 1.4% from pediatricians). • Specialists provided 18.8% visits for adults, less than youth with CP (28.4%). • Adults received 6.4% of outpatient physician visits in the emergency department, higher than youths with CP (5.6%). • Compared to the general population, adults with CP received annual physicals at a rate similar to the general population, except males with CP who received annual physicals 2.2 times less often than males in the general population. • Adults were more likely than youth to receive a pattern of care that was consistent with primary care clinical standards for the general population. • Although youth with CP were more likely to be hospitalized, adult women with CP had the longest mean length of stay ($M = 7.88$ days). • Respiratory system concerns were the most common reason for hospital admission, followed by digestive system issues, injury and poisoning. • Higher rates of admission for endocrine/nutritional/metabolic, mental disorders, and genitourinary were noted among youth with CP.

(*Continued*)

Table 3 Literature Review Findings: Health Service Use—cont'd

Study Reference (Authors, Year)	CP Sample Size (n) and Study Design (Admin Data, Chart Review, Survey etc.)	Demographic Information (Age, Gender etc.)	CP Type, CP Severity, and Presence and Severity of ID	Study Objectives and Findings
Young et al. (2011) Archives of Physical and Medical Rehabilitation *Location*: Canada	Adults with CP ($N = 477$) Sex: Females = 202; males = 275 Admin data between 1999 and 2002	Mean age: 26.3 (2.6 years) 42.3% females	CP (ID status unknown) Severity in CP groups was assessed using the GMFCS levels and only available for 18% of the total CP sample (adult and youth) Adult CP severity: 36% mild; 19% moderate; 45% severe ⋆ Study did not report on CP type, CP severity, or presence or severity of ID in adults sample specifically	**Study objective:** To determine the most common reasons for hospital admission among youth and young adults with CP. **Findings:** • During the study period, 19.3% of young adults were admitted to an acute care hospital at least once. • Annual rates of admission for young adults were 98 per 1000. • Mean length of stay was 9.6 days for young adults. • Top five reasons for hospital admission among adults with CP: pneumonia (15.5% of admissions), epilepsy (7.5%), mental illness (6.4%), lower GI problems or constipation (6.4%), and malnutrition or dehydration (5.3%). • LOS among adults with CP tended to be longer (20.8 days) than among youth and was attributed to mental health issues. • Health issues/admissions that were unique to adults with CP fractures and urinary tract infections.

CP, cerebral palsy; ID, intellectual disability; SD, standard deviation; SB, stereotyped behavior; GMFCS, Gross Motor Function Classification System; ER, emergency room department; LOS, length of stay; ABI, Acquired Brain Injury.

apply to another. What needs to be determined is whether a condition is due to ID, due to CP regardless of ID status, or because of how the presence of CP and ID interact. For example, if it is the presence of CP that triggers self-injurious behavior, then rates of self-injury would be similar across functioning levels. If, however, it were attributed to ID, then rates of self-injury in those with ID would be similar to what is observed among those with CP and ID.

3. *What is the incidence of these physical health issues in the CP population?* Only a proportion of the studies reviewed were population based. There are risks to generalizing at the population level with samples that are either exclusive to the community, or exclusive to clinic populations. Both types of studies have their place, but are not enough to develop population-based interventions.
4. *What is the incidence of mental health diagnoses in the CP population?* The majority of research on adults with CP focuses on physical health conditions, perhaps because they are more obviously associated with CP. However, mental health issues can be as debilitating or even more debilitating if they remain unaddressed, particularly among adults with disabilities. Further research is required which focuses on mental health issues, as well as mental health treatment in this population. For example, are anxiety disorders no more likely in those with CP compared to other groups, or have they just not been studied? Similarly, do treatments for mental health issues need to be modified or tailored to the CP population, both in terms of psychosocial interventions and pharmacological interventions?

4.1 Health Disparities among Adults with CP

Research on health and health service use among adults with CP is clearly in its infancy, with only 18 studies compared to numerous studies focused on children with CP. This may be influenced in part by the fact that in the past, individuals with CP did not live as long as they do now. That said, we now know that given the right supports, individuals with CP can live well into adulthood, particularly if their health issues are well understood and managed. This is why research on adult health issues is so important, and why we chose to focus this section of the review on health disparities among adults with CP.

In order to discuss health disparities, there needs to be evidence that health problems or health services differ between adults with CP and a relevant comparison group. In this review, we consider disparities between children and adults with CP; adults with CP and the general population; and adults with CP and other clinical populations. For the purpose of this chapter, we also define health disparities as population-specific differences in key health indicators between people with and without CP, without inference to the cause of these differences (Krahn, Hammond, & Turner, 2006).

4.1.1 Adults with CP and Children with CP

Compared to studies of children, very few studies have examined the physical health, mental health, or health service use patterns of adults with CP. In terms of physical health issues, we identified only one study (Murphy et al., 2012) that examined medical issues between children and adults with CP. Results suggested that individuals with CP may experience different medical conditions based on their age. While some studies have examined the physical health issues of children with CP (Beckung & Hagberg, 2002; Kennes et al., 2002; Koman, Smith & Shilt, 2004; Liptak et al., 2001; Stiers, Vanneste, Coene, & Vandenbussche, 2002), few have studied these issues in adults (Henderson et al., 2009; van der Slot et al., 2013; Turk et al., 1997). Another considerable gap remains in our understanding of these issues longitudinally. Evidence from the literature to date would suggest that children and adults face unique and significant physical health challenges, but further work is needed to better understand why this is the case and what can be done about it. For example, certain physical health issues, such as bladder issues and chronic pain, become more pronounced in adulthood. As such, it is essential that research examines these physical health challenges at different life stages and raises awareness about how best to diagnosis and treat these issues in this population. Additionally, it will be particularly important to understand the needs and health issues of young adults with CP transitioning from the pediatric to adult health system, where they may encounter considerable changes in service eligibility or accessibility.

In terms of mental health issues affecting adults with CP, our search yielded no studies comparing children and adults. While some studies examined mental health and behavior problems in adults with CP (Lundqvist, 2013; McDermott et al., 2005; van der Slot et al., 2012), this limited research focused on symptoms of depression or challenging behavior, but not other mental health issues such as psychosis, anxiety, or substance-abuse disorders, which may also impact individuals with CP. Similarly, although research to date has identified a link between individuals with CP and those with ID or

ASD, little is known about their mental health. Understanding which mental health and developmental issues are most common at different ages in individuals with CP, and among those with and without ID, is critical in identifying how best to support the mental health needs of individuals with CP across the life span. It is also important that we study whether the onset of psychiatric issues in those with CP is similar to individuals without CP.

Our search identified four studies comparing the health service use patterns of children/youth and adults with CP (Goodman et al., 2011; Young et al., 2006, 2007, 2011). Findings were generally inconsistent, and while this literature represents an important first step toward understanding health utilization among individuals with CP, a number of critical areas have yet to be studied including indicators of primary care and specialist visits. For example, Strauss et al. (1999) found that breast cancer was three times more prevalent in adults with CP than women in the general population. This finding highlights the importance of examining primary care indicators, such as cancer screening, in this population.

4.1.2 Adults with CP and Other Clinical Populations

To date, no studies have compared the physical and mental health issues in individuals with CP to other, clinically relevant populations, such as those with epilepsy or spina bifida. Such research would help inform whether difficulties accessing health services are unique to the CP population or whether individuals with similar disabilities experience the same health issues and health needs. Research comparing these three populations has tended to focus on similarities in the etiology or risk factors for developing these conditions, as well as commonalities in deficits or symptoms (Wallace, 2001; Wu et al., 2013); however, further research is needed that contrasts these populations using comparable methodologies. The same argument can be made with regard to health services utilization research among these three populations.

4.1.3 Adults with CP and the General Population

There are clear differences between individuals with CP and the general population, but the question remains as to how unique these issues are to CP, as opposed to other types of disability. It is also unknown how much of the differences are a result of discrimination from having a disability. Most studies comparing individuals with CP to the general population have focused on differences in mortality (Duruflé-Tapin et al., 2014), physical health issues (Day et al., 2007; Jahnsen, Villien, Aamodt, Stanghelle, & Holm, 2004; Jahnsen, Villien, Stanghelle, & Holm, 2003; Liptak et al., 2001), and patterns of health service use (Young et al., 2006, 2007, 2011). In terms of mortality, because of their complex medical and physical health issues, individuals with CP tend to die at a younger age than the general population (Duruflé-Tapin et al., 2014). Compared to the general population, individuals with CP across all ages, also tend to use health services more often (Young et al., 2006, 2007, 2011). However, no studies were identified that examined the mental health issues of individuals with CP compared to the general population. It may be that medical, cognitive, or communication issues inherent to this population make it challenging to tease apart mental health issues, however, identifying and supporting mental health problems among individuals with CP should be an important clinical and research focus going forward.

5. CONCLUSIONS

Overall, our review showed that common chronic physical health issues frequently seen in adults with CP included bladder issues, musculoskeletal problems, and chronic pain. Additionally, in some studies gender impacted the prevalence of, and risk for, certain comorbid physical issues, such as fragility fractures from osteopenia in women (Henderson et al., 2009). Findings indicate that adults with CP are also at risk for depression and self-injurious behavior, although it is not known how in particular mental health issues are related to the presence of ID. Lastly, research to date fails to demonstrate a consistent pattern of health service use among adults with CP.

While there is an emerging literature examining differences in the health and health service utilization patterns of individuals with CP, a number of gaps remain. First, studies clarifying what physical and mental health issues are comorbid versus secondary to adults with CP. Second, how does the presence of an ID impact the physical, mental health, and health utilization patterns of this population. Third, population-level studies are needed to ensure that representative, generalizable samples of the population are obtained. Fourth, studies which consider the mental health issues of adults with CP, beyond depression and self-injury. Lastly, there is a need for studies that compare adults with CP to children with CP, and to the general population and other clinically relevant groups.

ACKNOWLEDGMENTS

This paper was funded by the Ministry of Health and Long-Term Care Health Services Research Fund program award (Ministry Grant #06671) and is part of the Health Care Access Research and Developmental Disabilities (H-CARDD) program. The opinions, results, and conclusions reported in this paper are those of the authors and are not necessarily those of the funding sources. No endorsement by the Ontario Ministry of Health and Long-Term Care is intended or should be inferred.

REFERENCES

Bax, M., Goldstein, M., Rosenbaum, P., Leviton, A., Paneth, N., Dan, B., et al. (2005). Proposed definition and classification of cerebral palsy. *Developmental Medicine and Child Neurology, 47*(8), 571–576.

Beckung, E., & Hagberg, G. (2002). Neuroimpairments, activity limitations, and participation restrictions in children with cerebral palsy. *Developmental Medicine and Child Neurology, 44*(5), 309–316.

Day, S. M., Strauss, D. J., Vachon, P. J., Rosenbloom, L., Shavelle, R. M., & Wu, Y. W. (2007). Growth patterns in a population of children and adolescents with cerebral palsy. *Developmental Medicine and Child Neurology, 49*(3), 167–171.

Dodd, K. J., Taylor, N. F., & Damiano, D. L. (2002). Systematic review of the effectiveness of strength-training programs for people with cerebral palsy. *Archives of Physical Medicine and Rehabilitation, 83*(8), 1157–1164.

Duruflé-Tapin, A., Colin, A., Nicolas, B., Lebreton, C., Dauvergne, F., & Gallien, P. (2014). Analysis of the medical causes of death in cerebral palsy. *Annals of Physcial and Rehabilitation Medicine, 57*, 24–37.

Goodman, D. M., Hall, M., Levin, A., Watson, S., Williams, R. G., Shah, S. S., et al. (2011). Adults with chronic health conditions originating in childhood: inpatient experience in children's hospitals. *Pediatrics, 128*(1), 5–13.

Hemming, K., Hutton, J. L., & Pharoah, P. O. (2006). Long-term survival for a cohort of adults with cerebral palsy. *Developmental Medicine and Child Neurology, 48*(2), 90–95.

Henderson, C. M., Rosasco, M., Robinson, L. M., Meccarello, J., Janicki, M. P., Turk, M. A., et al. (2009). Functional impairment severity is associated with health status among older persons with intellectual disability and cerebral palsy. *Journal of Intellectual Disability Research, 53*(11), 887–897.

Houtrow, A., Kang, T., & Newcomer, R. (2012). In-home supportive services for individuals with cerebral palsy in California. *Journal of Pediatric Rehabilitation Medicine, 5*(3), 187–195.

Jahnsen, R., Villien, L., Aamodt, G., Stanghelle, J., & Holm, I. (2004). Musculoskeletal pain in adults with cerebral palsy compared with the general population. *Journal of Rehabilitation Medicine, 36*(2), 78–84.

Jahnsen, R., Villien, L., Stanghelle, J. K., & Holm, I. (2003). Fatigue in adults with cerebral palsy in Norway compared with the general population. *Developmental Medicine and Child Neurology, 45*(5), 296–303.

Kennes, J., Rosenbaum, P., Hanna, S. E., Walter, S., Russell, D., Raina, P., et al. (2002). Health status of school-aged children with cerebral palsy: information from a population-based sample. *Developmental Medicine and Child Neurology, 44*(4), 240–247.

Ketelaar, M., Vermeer, A., & Holders, P. J. (1998). Functional motor abilities of children with cerebral palsy: a systematic literature review of assessment measures. *Child Rehabilitation, 12*(5), 369–380.

Koman, L. A., Smith, B. P., & Shilt, J. S. (2004). Cerebral palsy. *Lancet, 363*(9421), 1619–1631.

Koritsas, S., & Iacono, T. (2009). Limitations in life participation and independence due to secondary conditions. *American Association on Intellectual and Developmental Disabilities, 114*(6), 437–448.

Krahn, G. L., Hammond, L., & Turner, A. (2006). A cascade of disparities: health and health care access for people with intellectual disabilities. *Mental Retardation and Developmental Disabilities Research Reviews, 12*(1), 70–82.

Krigger, K. (2006). Cerebral palsy: an overview. *American Family Physician, 73*(1), 91–100.

Kroll, T., & Neri, M. T. (2004). Use of primary prevention services among male adults with cerebral palsy, multiple sclerosis, or spinal cord injury in managed care and fee-for-service. *Managed Care Quarterly, 12*, 6–10.

Liptak, G. S., O'Donnell, M., Conaway, M., Chumlea, W. C., Worley, G., Henderson, R. C., et al. (2001). Health status of children with moderate to severe cerebral palsy. *Developmental Medicine and Child Neurology, 43*(6), 364–370.

Lundqvist, L. (2013). Prevalence and risk markers of behavior problems among adults with intellectual disabilities: a total population study in Orebro County, Sweden. *Research in Developmental Disabilities, 34*(4), 1346–1356.

McDermott, S., Moran, R., Platt, T., Issac, T., Wood, H., & Dasari, S. (2005). Depression in adults with disabilities, in primary care. *Disability and Rehabilitation, 27*(3), 117–123.

Mesterman, R., Leitner, Y., Yifat, R., Gilutz, G., Levi-Hakeni, O., Bitchonsky, O., et al. (2010). Cerebral palsy—long-term medical, functional, educational, and psychosocial outcomes. *Journal of Child Neurology, 25*(1), 36–42.

Murphy, K. P., Boutin, S. A., & Ide, K. R. (2012). Cerebral palsy, neurogenic bladder, and outcomes of lifetime care. *Developmental Medicine and Child Neurology, 54*(10), 945–950.

Mutch, L., Alberman, E., Hagberg, B., Kodama, K., & Perst, M. V. (1992). Cerebral palsy epidemiology: where are we now and where are we going. *Developmental Medicine and Child Neurology, 34*(6), 547–551.

Rosenbaum, P., Paneth, N., Leviton, A., Goldstein, M., & Bax, M. (2006). A report: the definition and classification of cerebral palsy April 206. *Developmental Medicine and Child Neurology, 49*(109), 8–14.

van der Slot, W. M. A., Nieuwenhuijsen, C., van der Berg-Emons, R. J. G., Bergen, M. P., Hilbernik, S. R., Stam, H. J., et al. (2012). Chronic pain, fatigue, and depressive symptoms in adults with spastic bilateral cerebral palsy. *Developmental Medicine and Child Neurology, 54*(9), 836–842.

van der Slot, W. M. A., Roebroeck, M. E., Nieuwenhuijsen, C., Bergen, M. P., Stam, H. J., Burdof, A., & The MoveFit and Lifespan Research Group. (2013). Cardiovascular disease risk in adults with spastic bilateral cerebral palsy. *Journal of Rehabilitation Medicine, 45*, 866–872.

Stevenson, C. J., Pharoah, P. O. D., & Stevenson, R. (1997). Cerebral palsy—the transition from youth to adulthood. *Developmental Medicine and Child Neurology, 39*(5), 336–342.

Stiers, P., Vanneste, G., Coene, S., & Vandenbussche, E. (2002). Visual-perceptual impairment in a random sample of children with cerebral palsy. *Developmental Medicine and Child Neurology, 44*(6), 370–382.

Strauss, D., Cable, W., & Shavelle, R. (1999). Causes of excess mortality in cerebral palsy. *Developmental Medicine and Child Neurology, 41*(9), 580–585.

Turk, M. A., Geremski, C. A., Rosenbaum, P. F., & Weber, R. J. (1997). The health status of women with cerebral palsy. *Archives of Physical Medicine and Rehabilitation, 78*, s-10–17.

Vincer, M. J., Allen, A. C., Joseph, K. S., Stinson, D. A., Scott, H., & Wood, E. (2006). Increasing prevalence of cerebral palsy among very preterm infants: a population-based study. *Pediatrics, 118*(6), e1621–1626.

Wallace, S. J. (2001). Epilepsy in cerebral palsy. *Developmental Medicine and Child Neurology, 43*(10), 713–717.

Wu, Y. W. (2002). Systematic review of chorioamnionitis and cerebral palsy. *Mental Retardation and Developmental Disabilities Research Reviews, 8*(1), 25–29.

Wu, C. S., Pedersen, L. H., Miller, J. E., Sun, Y., Streja, E., Uldall, P., et al. (2013). Risk of cerebral palsy and childhood epilepsy related to infections during pregnancy. *PLoS One, 8*(2), 1–7.

Young, N. L., Gilbert, T. K., McCormick, A., Ayling-Campos, A., Boydell, K., Law, M., et al. (2007). Youth and young adults with cerebral palsy: their use of physician and hospital services. *Archives of Physical Medicine and Rehabilitation, 88*(6), 696–702.

Young, N. L., McCormick, A. M., Gilbert, T., Ayling-Campos, A. N., Burke, T., Fehlings, D., et al. (2011). Reasons for hospital admissions among youth and young adults with cerebral palsy. *Archives of Physical Medicine and Rehabilitation, 92*(1), 46–50.

Young, N. L., McCormick, A., Mills, W., Barden, W., Boyden, K., Law, M., et al. (2006). The transition study: a look at youth and adults with cerebral palsy, spina bifida, and acquired brain injury. *Physical & Occupational Therapy in Pediatrics, 26*(4), 25–45.

CHAPTER SIX

A Review of Health Surveillance in Older Adults with Intellectual and Developmental Disabilities

Hélène Ouellette-Kuntz[*,§,1], **Lynn Martin**[¶],
Katherine McKenzie[*]
[*]Department of Public Health Sciences, Queen's University, Kingston, ON, Canada
[§]Ongwanada, Kingston, ON, Canada
[¶]Department of Health Sciences, Lakehead University, Thunder Bay, ON, Canada
[1]Corresponding author: e-mail address: helene.kuntz@queensu.ca

Contents

International Review of Research in Developmental Disabilities, Volume 48
ISSN 2211-6095
http://dx.doi.org/10.1016/bs.irrdd.2015.03.004

Abstract

Increasing life expectancy, shifts to supporting people with intellectual and developmental disabilities in the community, their increased vulnerability to poor health, and the need for greater accountability call for more than occasional studies of aging in this population. Ongoing monitoring of health indicators is feasible in various capacities in different jurisdictions. In this chapter, we first situate the literature about aging with intellectual and developmental disabilities in the context of aging in the general population, and identify key indicators for consideration in health surveillance in older adults with intellectual and developmental disabilities. We then report on a population-based study in Ontario, Canada, which confirms earlier reports of increasing numbers of older adults with intellectual and developmental disabilities, premature aging in this population, and expected trends in use of home care and admission to long-term care. The review concludes with recommendations for future surveillance activities in Ontario and beyond. Concerned researchers should partner with knowledge users/decision-makers to maximize the use of electronic administrative and clinical data available to them. In time, the international research community may identify common indicators and methods thereby generating comparators across systems that can further inform policy development.

1. INTRODUCTION

This review of special considerations in the health surveillance of older adults with intellectual and developmental disabilities is comprised of two main parts. Part 1 consists of a review of the literature blending findings related to population aging, including life expectancy, changes in living arrangements and health care needs, for the general population and the subset who live with intellectual and developmental disabilities. This part concludes with a review of studies which provide insights into the elaboration of a framework of indicators for health surveillance in older adults with intellectual and developmental disabilities. Part 2 describes the methods and results of a population-based study in Ontario, Canada, which shows promise for use in ongoing monitoring of health in older adults with intellectual and developmental disabilities. The review concludes with recommendations for future surveillance activities in Ontario and beyond.

2. PART 1: LITERATURE REVIEW

2.1 Population Aging

Interest in population aging is recognized as a global issue, affecting all developed and developing countries. Population aging is attributed to decreasing childhood and adult mortality, as well as to decreasing fertility rates (United Nations, 2013). Though rates are higher in developed than in developing areas (Mirkin & Weinberger, 2001), in 2010, persons 65 years of age or older made up approximately 8% of the population worldwide; this rate is expected to triple by 2050 (National Institute of Aging (NIA), National Institutes of Health (NIH), US Department of Health and Human Services (USDHHS), & World Health Organization (WHO), 2011). Similarly, the World Population Ageing 2013 report projects that the number of adults aged 60 years or more will grow to more than double by 2050—from 841 million to over 2 billion (United Nations, 2013). It is also believed that the proportion of "oldest old" (i.e., persons aged 80 years or more) will also grow (United Nations, 2013).

Just as the general global population is aging, so too is the subset of the population with intellectual and developmental disabilities. Decreasing childhood mortality, technological advances, and increasing life expectancy have led to growth in the population of adults with intellectual and developmental disabilities (Janicki, Dalton, Henderson, & Davidson, 1999; Marks, Sisirak, & Hsieh, 2008). Overall, intellectual and developmental disabilities are estimated to affect between 1.5% and 2.5% of adults in the United States (Department of Health and Human Services, 2000) and between 1% and 3% in Canada (Sullivan et al., 2011). About 10 years ago, it was estimated that adults aged 65 years or more made up approximately 12% of the population of persons with intellectual and developmental disabilities in the United States; this was projected to reach 25% by 2040 (Davidson, Prasher, & Janicki, 2003).

2.1.1 Changes in Life Expectancy

Life expectancy in the general population is 78 years in developed and 68 years in developing regions (United Nations, 2013). The United Nations (2013) predict that life expectancy will reach 83 years and 75 years in developed and developing regions, respectively, as early as 2045. Life expectancy among persons with intellectual and developmental disabilities has increased from 19 years of age in the 1930s to approximately 66 years in the 1990s (Bittles et al., 2002; Janicki et al., 1999), though this gain is not seen equally across the entire population. For example, life expectancy among persons with Down syndrome in the 1990s was only 56 years (Coppus, 2013). It is generally accepted that life expectancy among persons with intellectual and developmental disabilities has continued to increase since the 1990s although it remains lower than in the general population (Coppus, 2013). More recent life expectancy figures for this population were not identified through our review.

Globally, women live longer than men. The World Population Ageing 2013 report finds that there are 85 men to every 100 women 60 years of age or older, and 61 men per 100 women 80 years of age or older (United Nations, 2013). Stancliffe et al. (2012) found a similar trend among adults with Down syndrome (i.e., men with Down syndrome have a shorter life expectancy than women with Down syndrome), but a different pattern among persons with intellectual and developmental disabilities without Down syndrome (i.e., women have a shorter life expectancy).

2.1.2 Changes in Living Arrangements

Approximately 74% of older adults (>59 years) in the general population of more developed regions live in the community, either alone or with their spouse only (United Nations, 2013). In Canada, approximately 93% of older adults in the general population live in their home, many of whom live alone (Canadian Institute for Health Information (CIHI), 2011a). Based on information from the 2006 Canadian census, CIHI (2011a) reported that 37% of adults aged 75 years or more lived alone and that 49% of those 85 years and older lived alone.

The process of deinstitutionalization of persons with intellectual and developmental disabilities is complete, in progress, or planned in many jurisdictions around the world. As such, in many nations, all persons with intellectual and developmental disabilities live in the community. When these individuals live in their family home, the ability of their parents to provide ongoing support will certainly be affected by their own age-related health conditions and physical impairments. At some point, it is likely that both parents and their aged children with intellectual and developmental disabilities will require some type of formalized support to remain in the home. As such, health and social service agencies in the community should expect to see a further rise in the number of aged persons with intellectual and developmental disabilities who require support.

2.2 Aging and Health

Population aging is associated with increases in rates of disability and chronic conditions (United Nations, 2013). Women, on average, live longer than men but experience higher rates of poor health (NIA, NIH, USDHHS, & WHO, 2011).

Adults with intellectual and developmental disabilities are known to have distinctive health care needs (Ouellette-Kuntz, 2005), and care needs are known to increase with age. While it is estimated that approximately 12% of adults with intellectual and developmental disabilities are currently aged 65 years or more (Davidson et al., 2003), the proportion requiring aging-related care is likely to be much higher given that intellectual and developmental disabilities are associated with premature aging (Béange, 2002)—starting as early as at 40 years of age (Lifshitz & Merrick, 2004; Stax, Luciano, Dunn, & Quevedo, 2010).

In their review of the literature published between 1999 and 2009, Haveman et al. (2010) report that "there was almost a total lack of information about the aging process and its consequences for persons with [intellectual and developmental disabilities] in low- and middle-income countries" (p. 64). The studies that do exist are therefore biased in that they reflect the context of higher income countries, such as Canada, the United States, Europe, Australia, and New Zealand (Haveman et al., 2010). The knowledge gained from these studies is often further biased by use of samples, rather than population-level data. Consequently, the findings are often not representative beyond the setting (e.g., institutions) or condition (e.g., Down syndrome) studied.

Though the evidence base focusing on age-related health conditions among persons with intellectual and developmental disabilities is relatively small, it suggests that persons with intellectual and developmental disabilities experience higher rates of age-related health conditions than the general population (Cooper, 1997; Haveman et al., 2010; Krahn, Hammond, & Turner, 2006; World Health Organization, 2000)—most often at earlier ages (see Marks et al., 2008). For example, older adults with intellectual and developmental disabilities are known to have higher rates of **dementia** than the general population (Strydom, Chan, King, Hassiotis, & Livingston, 2013; Torr, 2005). In their study, Strydom, Hassiotis, King, and Livingston (2008) reported a prevalence of dementia of 18.3% among older adults with intellectual and developmental disabilities, compared to 2.8% in the general population. The incidence of dementia among older adults with intellectual and developmental disabilities was reported to be up to five times that in the general aging population (Strydom et al., 2013). The overall incidence rate was 54.6/1000 person years for adults with IDD 60 years of age or more and 97.8/1000 person years among those aged 70–74 years.

The prevalence of dementia is even higher among those with Down syndrome (see Coppus et al., 2006), who have a genetic predisposition for dementia (Cooper, 1997). It is believed that by the age of 40 years, almost all adults with Down syndrome show neuropathological signs of Alzheimer disease (Wisniewski, Wisniewski, & Wen, 1985). Coppus et al. (2006) found that, among persons with Down syndrome, the prevalence of dementia doubled with every increment of 5 years in age up to the age of 60 years (8.9% in 45–49 years; 17.7% in 50–54 years; 32.1% in 55–59 years). The prevalence of dementia decreased among those with Down syndrome aged 60 years or more (to 25.2%), likely as the result of increased mortality (Coppus et al., 2006).

Falls are a major cause of both morbidity and mortality among older adults in the general population (Ambrose, Paul, & Hausdorff, 2013), and as such, have been widely studied. Older adults with intellectual and developmental disabilities are known to experience higher rates of falls compared to the general population (rate of 1.00 fall per person per year vs 0.45–0.65 in the general population) (Enkelaar, Smulders, van Schrojenstein Lantman-de Valk, Weerdesteyn, & Geurts, 2013). Older adults with intellectual and developmental disabilities are also more likely to have many risk factors for falls. For example, **balance** is an important intrinsic risk factor for falls, and older adults with intellectual and developmental disabilities experience problems in balance similar to what is seen among persons 20 years older in the general population (Hilgenkamp, van Wijck, & Evenhuis, 2013). Bastiaanse, Mergler, Evenhuis, and Echteld (2014) reported that 43.9% of adults with intellectual and developmental disabilities 50 years or more in the Healthy Ageing with Intellectual Disability (HA-ID) study had **low bone quality**, thereby increasing risk for fractures. They also report that age, sex (female), level of intellectual and developmental disabilities (severe), **impaired mobility**, low body mass index (BMI), and use of anticonvulsant drugs were positively associated with low bone density. **Medications, and polypharmacy** in particular, represent an extrinsic factor linked to increased risk of falls (Slattum & Ansello, 2013). That persons with intellectual and developmental disabilities are at increased risk of polypharmacy is well known. A recent study found that rates of polypharmacy increase with age among persons with intellectual and developmental disabilities 18–64 years old (Cobigo, Ouellette-Kuntz, Lake, Wilton, & Lunsky, 2013). It has also been shown that medication errors are high among older adults with intellectual and developmental disabilities. A recent study reported that 47.5% of a sample of 600 adults with intellectual and developmental disabilities aged 50+ years had one or more medication errors in a one-year period (Zaal, van der Kaaij, Evenhuis, & van den Bemt, 2013). This same study reported that the likelihood of prescription errors increased significantly with age (adjusted odds ratio = 1.03 with each year; 95% confidence interval (CI) 1.01–1.06). **Prevention practices** are important to minimize the occurrence of falls and fractures. In the general population, **bone mineral density testing** is recommended among postmenopausal women and men over the age of 50 who have experienced a previous low-trauma fracture as a method of monitoring ongoing risk (Brown & Josse, 2002). While adults with intellectual and developmental disabilities are not identified as a high-risk group, an analysis of adults aged 40–64 years in Ontario revealed a significant discrepancy between adults with and without intellectual and developmental disabilities who received the recommended bone mineral density test in the year following a low-trauma fracture (Balogh et al., 2013).

A number of studies of aging and health have focused on **cardiovascular disease**, as it is among the leading causes of morbidity worldwide (World Health Organization, 2014). A recent large-scale study showed that rates of cardiovascular disease and many of its risk factors were similarly distributed across populations of aging adults with and without intellectual and developmental disabilities (de Winter, Bastiaanse, Hilgenkamp, Evenhuis, & Echteld, 2012a), others have found that older adults with intellectual and developmental disabilities actually fared better than the general aging population in terms of risk factors for cardiovascular disease (Wallace & Schluter, 2008), though risk factors often go unnoticed among those with intellectual and developmental disabilities (de Winter et al., 2012a).

While there has been attention to a number of different age-related health conditions in the literature, there is also recognition that few people will experience a single health condition. In their review, Haveman et al. (2010) noted the complete lack of articles focused on co/multimorbidity, which is surprising given that **co/multimorbidity** is known to be high among adults with intellectual and developmental disabilities and to increase with age. Since then, discussions of comorbidity (e.g., mental health and cardiovascular disease—see de Winter, Hermans, Evenhuis, & Echteld, 2015) and multimorbidity (see Hermans & Evenhuis, 2014) have appeared in the literature.

2.2.1 Multimorbidity

Given the range of health issues that are frequently present in older adults with intellectual and developmental disabilities, the adoption of a framework and the identification of a measure that encompasses overall health are warranted. In the general population, multimorbidity (also called comorbidity) is often used as an indicator of overall health and to characterize health complexity. In epidemiological studies, it is often defined as the presence of two or more concurrent, chronic conditions which may or may not negatively influence daily functioning (Marengoni et al., 2011). Multimorbidity is common among persons with intellectual and developmental disabilities. Hermans and Evenhuis (2014) reported that as many as 80% of adults with intellectual and developmental disabilities (≥50 years of age) in the Netherlands experienced at least two chronic conditions, and 47% had at least four conditions. Similarly, McCarron et al. (2013) estimated that 71% of adults with intellectual and developmental disabilities (≥40 years of age) in Ireland had multimorbidity, with the proportion being highest among those aged 40–49 years.

Valderas, Starfield, Sibbald, Salisbury, and Roland (2009) provide a framework for understanding comorbidity, multimorbidity, and complexity which is particularly applicable to intellectual and developmental disabilities. In their model, a number of conditions (condition 2 to condition *n*) occur in the presence of an index condition (condition 1). Conditions 2 to *n* are the comorbidities (e.g., dementia, cardiovascular disease) which combined with the index condition create multimorbidity. Multimorbidity affects individuals differently depending on health-related attributes such as age, sex, and other vulnerabilities. While there has been a practice in our field to treat intellectual and developmental disabilities as a comorbidity as in the case of dual diagnosis, the social model of disability places these as vulnerabilities rather than medical conditions. The experience of multimorbidity can then be described as the morbidity burden. Recognizing that nonhealth-related attributes (e.g., living arrangement, informal supports) also have an impact on an individual's need for care, the term complexity is used to capture the unique needs of individuals with multimorbidity given their individual circumstances (see Figure 1) (Valderas et al., 2009).

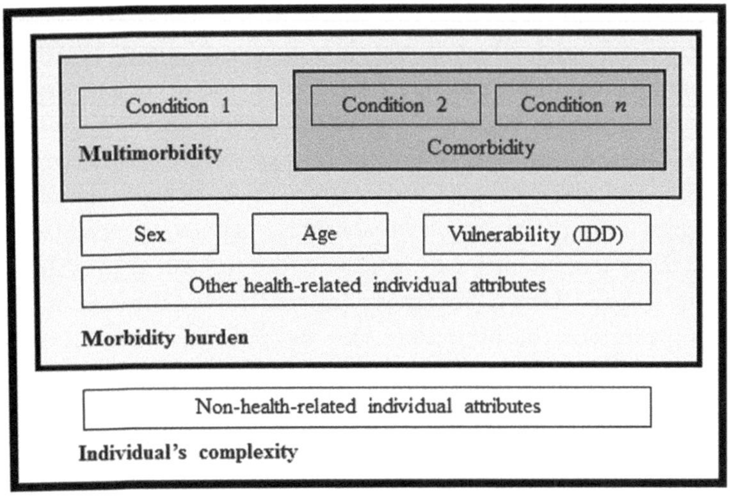

Figure 1 Model to understand health complexity in older adults with intellectual and developmental disabilities. *Adapted from Valderas et al. (2009).*

2.2.2 Frailty

Frailty is another method used to characterize health complexity, particularly among the elderly. It has been shown to be a useful predictor of adverse outcomes, such as use of long-term care (LTC) services, falls, or death (Ensrud et al., 2008; Rockwood, Mitnitski, Song, Steen, & Skoog, 2006). While there is no agreed-upon consensus on the definition and measurement of frailty (Clegg, Young, Iliffe, Rikkert, & Rockwood, 2013), it is generally accepted that frailty incorporates vulnerabilities within and across multiple domains, including cognitive, biological, social, psychological, and environmental (Rockwood et al., 2005). With respect to measurement, two multidimensional approaches to assessing frailty are frequently described in the literature.

The first involves the "frailty phenotype," developed for the Cardiovascular Health Study (Fried et al., 2001). According to this model, frailty is defined as the presence of at least three of the following characteristics: weight loss, weakness, poor endurance and exhaustion, low physical activity, and slowness. The presence of two of these features is characteristic of pre-frailty. It should be noted that this model has been criticized for its exclusive focus on the physical aspects of frailty (Rothman, Leo-Summers, & Gill, 2008; Sternberg, Schwartz, Karunananthan, Bergman, & Clarfield, 2011). The frailty phenotype approach has been used to evaluate frailty among persons with intellectual and developmental disabilities—in particular, in the

HA-ID study, which included 1050 adults with intellectual and developmental disabilities aged 50 years or older in the Netherlands (Evenhuis, Hermans, Hilgenkamp, Bastiaanse, & Echteld, 2012). The authors reported that 13% of participants were frail, and 60% were prefrail. Evenhuis et al. (2012) also found that age was positively associated with frailty, where those aged 65 years and older were 1.7 times more likely to be frail compared to their younger counterparts. Approximately 11% of persons aged 50–64 years were considered frail, which was similar to the published prevalence estimates in the general Dutch population of adults over the age of 65 years. This finding supports the hypothesis that individuals with intellectual and developmental disabilities experience frailty earlier.

The second approach to measuring frailty is the accumulation of deficits model (Rockwood et al., 2006), which proposes that individuals become increasingly frail based on the number of health deficits present. Here, deficits refer to any sign, symptom, disability, disease, or abnormal laboratory measurement, and there is no set list of deficits. Instead, the emphasis is on the proportion of deficits present out of the total number of deficits measured. Therefore, unlike the frailty phenotype model which requires specific information, this approach can be more easily used when relying on secondary data. It can be applied to a range of data sets that collect health-related information, even those that may not have been designed to measure frailty per se. A recent systematic review of 20 frailty instruments reported that use of an accumulation of deficits approach is the most promising in that it permits inclusion of all potential factors leading to frailty (De Vries et al., 2011). The accumulation of deficits approach was also applied to a subset of the HA-ID cohort of older adults (Schoufour, Mitnitski, Rockwood, Evenhuis, & Echteld, 2013). Schoufour et al. (2013) reported that individuals with intellectual and developmental disabilities had similar rates of frailty at age 50 as did the European general population at age 70, again reinforcing the notion that frailty occurs earlier among persons with intellectual and developmental disabilities. In following this cohort over time, it was found that age-related **frailty** was related to an increase in care intensity, even after controlling for skills related to activities of daily living (ADLs—e.g., eating and bathing) and instrumental activities of daily living (IADLs—e.g., housework and meal preparation) (Schoufour, Evenhuis, & Echteld, 2014).

Individuals with intellectual and developmental disabilities have preexisting and life-long disabilities which may incorrectly appear as age-related deficits in such frailty measures. It is therefore important to reevaluate both the conceptualization and measurement of frailty to ensure they emphasize change and vulnerability to stressors, rather than merely counting or acknowledging preexisting limitations (Rockwood, Hogan, & MacKnight, 2000). As it has been recognized that not all measures of health suitable for the general population will produce accurate results among persons with intellectual and developmental disabilities (Brehmer-Rinderer, Zeilinger, Radaljevic, & Weber, 2013), measurement of frailty may need to be reconsidered in this population.

Recognizing the importance of a frailty measure designed specifically for individuals with intellectual and developmental disabilities, Brehmer and Weber (2010) used the POMONA II study to create a new frailty measure—the Vienna Frailty Questionnaire for persons with Intellectual Disabilities (VFQ-ID), revised a few years later to become the VFQ-ID-R (Brehmer-Rinderer et al., 2013). This measure consists of a total of 34 symptoms related to change in four domains, physical, psychological, cognitive, and social aspects of health, rather than the mere presence or counting of deficits. Frailty is indicated by the presence of (1) symptoms in three or four of these domains and (2) a minimum of six symptoms. Fulfilling only one of these two criteria indicates prefrailty. Using this measure, Brehmer-Rinderer et al. (2013) reported a prevalence of frailty of 17.7% in their sample of 147 adults with intellectual and developmental disabilities aged 20–72 years; a further 17.7% were considered prefrail. Though these findings are based on a relatively small sample, they build on previous work reporting high proportions of frail individuals among adults with intellectual and developmental disabilities compared to the general population, and at younger ages. Such findings corroborate the widely-held perception of premature aging among adults with intellectual and developmental disabilities, as well as the subsequent use of age-related care and services much earlier in life. However, as the health care needs of persons with intellectual and developmental disabilities are better addressed (for example through prevention, early detection, and improved management), the apparent inevitability of premature aging and frailty should be reconsidered.

2.3 Aging and Health Care

Older adults tend to be frequent users of health care services; as a result, more health care dollars are spent on this segment of the population than any other (CIHI, 2011a). It is believed that more frequent use of hospital services, community-based health care, long-term care, and prescription medication contribute to increased health care costs among older adults in the general population (CIHI, 2011a). As stated earlier, adults with intellectual and developmental disabilities experience higher rates of various age-related health issues at earlier ages than in the general aging population. Therefore, it follows that their health care costs could be even higher than in the general aging population. Interestingly, a recent study found that older adults with intellectual and developmental disabilities, who comprise 0.15–0.25% of the population of England, consume 5% of the total personal care budget (Strydom et al., 2010). However, these authors found no relationship between age (among those 60+) and cost. They attribute this to their view that "lifelong complex disability associated with (intellectual and developmental disabilities) means that people have longstanding care needs and the additional problems of ageing do not add significantly to this" (Strydom et al., 2010, p. 137). However, there is a need to further understand use of health care services in this population.

2.3.1 Hospital Services

Adults with intellectual and developmental disabilities are known to be frequent users of hospital services. A population-based study of ambulatory care sensitive conditions (such as asthma and congestive heart failure) reported that individuals with intellectual and developmental disabilities of all ages were consistently hospitalized at a higher rate compared to individuals without intellectual and developmental disabilities (Balogh, Brownell, Ouellette-Kuntz, & Colantonio, 2010). In their representative sample of 212 older adults with intellectual and developmental disabilities (i.e., aged 60 years or more), Strydom et al. (2010) reported that 51% had used hospital-based services in the last 6 months. More specifically, 21% had used **inpatient services**, 39% had used **outpatient services**, and 10% had used **emergency** or accident **services**. The authors note that while older adults with intellectual and developmental disabilities in their study were accessing an increasing proportion of resources, it was likely not as much as their conditions would indicate is needed (Strydom et al., 2010). Marks et al. (2008) similarly remarked that needs do not always translate into relevant health care services. These authors note, for example, inequities in receipt of **palliative** or **end-of-life care** services (which may be provided in hospital or in the community) among older adults with intellectual and developmental disabilities, in spite of the increasing life expectancy in this population.

2.3.2 Community-Based Health Care

Strydom et al. (2010) found high rates of contact with health care professionals in the community in their English study of adults with intellectual and developmental disabilities 60 years of age or more. Specifically, they found that 72% of older adults in their sample had visited their general practitioner and 21% had seen a community-based nurse. They also reported that a nontrivial subset had seen a mental health professional (i.e., 20% psychiatrist, 4% clinical psychologist, and 12% community psychiatric nurse).

In Canada, approximately 93% of older adults in the general population live in their home, many of whom live alone (CIHI, 2011a). The ability for many older adults to remain in their home is likely due to the receipt of informal support (i.e., support from family and friends) as well as community-based home health care services. It is estimated that just about one million Canadians are receiving home care services (Leatt, Pink, & Guerriere, 2000), the majority of whom are 65 years of age or more (Canadian Health Services Research Foundation, 2011). The types of services provided to older adults are varied, and include nursing, social work, and therapy (e.g., physical, occupational, speech, or respiratory) services, personal care services (e.g., bathing, dressing, eating), and home support services (e.g., meal preparation, housework) (CIHI, 2011a). CIHI (2011a) found that home health aide services, visits with nurses, and homemaking and meal services were received by similar proportions of adults in the 20–64 and 65–74 age groups; receipt of these services were much higher among the oldest age groups (75–84 years and 85+ years). As an example, meal services were received by 5% of home care recipients aged 20–64 years and 65–74 years, by 9% of those aged 75–84 years, and by 15% of those 85 years of age or more. Strydom et al. (2010) reported that only 3% of older adults with intellectual and developmental disabilities in their representative sample in England had received **community-based support with meals**.

2.3.3 Long-Term Care Services

In spite of the move toward community living in many jurisdictions worldwide, community-based residential arrangements may be jeopardized by medical complexity—or increasing medical complexity, and decreasing mobility (Martin, Fries, Hirdes, & James, 2011). Just as in the general population, older adults with intellectual and developmental disabilities with such needs may end up in LTC settings, also called nursing homes. The ability of such settings to provide supports that promote integration and inclusion—largely the reasons supporting deinstitutionalization efforts—has been questioned (Eley, Boyes, Young, & Hegney, 2009; Lakin, Hill, & Anderson, 1991; Lakin, White, Hill, Bruininks, & Wright, 1990).

Using a broad, nationally representative sample of 9707 nursing homes in the United States, Martin et al. (2011) found that persons with intellectual and developmental disabilities constituted approximately 2.4% of the resident population. **Nursing home** residents with intellectual and developmental disabilities were on average much younger than residents without intellectual and developmental disabilities (65.3 years vs 78.4 years, respectively), showed higher levels of cognitive impairment and aggression, and lower rates of **health instability** and pain (Martin et al., 2011). In Australia, a survey to identify individuals residing in residence aged care facilities also revealed that residents with intellectual and developmental disabilities were admitted at a younger age than other residents (59.4 years and 84.3 years, respectively), often because of the death or poor health of the primary informal caregiver, or because the supporting living environment was unable to provide adequate support (Bigby, Webber, Bowers, & McKenzie-Green, 2008). This survey also found that adults with intellectual and developmental disabilities remained in care, on average, 3.9 years longer than residents without intellectual and developmental disabilities.

2.3.4 Prescription Medication

Prescription medications are a significant driver of health care costs. In Canada, medications account for the second largest share of health care costs after hospitals (16.2% vs 29.1%, respectively) (CIHI, 2011b). The number of older adults in the general population who are taking multiple medications (i.e., polypharmacy) is increasing, as is the number of drug classes used (CIHI, 2011c). Adults with intellectual and developmental disabilities have high rates of polypharmacy. In their study in England, Strydom et al. (2010) reported that approximately 85% of older adults (55 years and over) with intellectual and developmental disabilities were taking at least one long-term medication—59% were taking at least three medications, 42% were taking four or more medications, and 5% were taking eight or more medications.

2.4 Health Surveillance of Aging with IDD

As the population of persons with intellectual and developmental disabilities grows, and their life expectancy increases, many are living longer with multiple, life-long conditions. It is therefore important to consider how best to monitor health and health care use in older cohorts with intellectual and developmental disabilities.

"Surveillance is the tracking and forecasting of health events and determinants through the collection, analysis and reporting of data" (Public Health Agency of Canada, 2012). Surveillance makes it possible to create practical, evidence-based policies and programs, and as such serves as a tool to help address health disparities/inequities. It assumes ongoing data collection, analysis, and use. Surveillance relies on indicators which are summary statistics that can be used to describe a situation concisely and comprehensively to "measure health status and health system performance and characteristics across different populations and between jurisdictions, or over time" (CIHI, 2006, p. 5) Indicators must be relevant, accurate, meaningful and useful, amenable to change, and feasible to collect and report on an ongoing basis (Betancourt, 2012).

Our review identified models which can inform health surveillance specific to aging with intellectual and developmental disabilities; these include ongoing surveys (the National Core Indicators in the United States of America), disability registries (namely in Denmark and Leicestershire, England), large-scale epidemiological studies (e.g., Finnish Survey, HA-ID in the Netherlands, and POMONA across Europe), and one-time projects (e.g., UK Confidential Inquiry). Methods and results from each are briefly described below. Table 1 lists indicators relevant to health surveillance of aging in intellectual and developmental disabilities revealed through these efforts and the above literature review.

2.4.1 Ongoing Surveys: National Core Indicators in the United States of America

The National Core Indicators (NCI) program is a partnership between the Human Services Research Institute (HSRI) in Cambridge, Massachusetts and the United States National Association of State Directors of Developmental Disabilities Services (NASDDDS). The program was launched in 1997 in 13 states. In 2011, 25 states and four substate regions were contributing information on an annual basis. Today, there exists a multiyear database capturing information from over 12,000 individuals supported.

Multiple data sources are used including interviews with consumers, family self-administered surveys, and collated agency or government-held data. The valid and reliable consumer survey gathers about 50% of the annual data on 114 indicators across five domains (http://www.nationalcoreindicators.org/indicators/). One of the domains concerns health, welfare, and rights. It includes the subdomains of safety, respect/rights, health, medications, wellness, and restraints. Indicators ranging from living arrangement, obesity,

Table 1 Key Indicators for Health Surveillance in Older Adults with Intellectual and Developmental Disabilities

Social and Environmental Determinants	Risk Conditions	Disease Prevention Practices	Health Care Use	Quality of Care	Health Outcomes
1. Living accommodation 2. Geography (developed or developing nation)	1. Age 2. Sex 3. IDD etiology 4. IDD severity 5. Obesity 6. Long-term medication use 7. Poly-pharmacy	1. Diet 2. Exercise 3. Bone density-screening 4. Fall risk assessment 5. Physical exam 6. Vaccination 7. Mammography 8. PSA test 9. Dental exam	1. Hospitalization (inpatient, outpatient emergency) 2. Days of hospitalization 3. Reasons for hospitalization 4. Admission to residential aged care facilities 5. Age at admission to residential aged care facility 6. Length of admission to residential aged care facility 7. Reason for admission to residential aged care facility 8. Use of community-based services 9. Use of psychiatric services 10. Use of palliative care 11. Treatment for osteoporosis	1. Advanced care planning 2. Adherence to Mental Capacity Act 3. Adjustment to changing care needs 4. Carers feeling listened to	1. Body mass index 2. Reduction in mobility 3. New or worsening sensory impairments 4. Dementia 5. Anxiety 6. Cardiovascular disease/metabolic syndrome/diabetes 7. Falls 8. ADLs/iADLs 9. Osteoporosis 10. Osteoarthritis 11 .Arthrosis 12. Kidney disease 13. Multimorbidity 14. Complexity/frailty/medical instability 15. Death/life expectancy/excess mortality 16. Age at death 17. Cause of death 18. Amenable death 19. Preventable death

mobility and sensory impairments, dementia, and mortality can be tracked over time and across subgroups.

The cross-sectional analysis by Stancliffe et al. (2012) comparing health conditions among adults with Down syndrome (n = 1199) versus adults with non-Down syndrome intellectual and developmental disabilities (n = 11,182) is one example of use of the NCI for health research related to aging with intellectual and developmental disabilities. As stated earlier, these authors reported shorter **life expectancy** in males with Down syndrome compared to females with Down syndrome, but longer life expectancy in males versus females with intellectual and developmental disabilities without Down syndrome. The study, which included 2420 individuals with intellectual and developmental disabilities 50—59 years of age and 1565 adults 60 years and older, found that 13.6% of 50—59 year olds and 7.9% of 60+ year olds **lived with family**.

Bershadsky and colleagues (Bershadsky, Hiersteiner, Fay, & Bradley, 2014; Bershadsky et al., 2012) used National Core Indictors data to identify disparities in **preventive care** among adults with intellectual and developmental disabilities. They found that older individuals were more likely to have had a **physical examination**, and a flu or pneumonia **vaccine** but they were less likely to have seen a **dentist**. They also reported that **mammography** among women 40 years and older and **PSA test** among men 50 years and older varied significantly based on one's living arrangement. Uptake was highest among those living in institutions and lowest among those living with relatives.

Also, relying on data from National Core Indicators, Lakin et al. (2008) found that age did not significantly contribute to variances in annualized expenditures for Medicaid **home and community-based services** across US states.

2.4.2 Registries: Denmark and Leicestershire, England

2.4.2.1 Denmark

Using the Danish Cytogenetic Register and the National Hospital Register, Zhu et al. (2013) compared **hospitalization** patterns for persons with Down syndrome born between 1910 and 2007 matched 20:1 on birth year to individuals identified through the Civil Registration System. This 30-year retrospective cohort study found increased risk among of **hospitalization** among those 50 years and older with Down syndrome compared to younger individuals with Down syndrome as well as compared to those 50 years and older without Down syndrome. The latter was most pronounced for admissions due to diseases of the nervous system and sensory organs (relative risk: 4.7). In this age group with Down syndrome, **days of hospitalization** were longer than for those without Down syndrome when the reasons for admission were related to diseases of the nervous system and sensory organs (relative risk: 2.8), and diseases of the respiratory system (relative risk: 2.2).

2.4.2.2 Leicestershire

The Leicestershire Learning Disability Register is an open cohort of adults with intellectual and developmental disabilities who live in Leicestershire and Rutland, UK (McGrother, Thorp, Taub, & Machado, 2001). The register includes adults (≥19 years) living and using specialist services in the region. Extensive data collection for cohort members occurs every 5 to 7 years through structured interviews with carers. The prevalence reported is considered an administrative prevalence of intellectual and developmental disabilities, as only individuals receiving support from social, health, voluntary, or independent sector services are included. The identification of the entire population of persons with intellectual and developmental disabilities is not possible (Bhaumik, Tyrer, McGrother, & Ganghadaran, 2008); however, the register is estimated to capture 95% of individuals with moderate to profound disabilities (Tyrer, Smith, McGrother, & Taub, 2007).

Mortality data from the Office for National Statistics is used to identify death among the cohort. Using the register, Tyrer, Smith, and McGrother (2007) reported on all cause and disease-specific **mortality** over 23,000 person-years of follow-up. Through indirect standardization, they identified excess mortality across all age groups. Of relevance to this review is their finding that adults with intellectual and developmental disabilities 50–59 years of age were 5.59 more likely to die than their counterparts without intellectual and developmental disabilities. This risk dropped to 3.45 and 1.39 for 60–69 and 70+ groups. Adults with intellectual and developmental disabilities reportedly had high mortality due to congenital abnormalities, mental disorders, bronchopneumonia, and diseases of the nervous system and sense organs. Only 41% of death records listed intellectual and developmental disabilities as a factor to contributing death (Tyrer & McGrother, 2009).

The register captures several other indicators relevant to health surveillance of aging in this population. In an analysis of **BMI**, Bhaumik, Watson, Thorp, Tyrer, and McGrother (2008) found that being older was associated with reduced risk of being underweight: 32% of men (20–29 years old) were underweight (BMI ≤20) compared to 15% of men over the age of 50 years. The same relationship existed between younger women and older women (25% and 9%, respectively). McGrother et al. (2006) reported that the prevalence of **epilepsy** decreased with age with approximately 20% of 40–69 year olds being affected compared to only 10% of those 70 years and older. The Leicestershire Learning Disability Register also provides the opportunity to study service utilization. Bhaumik, Tyrer, et al. (2008) reported that individuals accessing **specialist psychiatric services** were more likely to be older ($p < 0.001$) and living in residential settings ($p < 0.001$).

2.4.2.3 Finnish Survey

A population-level study conducted in Finland (Patja, Mölsä, & Iivanainen, 2001), which focused on **causes of mortality** among persons with intellectual and developmental disabilities over a period of 35 years. The original survey in 1962 resulted in the identification of 2369 individuals 2–97 years of age. In 1997, the data were linked to national databases whereby 1111 deaths were noted among the cohort. These authors found that causes of mortality were similar to those in the general population, but that mortality from cancers and external causes were lower among persons with intellectual and developmental disabilities.

2.4.2.4 HA-ID in the Netherlands

The HA-ID study used a cross-sectional design to obtain information on the health of 2322 persons with intellectual and developmental disabilities 50 years of age or older across three large care providers in different regions of the Netherlands. The resulting sample is considered to be representative of the overall Dutch population of older adults with intellectual and developmental disabilities (Hilgenkamp et al., 2011). A number of measures were used to assess various aspects of health, taking care to ensure that measures chosen were feasible for a large-scale study (e.g., relatively brief, easily administered, noninvasive, low cost) (Hilgenkamp et al., 2011). Hilgenkamp et al. (2011) provide the list of specific measures used in the study; these included physical examinations, fitness assessments, diaries, observations, biochemical markers, surveys, and chart reviews. Several studies on a wide range of health-related topics have been published using results from the HA-ID study.

In their study applying the **frailty** phenotype criteria to their sample of older adults, Evenhuis et al. (2012) found that the proportion of persons with intellectual and developmental disabilities 50–64 years of age who were frail was similar to that in older adults in the general population aged 65 years or more (11% vs 7% to 9%, respectively). These authors also report that frailty increased with age (i.e., to 18% in the 65+ age group), and that in addition to age, frailty was also associated with the presence of Down syndrome, dementia, motor disability, and severity of intellectual and developmental disabilities. In a 3-year follow-up study, it was found that after controlling for demographic characteristics (i.e., age, sex, level of intellectual and developmental disabilities, presence of Down syndrome), frailty was predictive of impairment in activities and instrumental activities of daily living (**ADLs and IADLs**) and mobility (Schoufour, Mitnitski, et al., 2014).

Data from the HA-ID study have also been used to examine specific health conditions as well as risk factors among older adults with intellectual and developmental disabilities. de Winter, Echteld, and Evenhuis (2014) studied chronic **kidney disease**, and found that overall rates were equal to the general population (i.e., 15.3%). They also reported that kidney disease was significantly associated with age, as well as with Down syndrome, obesity, hypercholesterolemia, and hypothyroidism. Mental health conditions have also been studied using HA-ID data. Hermans, Beekman, and Evenhuis (2013, 2014) examined symptoms of **anxiety** using the general anxiety subscale of the Hospital Anxiety and Depression Scale. They found that older adults with intellectual and developmental disabilities scored significantly higher on symptoms of anxiety compared to a sample of older adults without intellectual and developmental disabilities.

de Winter et al. (2012a) found that several **risk factors for cardiovascular disease** (e.g., hypertension, diabetes, and metabolic syndrome) were distributed similarly as in the general population of older adults. However, these authors noted that risk factors had not been previously diagnosed among a significant proportion of older adults with intellectual and developmental disabilities. In particular, **hypertension** had gone undetected in 50% of older adults with intellectual and developmental disabilities, **diabetes** was undetected in 45%, **hypercholesterolemia** in 46%, and **metabolic syndrome** had not been detected in 94% of those who met the criteria. In their work related to **overweight and obesity**, de Winter, Bastiaanse, Hilgenkamp, Evenhuis, and Echteld (2012b) found that prevalence was higher among older adults with intellectual and developmental disabilities than in the general older Dutch population (26% vs 10%, respectively). They also found that higher age was associated with higher risk of being overweight or obese; sex (female), presence of Down syndrome, autism, severity of intellectual and developmental disabilities (lesser), and independence in ADLs and IADLs (i.e., eating, meal preparation, shopping), inactivity, and use of atypical antipsychotics also increased the risk. With respect to **physical activity**, Hilgenkamp, van Wijck, and Evenhuis (2012) reported that physical activity levels were quite low among adults with intellectual and developmental disabilities across all age ranges. In fact, they report that the level of activity in the youngest age groups (50–59 years) equaled that of 20–30 year olds in the general population.

2.4.2.5 POMONA in Europe

The POMONA I (2002–2004) and II (2005–2008) population-based studies aimed to better understand age-specific differences in health among adults with intellectual and developmental disabilities in 13 and 14 European countries, respectively (Haveman et al., 2011). All participating countries collected information on 18 indicators, including five related to demographics (i.e., prevalence of intellectual and developmental disabilities, living arrangements, daily occupation, income/socioeconomic status, and life expectancy), six related to health status (i.e., epilepsy, oral health, BMI, mental health, sensory, and mobility), three related to determinants of health (i.e., physical activity, challenging behaviour, and medication), and four related to health systems (i.e., hospitalization/health care, health checkups, health promotion, and training health professionals) (Linehan, Walsh, van Schrojenstein Lantman-de Valk, & Kerr, 2004). The final sample consisted of 1269 adults with intellectual and developmental disabilities from 14 countries; the average age was 41 years (range 19–90 years), there were slightly more males (51%), and 34% lived at home with family (47% in a residential setting, 12% independently, and 7% in a nursing home/psychiatric or other group home) (Linehan et al., 2004). In their report, Linehan et al. (2004) detailed findings related to each of the indicators by participating country, but not by age. One related study was identified that focused on aging. In this study, Haveman et al. (2011) reported that a number of **lifestyle risk factors** are higher among older adults (i.e., 55+ years) compared to younger age groups, including rates of daily smoking, any alcohol use, and sedentary lifestyle. They also found higher prevalence of **cataracts, hearing disorder, diabetes, hypertension, osteoarthritis, and arthrosis**, as well as **osteoporosis** in this older age group. Interestingly, they noted that the prevalence of allergies and epilepsy decreased with advancing age.

2.4.3 Confidential Inquiry into Premature Deaths in the UK

Over a two-year period, 247 deaths among a population of 15,505 persons with intellectual and developmental disabilities 4 years of age and older were reported by agencies, detailed information surrounding the deaths were collected through interviews, and cause of death obtained from the Office of National Statistics (Heslop et al., 2014). Some of these deaths were compared to a sample of deaths occurring among individuals without intellectual and developmental disabilities during the same time period. Comparator cases were similar in age, sex, and cause of death.

Of relevance to the question of aging is the finding that 78% of deaths occurred after 50 years of age. Median **age at death** was comparable between males and females with intellectual and developmental disabilities (65 years and 63 years, respectively). The difference in median age at death between those with and without intellectual and developmental disabilities was most pronounced among females (63 years and 83 years, respectively) since females without intellectual and developmental disabilities lived, on average, longer than males without intellectual and developmental disabilities (78 years and 83 years, respectively).

Nearly half of the deaths among persons with intellectual and developmental disabilities were classified as avoidable which was more than twice as high as expected in England and Wales. The study identified problems in **advanced care planning** and **adherence to the Mental Capacity Act** as well as **living accommodation**, **adjustment to changing care needs**, and **carers not feeling listened** to as contributors to **premature death** among persons with intellectual and developmental disabilities.

2.4.4 Indicators for Health Surveillance of Aging in Intellectual and Developmental Disabilities

The above examples illustrate that monitoring the health of older adults with intellectual and developmental disabilities has proven to be feasible at the population-level to varying degrees in different locations. Indicators identified in the literature as relevant span from social and environmental determinants of health to health care use and health outcomes (see Table 1). In some instances, indicators can be framed under different components represented in the table. For example, obesity is considered a risk factor but it could also be considered a health outcome (BMI). Similarly, while diet and exercise are listed as disease prevention practices, poor diet or physical inactivity could be included under risk factors.

3. PART 2: A CANADIAN INITIATIVE

Canada is a federation of 10 provinces and 3 territories. While a national health policy establishes common principles that guide provincial management of health care by provinces and territories (Canada Health Act, 1985), the provision of health services for Canadians comes under the jurisdiction of the provincial and territorial governments. Each of the provinces and territories administers a health insurance plan that provides universal and comprehensive coverage for medically necessary hospital, inpatient and outpatient physician services. No national principles guide the provincial or territorial provision of disability services though Canada is signatory to the UN Convention on the Rights of Persons with Disabilities (Collin, 2012). Responsibility for disability supports vary across provinces and territories; typically spread across multiple and diverse government departments and service sectors. For example in Ontario, the responsibility for social policy development and funding of services for persons with intellectual and developmental disabilities falls to the Ministry of Community and Social Services for adults and to the Ministries of Children and Youth Services and Education for children. In Ontario, other government departments such as the Ministry of Health and Long-Term Care are responsible to provide generic services to all Ontarians including individuals with intellectual and developmental disabilities. The result is not only the lack of a national system or strategy related to the health care of persons with IDD but also the risk of fragmentation of services and supports within a provincial or territorial jurisdiction.

Furthermore, the fragmentation makes identification of the population of individuals with intellectual and developmental disabilities and health surveillance in particular very challenging. No registries exist. One solution is to create a cohort from administrative data sets. In this second part of the review, we describe research undertaken in partnership with the two key Ontario government departments responsible for services and supports to adults with intellectual and developmental disabilities as they age: the Ministry of Community and Social Services and the Ministry of Health and Long-Term Care.

In Ontario, interest in population aging has culminated in a $1.1 billion investment in the Aging at Home Strategy (Ontario's Ministry of Health and Long-Term Care) that allows people to remain healthy and live independently at home. Aging at home is not only a government priority, it is also a desire of persons with intellectual and developmental disabilities and their caregivers (Martin, Roy, & Wells, 1997). However, home care services were developed for the "average consumer," and adults with intellectual and developmental disabilities have distinct care needs. Further, the province's last specialized residential institution for people with intellectual and developmental disabilities was closed in 2009—all adults with intellectual and developmental disabilities are now aging in the community. For some, home is a group home; for many, home is with aging parents or siblings. Over the years, an unknown number have become residents of LTC facilities, and not all as seniors. Consequently, many have questioned the appropriateness of LTC for adults with intellectual and developmental disabilities.

3.1 Objectives

Our research sought to understand at what age the health care needs of adults with intellectual and developmental disabilities resemble those of aging persons without intellectual and developmental disabilities, examine rates of admission to home care services, and study patterns of admission to long term-care among adults with intellectual and developmental disabilities.

3.2 Methods

3.2.1 Cohort Creation

Five health administrative data sets and two clinical data sets were linked to create a cohort of adults with intellectual and developmental disabilities (18–99 years) living in Ontario in 2009/2010. These data sets capture province-wide Ministry of Health and Long-Term Care (MOHLTC)-funded services. These are held by the Institute for Clinical Evaluative Sciences (ICES; www.ices.on.ca) by arrangement with the MOHLTC. The administrative data sets capture information on the vast majority of physician-provided services available to all legal Ontario residents under the province's universal health care coverage including inpatient discharges from acute and psychiatric hospital beds (Discharge Abstract Database, Same Day Surgery Database, and Ontario Mental Health Reporting System), emergency department visit records (National Ambulatory Care Reporting System), and fee-for-service physician claims (Ontario Health Insurance Plan). The clinical data sets include data routinely collected in the provision of home care (Home Care Reporting System; CIHI, 2014a) and long-term care (Chronic Care Reporting System for Long-Term Care; CIHI, 2014b) using inter-RAI instruments and protocols (see www.interrai.org). These data sets are linkable at ICES using unique encoded identifiers.

Six of the above data sets were searched for diagnostic codes related to intellectual and developmental disabilities: Discharge Abstract Database, Same Day Surgery Database, Ontario Mental Health Reporting System, National Ambulatory Care Reporting System, Ontario Health Insurance Plan, and Home Care Database. The choice of codes to include was informed by other studies (Balogh, Hunter, & Ouellette-Kuntz, 2005; Ouellette-Kuntz et al., 2009; Westerinen, Kaski, Virta, Almqvist, & Iivanainen, 2007). Individuals with intellectual and developmental disabilities were defined as anyone who had at least one of the listed codes during a hospital stay, emergency room visit, or home care assessment, or who had at least two physician claims with such codes or who had a designation within a list of "conditions related to developmental disability status" in the Chronic Care Reporting System for Long-Term Care. All data sets were searched from their inception. Further details regarding the data sets, the diagnostic codes used, and the linkage process are provided in Lin et al. (2014) and Ouellette-Kuntz and Martin (2014).

3.2.2 Indicators

Once the cohort was identified, we examined key indicators related to aging commonly reported for all Ontarians. These included social and environmental determinants (rurality, neighborhood income), risk conditions (age, sex, mental illness, or addiction), health care use (home care and long-term care), and health outcomes (frailty, medical instability) indicators.

Rurality was attributed to individuals whose postal code corresponded to a 2006 census community-size category 5; that is, a census agglomeration with a population of less than 10,000 or designated rural.

Neighborhood income quintiles were assigned based on the individuals' residential postal code. Postal codes were lined to 2006 census data where Statistics Canada has adjusted income for household size and community size such that each community would be expected to have 20% of its population in each income quintile.

Mental illness or addiction was identified if an individual had a physician visit, mental health admission, hospital discharge, or emergency department visit between April 1, 2007 and March 13, 2009 coded as ICD-9: 290-298, 300-314, 316 or ICD-10:F00-F69, F99 or DSM-IV: 206.90, 290, 293-296.89, 297-298, 300-307, 308.3, 309.81, 310-314, 316; or if there was any provisional diagnosis, excluding those related to

IDD or learning disabilities, recorded in the Ontario Mental Health Reporting System between April 1, 2007 and March 13, 2009.

Home care use was coded as "yes" when an individual's health insurance number appeared in the interRAI Home Care database during specified periods.

Long-term care admission was coded as "yes" **when** an individual's health insurance number appeared in the RAI 2.0 for LTC (as per facility number) during specified periods.

Frailty was derived from The Johns Hopkins University Adjusted Clinical Group (ACG) System. The marker classifies a person as frail if he/she has any one of 81 diagnostic codes (grouped into 11 clusters of medical issues) known to be highly associated with limited functioning among older adults (Bronskill et al., 2010). No information is available that specifies the diagnostic codes used in the ACG System.

Medical instability was assessed using the Changes in Health, End Stage disease, Signs, and Symptoms (CHESS) scale which is a measure embedded in the assessment instruments used as part of regular clinical practice in home care (i.e., the RAI-HC assessment) and LTC (i.e., the RAI 2.0) settings in Ontario and elsewhere. The algorithm to derive the CHESS is based on the presence or absence of nine issues related to frailty in older populations, including cognitive decline, decline in performance of activities of daily living (ADLs, such as eating, dressing, bathing), shortness of breath, dehydration or insufficient fluid intake, edema, vomiting, weight loss, decrease in amount of fluid or food consumed, and instability of conditions (Hirdes, Frijters, & Teare, 2003). CHESS scale scores range between 0 and 4, where a score of 2 or more are used to indicate health instability. The CHESS has been shown to be a strong predictor of mortality, as well as of physician activity (e.g., visits, change orders), complex medical procedures, and pain among older adults (Hirdes et al., 2003).

3.2.3 Analysis

The cohort was compared to a random sample of 20% of the population without intellectual and developmental disabilities (18–99 years of age) eligible for MOHLTC-funded health services. Descriptive statistics comparing those with and without IDD are presented in tables and graphs. Changes over time in home care use and LTC admissions are examined by providing annual rates and 95% confidence intervals. Prevalence of frailty and medical instability are presented and logistic regression is used to examine the impact of intellectual and developmental disabilities on frailty while controlling for age, sex, and the presence of mental illness or addiction problem. Unless otherwise specified, the analyses presented reflect data for the 2009/2010 fiscal year (April 1 to March 31).

3.3 Results

3.3.1 The Cohort

The cohort included 51,138 adults (18–99 years of age) with intellectual and developmental disabilities living in Ontario in 2009/2010. The overall cohort with intellectual and developmental disabilities is younger than the comparison group mainly because of the higher proportion of 18–24 year olds (see Figure 2). Of particular note is the lack of change in the proportion of adults with intellectual and developmental disabilities across the two oldest age groups (5.9% in each for a total of 11.8% being 65 years and over).

As expected, there are more males in the cohorts with intellectual and developmental disabilities compared to the cohorts without intellectual and developmental disabilities (see Table 2). Adults with intellectual and developmental disabilities are slightly more likely to live in rural areas and in the poorest neighborhoods. They are significantly more likely to have a diagnosed mental illness or addiction problem.

3.3.2 Health Care Use (Home Care and Long-Term Care)

As shown in Table 2, 10,563 or 23% of adults with intellectual and developmental disabilities received **home care services** at some point between

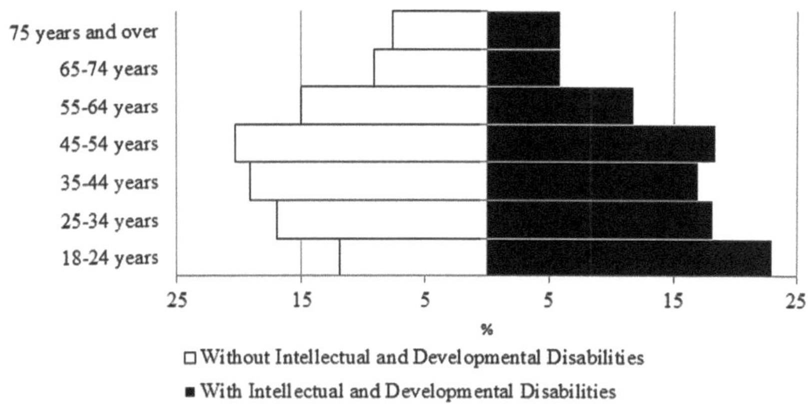

Figure 2 Baseline age distribution of individuals with and without intellectual and developmental disabilities studied.

Table 2 Baseline Characteristics (2009/2010) of Individuals with and without Intellectual and Developmental Disabilities Studied

	Overall[a]		**Home Care[b]**		**Long-Term Care[c]**	
	IDD[d]	**No IDD**	**IDD[d]**	**No IDD**	**IDD[d]**	**No IDD**
Number	51,138	3,323,408	10,563	321,193	2257	30,067
Age (%)						
18–24 years	23.0	11.9	8.5	2.9	1.3	0.0
25–34 years	18.1	17.0	11.6	5.0	2.6	0.1
35–44 years	17.0	19.1	15.9	7.7	6.2	0.4
45–54 years	18.4	20.3	25.3	13.3	16.4	1.7
55–64 years	11.8	15.0	19.3	18.0	25.3	4.8
65–74 years	5.9	9.1	10.2	20.6	19.9	13.9
>75 years	5.9	7.6	9.2	32.5	28.4	79.0
Male (%)	56.9	48.5	51.1	45.9	43.8	34.8
Rural (%)	15.0	11.5	17.2	14.3	18.2	14.7
Lowest neighborhood income quintile (%)	27.0	19.2	27.7	21.0	28.3	24.7
Mental illness and/or addiction (%)	49.7	26.6	55.1	35.8	66.6	54.4

[a]Residents of Ontario in 2009/2010.
[b]Residents of Ontario in 2009/2010 who were admitted to home care between April 1, 2009 and March 31, 2014.
[c]Residents of Ontario in 2009/2010 who were newly admitted to long-term care between April 1, 2009 and March 31, 2013.
[d]Intellectual and developmental disabilities.

April 1, 2009 and March 31, 2014. This proportion is greater than for adults without intellectual and developmental disabilities (9.8%). Since home care serves largely an aging population, we examined use across age groups (see Figure 3). While in both groups, the proportion using home care increases steadily with age, among those with intellectual and developmental disabilities, 8.2% of 18–24 year olds use home care whereas this proportion is only reached around age 55 among those without intellectual and developmental disabilities. In both groups, women are more likely to use such services (26.0% vs 20.6% in those with intellectual and developmental disabilities; 10.3% vs 9.3% in those without intellectual and developmental disabilities) as are individuals with mental health or addiction problems (25.4% vs 20.5% in those with intellectual and developmental disabilities; 13.3% vs 8.6% in those without intellectual and developmental disabilities).

Examination of rates of admission to home care between 2009 and 2014 shows that overall rates of admission are two to three times higher among

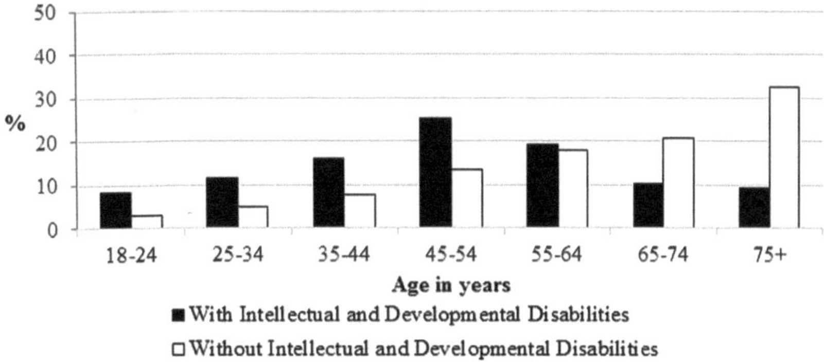

Figure 3 Baseline age distribution of individuals with and without intellectual and developmental disabilities who received home care services (2009–2014).

persons with intellectual and developmental disabilities (see Figure 4). A different pattern is also evident in admission rates between the two groups over time. Specifically, admission rates among persons with intellectual and developmental disabilities slightly decrease and then return to initial levels by the end of the 5-year period, whereas a steady (though small) increase is observed in the cohort without intellectual and developmental disabilities.

As also shown in Table 2, 2257 or 4.5% of adults with intellectual and developmental disabilities were newly admitted to **LTC** at some point between April 1, 2009 and March 31, 2013. This proportion is greater than for adults without intellectual and developmental disabilities (0.9%).

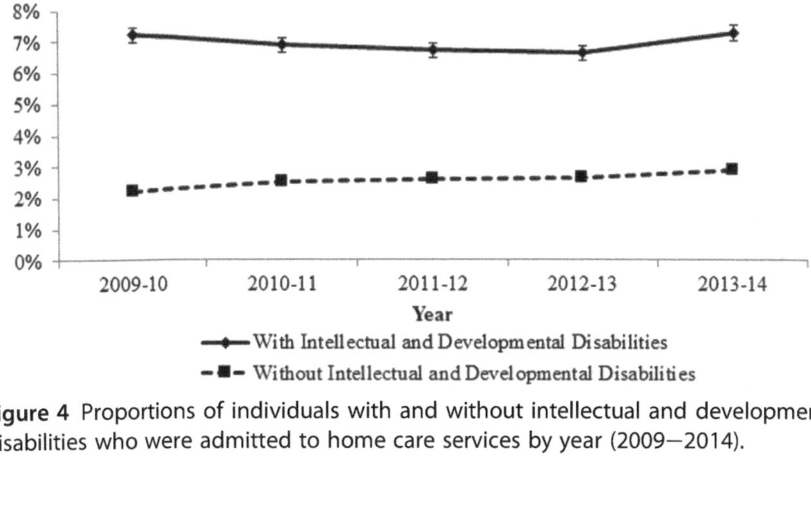

Figure 4 Proportions of individuals with and without intellectual and developmental disabilities who were admitted to home care services by year (2009–2014).

As with home care, long-term care is primarily intended to serve an older population; we therefore also examined admissions across age groups (see Figure 5). While in both groups, the proportion admitted to LTC increases steadily with age, among those with intellectual and developmental disabilities, 0.3% of 18–24 year olds use home care whereas this proportion is only reached around age 60 among those without intellectual and developmental disabilities. The data suggest that adults with intellectual and developmental disabilities are admitted to LTC approximately 25 years earlier than those without intellectual and developmental disabilities. In both groups, women are more likely to be admitted to long-term care, but the risk of admission for women is most marked in the cohort without intellectual and developmental disabilities (5.7% vs 3.5% in persons with intellectual and developmental disabilities; 1.0% vs 0.5% in those without intellectual and developmental disabilities). A similar pattern is seen for the presence of mental health or addiction problems where the ratio in the group with intellectual and developmental disabilities is not as large as that in the group without intellectual and developmental disabilities (5.9% vs 3.0% in group with intellectual and developmental disabilities; 1.8% vs 0.6% in group without intellectual and developmental disabilities).

Examination of rates of admission to LTC between 2009 and 2013 shows that overall rates of admission are three to nine times higher among persons with intellectual and developmental disabilities (see Figure 6). A different pattern is also evident in admission rates between the two groups over time. Specifically, admission rates among persons with intellectual and developmental disabilities slightly decrease over the 4-year period,

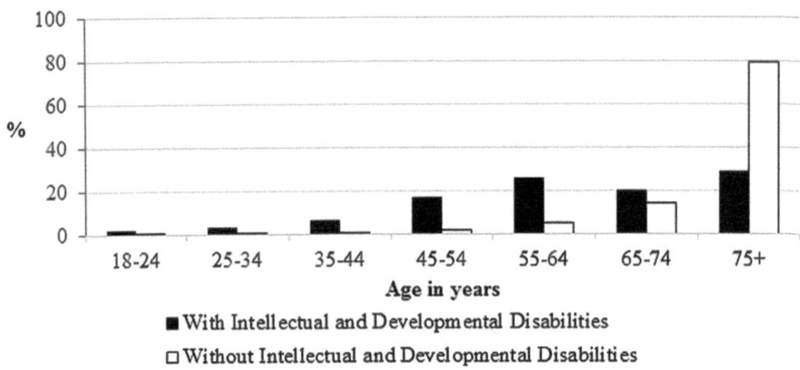

Figure 5 Baseline age distribution of individuals with and without intellectual and developmental disabilities who were admitted to long-term care (2009–2013).

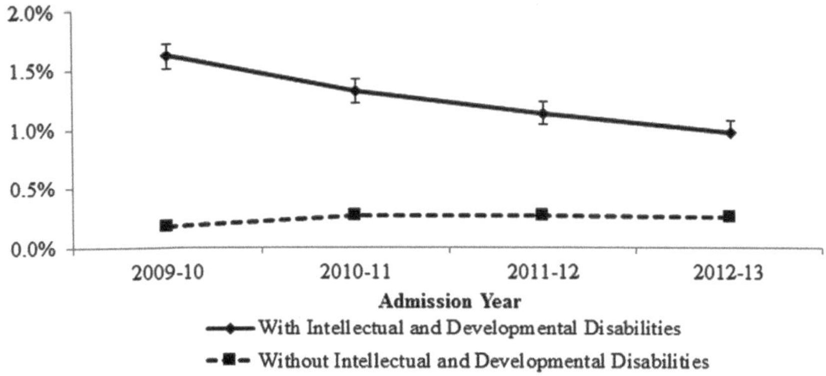

Figure 6 Proportions of individuals with and without intellectual and developmental disabilities who were admitted to long-term care by year (2009–2013).

whereas there is an initial increase after the first year observed in the cohort without intellectual and developmental disabilities that then remains stable.

3.3.3 Frailty and Medical Instability

Overall, the occurrence of frailty was much higher among adults (18–99 years) with intellectual and developmental disabilities (8.9%) than among those without (3.1%). Examination of frailty across age groups (see Figure 7) showed that the proportion of adults 18–24 years of age with intellectual and developmental disabilities who were frail was comparable to that among

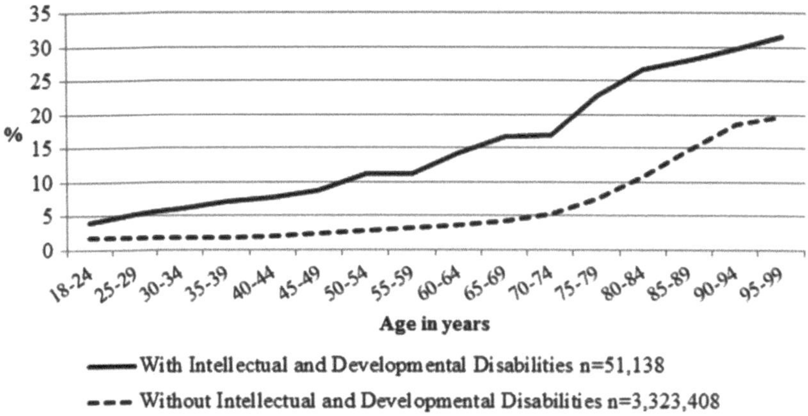

Figure 7 Proportion of adults with and without intellectual and developmental disabilities who are frail as per the frailty marker.

60–64 year olds without intellectual and developmental disabilities (3.9% and 3.6%, respectively).

As is found in the general population, women with intellectual and developmental disabilities are more likely to be frail (10.7% and 3.9% among women with and without intellectual and developmental disabilities, respectively, vs 7.6% and 2.3% among men with and without intellectual and developmental disabilities, respectively). Frailty increases steadily in both men and women with intellectual and developmental disabilities as they get older, ranging from 3.5% among men 18–24 years of age to 24.3% among men 75 years and older, and from 4.9% among women 18–24 years of age to 26.9% among women 75 years and older. We also found that frailty was associated with mental illness or addiction problems in both adults with and without intellectual and developmental disabilities (odds ratios: 3.06 and 2.71). After controlling for age, sex, and the presence of mental illness or addiction problems, adults with intellectual and developmental disabilities were almost three times more likely to be frail (odds ratio: 2.87; 95% CI: 2.78–2.97).

Medical instability was identified in 27.6% of adults with intellectual and developmental disabilities receiving home care. This is lower than the proportion of adults without intellectual and developmental disabilities in home care who score as medically unstable (37.9%). Medical instability was also identified in 31.7% of adults with intellectual and developmental disabilities admitted to LTC which was consistent with what was found in the cohort without intellectual and developmental disabilities (30.9%).

After controlling for age, sex, and the presence of mental illness or addiction problems, adults with intellectual and developmental disabilities receiving home care remained less likely to be medically unstable (odds ratio: 0.85; 95% CI:0.79–0.91). Among those admitted to long-term care, intellectual and developmental disabilities were not associated with medical instability after controlling for these same covariates.

3.4 Discussion

An important contribution of our study was the identification of a cohort of adults with intellectual and developmental disabilities to age 99 living in Ontario. We identified over 6000 adults with intellectual and developmental disabilities 65 years and older (the age of pensioners/seniors in Ontario). They represent 11.8% of the entire cohort identified. This sizable group highlights the importance of ensuring adequate senior/aged care services are in place to meet the needs of this vulnerable group of older adults. Of note is the similarity observed in the sex difference in risk of frailty among adults with and without intellectual and developmental disabilities.

Furthermore, senior/aged care may be appropriate at an earlier age as a number of adults with intellectual and developmental disabilities show patterns of frailty and medical instability at an earlier age than those typically supported in that sector. While frailty among adults without intellectual and developmental disabilities becomes more prominent after age 80 (>10%), among those with intellectual and developmental disabilities, frailty is seen in more than 10% of 50 year olds. It is important, however, to recognize that aged care in the form of admission to LTC facilities/nursing homes may not be appropriate for individuals with intellectual and developmental disabilities who, while they may be frail, have many more years of life ahead of them. We have observed a significant decrease in the proportion of adults with intellectual and developmental disabilities newly admitted to such facilities over the past 4 years and we have found that they have comparable levels of medical instability as others admitted without intellectual and developmental disabilities; this is promising.

An alternative to admission to LTC in Ontario is home care. We have observed a much higher use of home care by adults with intellectual and developmental disabilities consistently over the past 5 years. Adults with intellectual and developmental disabilities access home care at an earlier age and are more likely to do so without being medically unstable. It appears that home care services are responding, at least in part, to the unique needs of this population. We recognize, however, that some individuals in need of LTC in Ontario remain hospitalized in acute care hospitals due to the lack of space in LTC facilities. Hospitalizations where patients who no longer need acute services, but who continue to use limited, expensive acute care resources while they wait to be discharged to a more appropriate setting, are termed "alternate level of care." In 2007–2008, 41% of alternate level of care hospitalizations resulted in a discharge to a LTC facility (Canadian Institute for Health Information, 2009). It will be important to determine the extent to which adults with intellectual and developmental disabilities comprise this group who wait in acute care hospitals for proper residential supports. In addition to the identification of alternate level of care hospitalizations, we have identified other key indicators to examine using our cohort and the rich data sets available to us. These include mortality, caregiver distress, and access to palliative care.

While the frailty marker and medical instability indicator we have used to date are informative, we are not convinced that these are the best measures for this population. Consequently, we are exploring different ways of capturing the medical complexity seen in older adults with intellectual and developmental disabilities. We are particularly concerned that the frailty marker, which is more easily and commonly used, does not capture changes in status; while instability is captured by the CHESS, this measure is only available for those who are receiving home care and long-term care services, where interRAI instruments are mandated. The ability to measure change in status is most important when attempting to untangle disability-related needs and aging-related needs as individuals get older. Our ongoing work in this area attempts to combine the accumulation of deficit approach while focusing on changes in vulnerability.

As noted earlier, surveillance requires not only the collection, analysis, and interpretation of data based on relevant indicators, but also the application of findings to improve policy and practice. Our research is funded by two unique research funding programs in Canada: a Canadian Institute of Health Research Partnership for System Improvement Grant and the Ministry of Health and Long-Term Care Health System Research Fund. Both are integrated knowledge translation programs requiring researchers and knowledge users/decision-makers to work together throughout the research process (see Canadian Institutes of Health Research, 2012). It is unclear whether the type of work that we are doing would be possible without the involvement of researchers, as the health status of persons with intellectual and developmental disabilities may not be as high a priority as other issues facing decision- and policy-makers.

Our work is not, however, without limitations. In particular, the cohort created is closed. As such over time the individuals studied are getting older, sicker and the likelihood of dying increases. Results, particularly related to trends over time, must be interpreted with this caution. Also, much of the data we rely on are administrative, meaning they are collected to enroll residents eligible for health care and to reimburse for services. Iezzoni (1997) cautions that such data "allow limited insight into the quality of processes of care, errors of omission or commission, and the appropriateness of care" (p. 666). Fortunately, for subsets of individuals in our cohort, home care recipients and those admitted to long-term care, electronic clinical information is available through the interRAI assessment protocols adopted to support clinical decision-making and care planning in these sectors.

3.5 Conclusion

3.5.1 Special Considerations

A few examples of ongoing monitoring of health among individuals with intellectual and developmental disabilities, including older individuals, have been identified. A major issue for researchers is the lack of consensus on how to stratify results by age in order to allow for comparisons across studies and to perform meta-analyses which could contribute to a better understanding of aging in this population. We recommend including all adults (if possible) and reporting in 10 year increments starting at <25 and extending to ≥ 75 years.

A second consideration is the inconsistent reporting of chronic conditions in terms of lifetime prevalence. By combining lifelong conditions along with new emerging conditions such as mental illness, epilepsy, sensory impairments, etc., it becomes impossible to untangle the contribution of aging on the risk of developing these conditions.

In a similar way, it is important to understand the extent to which some age-related conditions can be measured in the same way as in the general population. Frailty, for example, has been widely studied because of its link with numerous negative health outcomes among older adults. However, frailty may not be understood in the same way among persons with intellectual and developmental disabilities because of preexisting, life-long conditions and vulnerabilities. As such, among persons with intellectual and developmental disabilities, the need to capture age-related complexity, frailty, or medical instability as a function of changes in vulnerabilities is even more important.

In order to convince knowledge users/decision-makers of the need to act, comparators are often needed. Attention can be brought to surveillance results when changes over time or differences across groups are shown. It is important to control for potential confounders in such analyses. When comparing to the population of individuals without intellectual and developmental disabilities, it is critically important to control for difference in age and sex distributions. While our review did not identify rurality or socioeconomic status as social and environmental determinants, they are commonly identified as associated with health and health care in Canada and therefore they were included in the study. We recommend their inclusion in future work.

3.5.2 Future Directions for Surveillance in Ontario and Beyond

3.5.2.1 Ontario

As noted earlier, our work in Ontario continues. We can continue to examine an extensive list of indicators among our cohort at relatively low cost. Setting priorities for indicator selection will continue to be done in partnership with knowledge users/decision-makers.

3.5.2.2 Canada

To our knowledge, only the province of Manitoba currently has the ability to monitor health among older adults with intellectual and developmental disabilities at the population level like we have done in Ontario. This would be possible in Manitoba due to the unique data repository function of the Manitoba Center for Health Policy (Ouellette-Kuntz et al., 2009). As noted earlier, the challenge for a Canadian surveillance system of health in older adults with intellectual and developmental disabilities is the multitude of health and social service systems across 12 provinces and 3 territories that make up the country, each having its own administrative data systems.

However, since 1994, the Canadian Institute for Health Information (CIHI) has led "the development and maintenance of comprehensive and integrated health information that enables sound policy and effective health system management that improve health and health care" (CIHI, 2014c). To this end, CIHI maintains a wide range of health information that it obtains from key partners, such as Ministries of Health, Statistics Canada, and Health Canada. More specifically, CIHI's data holdings include databases related to hospital care, community care, specialized care, pharmaceuticals, patient safety, the workforce, spending, and access and wait times (CIHI, 2014d). Included among these are the clinical data collected as part of regular practice in home care and long-term care using interRAI instruments (i.e., the RAI-HC and RAI 2.0) that were used in our analyses. In addition to being used in Ontario, the RAI-HC is also used in Manitoba, British Columbia, and Yukon; the RAI 2.0 is even more widely used (i.e., in Newfoundland and Labrador, Nova Scotia, Manitoba, Saskatchewan, Alberta, British Columbia, Yukon, and the Northwest Territories) (CIHI, 2014e). As such, there is capacity in a number of jurisdictions across Canada to similarly monitor the health of older adults with intellectual and developmental disabilities using interRAI data.

3.5.2.3 International

interRAI is an international collaborative of researchers, clinicians, and decision-makers from over 30 countries that works to improve the health, health care, and quality of life of vulnerable persons (interRAI, 2014). Through use of individual assessment instruments designed for specific settings (e.g., home care, long-term care, inpatient, or community-based mental health) or populations (e.g., intellectual/developmental disability), high quality data about the characteristics, preferences, and needs of individuals may be collected and used to promote evidence-based practice and policy (interRAI, 2014). interRAI instruments are used in a number of jurisdictions worldwide—a map showing the use of interRAI instruments worldwide is available on their Web site (www.interrai.org). As these measures have been adopted globally, often as assessments mandated by governments or institutions, there is capacity in a number of jurisdictions worldwide to similarly monitor the health of older adults with intellectual and developmental disabilities using interRAI data.

In conclusion, while health surveillance among older adults with intellectual and developmental disabilities presents unique challenges, our review has demonstrated that it has become increasingly important. Increasing life expectancy, shifts to supporting people with intellectual and developmental disabilities in the community, their increased vulnerability to poor health, and the need for greater accountability call for more than occasional studies of aging in this population. Ongoing monitoring of key health indicators is feasible in various capacities in different jurisdictions. Concerned researchers should partner with knowledge users/decision-makers to maximize the use of electronic administrative and clinical data available to them. In time, the international research community may identify common indicators and methods thereby generating comparators across systems that can further inform policy development.

ACKNOWLEDGMENTS

The original research reported in this paper was funded by the Ontario Ministry of Health and Long-Term Care Health Systems Research Fund (Ministry Grant #06671). The opinions, results, and conclusions in this report are those of the authors and are not necessarily those of the funding source. No endorsement by the Ontario Ministry of Health and Long-Term Care, the Ministry of Community and Social Services, or the Institute for Clinical Evaluative Sciences is intended or should be inferred. The authors gratefully acknowledge the assistance of Sugeetha Nithiananthan in the initial stages of the literature review.

REFERENCES

Ambrose, A. F., Paul, G., & Hausdorff, J. M. (2013). Risk factors for falls among older adults: a review of the literature. *Maturitas, 75*(1), 51–61.

Balogh, R., Brownell, M., Ouellette-Kuntz, H., & Colantonio, A. (2010). Hospitalisation rates for ambulatory care sensitive conditions for persons with and without an intellectual disability—a population perspective. *Journal of Intellectual Disability Research, 54*(9), 820–832.

Balogh, R. S., Hunter, D., & Ouellette-Kuntz, H. (2005). Hospital utilization among persons with an intellectual disability, Ontario, Canada, 1995–2001. *Journal of Applied Research in Intellectual Disabilities, 18*(2), 181–190.

Balogh, R. S., Wood, J. R., Lunsky, Y., Ouellette-Kuntz, H. M. J., Wilton, A. S., Cobigo, V., et al. (2013). Chronic disease management. In Y. Lunsky, J. E. Klein-Geltink, & E. A. Yates (Eds.), *Atlas on the primary care of adults with developmental disabilities in Ontario*. Toronto, ON: Institute for Clinical Evaluative Sciences and Centre for Addiction and Mental Health.

Bastiaanse, L. P., Mergler, S., Evenhuis, H. M., & Echteld, M. A. (2014). Bone quality in older adults with intellectual disabilities. *Research in Developmental Disabilities, 35*(9), 1927–1933.

Béange, H. (2002). Epidemiological issues. In V. P. Prasher, & M. P. Janicki (Eds.), *Physical health of adults with intellectual disabilities* (pp. 1–20). Oxford, UK: Blackwell Publishing LTD.

Bershadsky, J., Hiersteiner, D., Fay, M. L., & Bradley, V. (2014). Race/ethnicity and the use of preventive health care among adults with intellectual and developmental disabilities. *Medical Care, 52*(10), S25–S31.

Bershadsky, J., Taub, S., Bradley, V., Engler, J., Moseley, C., Lakin, K. C., et al. (2012). Place of residence and preventive health care for developmental disabilities services recipients in twenty states. *Public Health Reports, 127*(5), 475–485.

Betancourt, M. T. (June 13, 2012). Indicator framework for the surveillance of chronic disease and associated determinants in Canada. In *Presentation given at the CPHA 2012 conference in Edmonton, Alberta.*

Bhaumik, S., Tyrer, F. C., McGrother, C., & Ganghadaran, S. K. (2008). Psychiatric service use and psychiatric disorders in adults with intellectual disability. *Journal of Intellectual Disability Research, 52*(11), 986–995.

Bhaumik, S., Watson, J. M., Thorp, C. F., Tyrer, F., & McGrother, C. W. (2008). Body mass index in adults with intellectual disability: distribution, associations and service implications: a population-based prevalence study. *Journal of Intellectual Disability Research, 52*(4), 287–298.

Bigby, C., Webber, R., Bowers, B., & McKenzie-Green, B. (2008). A survey of people with intellectual disabilities living in residential aged care facilities in Victoria. *Journal of Intellectual Disability Research, 52*(5), 404–414.

Bittles, A. H., Petterson, B. A., Sullivan, S. G., Hussain, R., Glasson, E. J., & Montgomery, P. D. (2002). The influence of intellectual disability on life expectancy. *Journals of Gerontology Series A, Biological Sciences and Medical Sciences, 57*, M470–M472.

Brehmer-Rinderer, B., Zeilinger, E. L., Radaljevic, A., & Weber, G. (2013). The Vienna frailty questionnaire for persons with intellectual disabilities—revised. *Research in Developmental Disabilities, 34*(6), 1958–1965.

Brehmer, B., & Weber, G. (2010). Frailty vs disability distinctions in people with intellectual disabilities. *Journal of Policy and Practice in Intellectual Disabilities,* 7(1), 49–58.

Bronskill, S. E., Carter, M. W., Costa, A. P., Esensoy, A. V., Gill, S. S., Gruneir, A., et al. (2010). *Aging in Ontario: An ICES chartbook of health service use by older adults – Technical report*. Toronto, ON: Institute for Clinical Evaluative Sciences.

Brown, J. P., & Josse, R. G. (2002). 2002 Clinical practice guidelines for the diagnosis and management of osteoporosis in Canada. *Canadian Medical Association Journal, 167*(Suppl. 10), S1–S34.

Canada Health Act. (1985, c. C-6). Retrieved from the Department of Justice Canada, website: http://laws-lois.justice.gc.ca/PDF/C-6.pdf.

Canadian Health Services Research Foundation. (2011). *Better with age: Health systems planning for the aging population – Synthesis report (a regional roundtable series)*. Ottawa, ON: Canadian Health Services Research Foundation.

Canadian Institute for Health Information. (2006). *Pan-Canadian primary health care indicators: Pan-Canadian primary health care indicator development project* (Report 1, Vol. 1). Ottawa, ON: CIHI.

Canadian Institute for Health Information. (2009). *Alternate level of care in Canada*. Ottawa, ON: CIHI.

Canadian Institute for Health Information. (2011a). *Health care in Canada, 2011—A focus on seniors and aging*. Ottawa, ON: CIHI.
Canadian Institute for Health Information. (2011b). *National health expenditure trends, 1975 to 2011*. Ottawa, ON: CIHI.
Canadian Institute for Health Information. (2011c). *Health care cost drivers: The facts*. Ottawa, ON: CIHI.
Canadian Institute for Health Information. (2014a). *Home care reporting system (HCRS)*. Retrieved from http://www.cihi.ca/CIHI-ext-portal/internet/en/document/types+of+care/community+care/home+care/hcrs_metadata.
Canadian Institute for Health Information. (2014b). *Continuing care reporting system (CCRS) metadata*. Retrieved from http://www.cihi.ca/CIHI-ext-portal/internet/en/document/types+of+care/hospital+care/continuing+care/ccrs_metadata.
Canadian Institute for Health Information. (2014c). *Vision and mandate*. Retrieved from http://www.cihi.ca/CIHI-ext-portal/internet/EN/SubTheme/about+cihi/vision+and+mandate/cihi010703.
Canadian Institute for Health Information. (2014d). *Data holdings*. Retrieved from http://www.cihi.ca/CIHI-ext-portal/internet/EN/Document/standards+and+data+submission/data+holding+metadata/data_holdings_metadata.
Canadian Institute for Health Information. (2014e). *Jurisdictional coverage of CIHI's data holdings (of latest year available), as of September 30, 2014*. Retrieved from http://www.cihi.ca/CIHI-ext-portal/pdf/internet/DATA_HOLD_JURIS_EN.
Canadian Institutes of Health Research. (2012). *Guide to knowledge translation planning at CIHR: Integrated and end-of-grant approaches*. Ottawa, ON: CHIR.
Clegg, A., Young, J., Iliffe, S., Rikkert, M. O., & Rockwood, K. (2013). Frailty in elderly people. *Lancet, 381*(9868), 752—762.
Cobigo, V., Ouellette-Kuntz, H., Lake, J., Wilton, A. S., & Lunsky, Y. (2013). Medication use. In Y. Lunsky, J. E. Klein-Geltink, & E. A. Yates (Eds.), *Atlas on the primary care of adults with developmental disabilities in Ontario*. Toronto, ON: Institute for Clinical Evaluative Sciences and Centre for Addiction and Mental Health.
Collin, C. (December 5, 2012). *Canada and the convention on the rights of persons with disabilities*. Library of Parliament Research Publications, 89E. Retrieved from http://www.parl.gc.ca/Content/LOP/ResearchPublications/2012-89-e.htm.
Cooper, S. A. (1997). Clinical study of the effects of age on the physical health of adults with mental retardation. *American Journal of Mental Retardation, 102*(6), 582—589.
Coppus, A. M. W. (2013). People with intellectual disability: what do we know about adulthood and life expectancy? *Developmental Disabilities Research Reviews, 18*(1), 6—16.
Coppus, A., Evenhuis, H., Verberne, G.-J., Visser, F., Van Gool, P., Eikelenboom, P., et al. (2006). Dementia and mortality in persons with Down's syndrome. *Journal of Intellectual Disability Research, 50*(10), 768—777.
Davidson, P. W., Prasher, V. P., & Janicki, M. P. (Eds.). (2003). *Mental health, intellectual disabilities and the aging process*. Oxford: Blackwell Publishing LTD.
De Vries, N. M., Staal, J. B., Van Ravensberg, C. D., Hobbelen, J. S. M., Olde Rikkert, M. G. M., & Nijhuis-Van der Sanden, M. W. G. (2011). Outcome instruments to measure frailty: a systematic review. *Ageing Research Reviews, 10*(1), 104—114.
Department of Health and Human Services. (2000). *Clinical guidelines series for area programs: VII. Evaluation and treatment of psychiatric and behavioral problems in persons with mental retardation*. Raleigh, NC: North Carolina Department of Health and Human Services.
Eley, D. S., Boyes, J., Young, L., & Hegney, D. G. (2009). Accommodation needs for carers of and adults with intellectual disability in regional Australia: their hopes for and perceptions of the future. *Rural and Remote Health, 9*(3), 1239.
Enkelaar, L., Smulders, E., van Schrojenstein Lantman-de Valk, H., Weerdesteyn, V., & Geurts, A. C. H. (2013). Prospective study on risk factors for falling in elderly persons

with mild to moderate intellectual disabilities. *Research in Developmental Disabilities, 34*(11), 3754–3765.

Ensrud, K. E., Ewing, S. K., Taylor, B. C., Fink, H. A., Cawthon, P. M., Stone, K. L., et al. (2008). Comparison of 2 frailty indexes for prediction of falls, disability, fractures, and death in older women. *Archives of Internal Medicine, 168*(4), 382–389.

Evenhuis, H. M., Hermans, H., Hilgenkamp, T. I. M., Bastiaanse, L. P., & Echteld, M. A. (2012). Frailty and disability in older adults with intellectual disabilities: results from the healthy ageing and intellectual disability study. *Journal of the American Geriatrics Society, 60*(5), 934–938.

Fried, L. P., Tangen, C. M., Walston, J., Newman, A. B., Hirsch, C., Gottdiener, J., et al. (2001). Frailty in older adults evidence for a phenotype. *The Journals of Gerontology Series A: Biological Sciences and Medical Sciences, 56*(3), M146–M157.

Haveman, M., Heller, T., Lee, L., Maaskant, M., Shooshtari, S., & Strydom, A. (2010). Major health risks in aging persons with intellectual disabilities: an overview of recent studies. *Journal of Policy and Practice in Intellectual Disabilities, 7*(1), 59–69.

Haveman, M., Perry, J., Salvador-Carulla, L., Noonan Walsh, P., Kerr, M., van Schrojenstein Lantman-de-Valk, H., et al. (2011). Ageing and health status in adults with intellectual disabilities: results of the European POMONA II study. *Journal of Intellectual and Developmental Disability, 36*(1), 49–60.

Hermans, H., Beekman, A. T. F., & Evenhuis, H. M. (2013). Prevalence of depression and anxiety in older users of formal Dutch intellectual disability services. *Journal of Affective Disorders, 144*(1–2), 94–100.

Hermans, H., Beekman, A. T. F., & Evenhuis, H. M. (2014). Comparison of anxiety as reported by older people with intellectual disabilities and by older people with normal intelligence. *The American Journal of Geriatric Psychiatry, 22*(12), 1391–1398.

Hermans, H., & Evenhuis, H. M. (2014). Multimorbidity in older adults with intellectual disabilities. *Research in Developmental Disabilities, 35*(4), 776–783.

Heslop, P., Blair, P. S., Fleming, P., Hoghton, M., Marriott, A., & Russ, L. (2014). The confidential inquiry into premature deaths of people with intellectual disabilities in the UK: a population-based study. *The Lancet, 383*(9920), 889–895.

Hilgenkamp, T. I., Bastiaanse, L. P., Hermans, H., Penning, C., van Wijck, R., & Evenhuis, H. M. (2011). Study healthy ageing and intellectual disabilities: recruitment and design. *Research in Developmental Disabilities, 32*(3), 1097–1106.

Hilgenkamp, T., van Wijck, R., & Evenhuis, H. (2012). Measuring physical activity with pedometers in older adults with intellectual disability: reactivity and number of days. *Intellectual and Developmental Disabilities, 50*(4), 343–351.

Hilgenkamp, T. I., van Wijck, R., & Evenhuis, H. M. (2013). Feasibility of eight physical fitness tests in 1050 older adults with intellectual disability: results of the healthy ageing with intellectual disabilities study. *Intellectual and Developmental Disabilities, 51*(1), 33–47.

Hirdes, J. P., Frijters, D. H., & Teare, G. F. (2003). The MDS-CHESS scale: a new measure to predict mortality in institutionalized older people. *Journal of the American Geriatrics Society, 51*(1), 96–100.

Iezzoni, L. I. (1997). Assessing quality using administrative data. *Annals of Internal Medicine, 127*(8 Pt 2), 666–674.

interRAI. (2014). *The interRAI organization: Who we are.* Retrieved from http://interrai.org/organization.html.

Janicki, M. P., Dalton, A. J., Henderson, C. M., & Davidson, P. W. (1999). Mortality and morbidity among older adults with intellectual disability: health services considerations. *Disability and Rehabilitation, 21*(56), 284–294.

Krahn, G. L., Hammond, L., & Turner, A. (2006). A cascade of disparities: health and health care access for people with intellectual disabilities. *Mental Retardation and Developmental Disabilities Research Review, 12*(1), 70–82.

Lakin, K. C., Doljanac, R., Byun, S., Stancliffe, R. J., Taub, S., & Chiri, G. (2008). Factors associated with expenditures for medicaid home and community based services (HCBS) and intermediate care facilities for persons with mental retardation (ICF/MR) services for persons with intellectual and developmental disabilities. *Intellectual and Developmental Disabilities, 46*(3), 200–214.

Lakin, K. C., Hill, B. K., & Anderson, D. (1991). Persons with mental retardation in nursing homes in 1977 and 1985. *Mental Retardation, 29*(1), 25–33.

Lakin, K. C., White, C. C., Hill, B. K., Bruininks, R. H., & Wright, E. A. (1990). Longitudinal change and interstate variability in the size of residential facilities for persons with mental retardation. *Mental Retardation, 28*(6), 343–351.

Leatt, P., Pink, G. H., & Guerriere, M. (2000). Towards a Canadian model of integrated healthcare. *Healthcare Papers, 1*(2), 13–35.

Lifshitz, H., & Merrick, J. (2004). Aging among persons with intellectual disability in Israel in relation to type of residence, age, and etiology. *Research in Developmental Disabilities, 25*(2), 193–205.

Lin, E., Balogh, R., Isaacs, B., Ouellette-Kuntz, H., Selick, A., Wilton, A. S., et al. (2014). Strengths and limitations of health and disability support administrative databases for population-based health research in intellectual and developmental disabilities. *Journal of Policy and Practice in Intellectual Disabilities, 11*(4), 235–244.

Linehan, C., Walsh, P. N., van Schrojenstein Lantman-de Valk, H. M. J., & Kerr, M. (2004). *POMONA: Health indicators for people with intellectual disability in the member states.* Final report. Retrieved from http://www.pomonaproject.org/report.php.

Marengoni, A., Angleman, S., Melis, R., Mangialasche, F., Karp, A., Garmen, A., et al. (2011). Aging with multimorbidity: a systematic review of the literature. *Ageing Research Reviews, 10*(4), 430–439.

Marks, B., Sisirak, J., & Hsieh, K. (2008). Health services, health promotion, and health literacy: report from the state of the science in aging and developmental disabilities conference. *Disability and Health Journal, 1*(3), 136–142.

Martin, L., Fries, B. E., Hirdes, J. P., & James, M. (2011). Using the RUG-III classification system for understanding the resource intensity of persons with intellectual disability residing in nursing homes. *Journal of Intellectual Disabilities, 15*(2), 131–141.

Martin, D. M., Roy, A., & Wells, M. B. (1997). Health gain through health checks: improving access to primary health care for people with intellectual disability. *Journal of Intellectual Disability Research, 41*(5), 401–408.

McCarron, M., Swinburne, J., Burke, E., McGlinchey, E., Carroll, R., & McCallion, P. (2013). Patterns of multimorbidity in an older population of persons with an intellectual disability: results from the intellectual disability supplement to the Irish longitudinal study on aging (IDS-TILDA). *Research in Developmental Disabilities, 34*(1), 521–527.

McGrother, C. W., Bhaumik, S., Thorp, C. F., Hauck, A., Branford, D., & Watson, J. M. (2006). Epilepsy in adults with intellectual disabilities: prevalence, associations and service implications. *Seizure, 15*(6), 376–386.

McGrother, C., Thorp, C., Taub, N., & Machado, O. (2001). Prevalence, disability and need in adults with severe learning disability. *Tizard Learning Disability Review, 6*(3), 4–13.

Mirkin, B., & Weinberger, M. B. (2001). The demography of population ageing. *Publicado en Population Bulletin of the United Nations, 42*(43), 37–53.

National Institute of Aging, National Institutes of Health, US Department of Health and Human Services, and World Health Organization. (2011). *Global health and aging.* Retrieved from http://www.nia.nih.gov/sites/default/files/global_health_and_aging.pdf.

Ontario's Ministry of Health and Long-Term Care. (n.d.). Ontario's aging at home strategy. Retrieved from http://www.health.gov.on.ca/en/public/programs/ltc/33_ontario_strategy.aspx.

Ouellette-Kuntz, H. (2005). Understanding health disparities and inequities faced by individuals with intellectual disabilities. *Journal of Applied Research in Intellectual Disabilities, 18*(2), 113–121.

Ouellette-Kuntz, H., & Martin, L. (2014). *Applied health research question report: Aging profiles of adults with and without developmental disabilities in Ontario.* Toronto, ON: Health Care Access Research and Developmental Disabilities Program.

Ouellette-Kuntz, H., Shooshtari, S., Temple, B., Brownell, M., Burchill, C., Holden, J. J. A., et al. (2009). Estimating administrative prevalence of intellectual disabilities in Manitoba. *Journal on Developmental Disabilities, 15*(3), 69–80.

Patja, K., Mölsä, P., & Iivanainen, M. (2001). Cause-specific mortality of people with intellectual disability in a population-based, 35-year follow-up study. *Journal of Intellectual Disability Research, 45*(1), 30–40.

Public Health Agency of Canada. (November 13, 2012). *Surveillance.* Retrieved from http://www.atlantique.phac.gc.ca/php-psp/surveillance-eng.php.

Rockwood, K., Hogan, D. B., & MacKnight, C. (2000). Conceptualisation and measurement of frailty in elderly people. *Drugs & Aging, 17*(4), 295–302.

Rockwood, K., Mitnitski, A., Song, X., Steen, B., & Skoog, I. (2006). Long-term risks of death and institutionalization of elderly people in relation to deficit accumulation at age 70. *Journal of the American Geriatrics Society, 54*(6), 975–979.

Rockwood, K., Song, X., MacKnight, C., Bergman, H., Hogan, D. B., McDowell, I., et al. (2005). A global clinical measure of fitness and frailty in elderly people. *Canadian Medical Association Journal, 173*(5), 489–495.

Rothman, M. D., Leo-Summers, L., & Gill, T. M. (2008). Prognostic significance of potential frailty criteria. *Journal of the American Geriatrics Society, 56*(12), 2211–2216.

Schoufour, J. D., Evenhuis, H. M., & Echteld, M. A. (2014). The impact of frailty on care intensity in older people with intellectual disabilities. *Research in Developmental Disabilities, 35*(12), 3455–3461.

Schoufour, J. D., Mitnitski, A., Rockwood, K., Evenhuis, H. M., & Echteld, M. A. (2013). Development of a frailty index for older people with intellectual disabilities: results from the HA-ID study. *Research in Developmental Disabilities, 34*(5), 1541–1555.

Schoufour, J. D., Mitnitski, A., Rockwood, K., Hilgenkamp, T. I. M., Evenhuis, H. M., & Echteld, M. A. (2014). Predicting disabilities in daily functioning in older people with intellectual disabilities using a frailty index. *Research in Developmental Disabilities, 35*(10), 2267–2277.

Slattum, P., & Ansello, E. F. (2013). Medications as a risk factor in falls by older adults with and without intellectual disabilities. *Age in Action, 28*(1), 1.

Stancliffe, R. J., Lakin, K. C., Larson, S. A., Engler, J., Taub, S., Fortune, J., et al. (2012). Demographic characteristics, health conditions, and residential service use in adults with Down syndrome in 25 US states. *Intellectual and Developmental Disabilities, 50*(2), 92–108.

Stax, T. E., Luciano, L., Dunn, A. M., & Quevedo, J. P. (2010). Aging and developmental disability. *Physical Medicine & Rehabilitation Clinics of North America, 21*(2), 419–427.

Sternberg, S. A., Schwartz, A. W., Karunananthan, S., Bergman, H., & Clarfield, A. M. (2011). The identification of frailty: a systematic literature review. *Journal of the American Geriatrics Society, 59*(11), 2129–2138.

Strydom, A., Chan, T., King, M., Hassiotis, A., & Livingston, G. (2013). Incidence of dementia in older adults with intellectual disabilities. *Research in Developmental Disabilities, 34*(6), 1881–1885.

Strydom, A., Hassiotis, A., King, M., & Livingston, G. (2008). The relationship of dementia and prevalence in older adults with intellectual disability (ID) to age and severity of ID. *Psychological Medicine, 39*(1), 13–21.

Strydom, A., Romeo, R., Perez-Achiaga, N., Livingston, G., King, M., Knapp, M., et al. (2010). Service use and cost of mental disorder in older adults with intellectual disability. *The British Journal of Psychiatry, 196*(2), 133–138.

Sullivan, W. F., Berg, J. M., Bradley, E., Cheetham, T., Denton, R., Heng, J., et al. (2011). Primary care of adults with developmental disabilities: Canadian consensus guidelines. *Canadian Family Physician, 57*(5), 541–553.

Torr, J. (2005). Dementia and intellectual disability. In A. Burns, J. T. O'Brien, & D. Ames (Eds.), *Dementia* (pp. 745–749). London, UK: Hodder Arnold.

Tyrer, F., & McGrother, C. (2009). Cause-specific mortality and death certificate reporting in adults with moderate to profound intellectual disability. *Journal of Intellectual Disability Research, 53*(11), 898–904.

Tyrer, F., Smith, L. K., & McGrother, C. W. (2007). Mortality in adults with moderate to profound intellectual disability: a population-based study. *Journal of Intellectual Disability Research, 51*(7), 520–527.

Tyrer, F., Smith, L. K., McGrother, C. W., & Taub, N. A. (2007). The impact of physical, intellectual and social impairments on survival in adults with intellectual disability: a population-based register study. *Journal of Applied Research in Intellectual Disabilities, 20*(4), 360–367.

United Nations. (2013). *World population ageing 2013*. New York, NY: United Nations.

Valderas, J. M., Starfield, B., Sibbald, B., Salisbury, C., & Roland, M. (2009). Defining comorbidity: implications for understanding health and health services. *The Annals of Family Medicine, 7*(4), 357–363.

Wallace, R. A., & Schluter, P. (2008). Audit of cardiovascular disease risk factors among supported adults with intellectual disability attending an ageing clinic. *Journal of Intellectual and Developmental Disability, 33*(1), 48–58.

Westerinen, H., Kaski, M., Virta, L., Almqvist, F., & Iivanainen, M. (2007). Prevalence of intellectual disability: a comprehensive study based on national registers. *Journal of Intellectual Disability Research, 51*(9), 715–725.

de Winter, C. F., Bastiaanse, L. P., Hilgenkamp, T. I. M., Evenhuis, H. M., & Echteld, M. A. (2012a). Cardiovascular risk factors (diabetes, hypertension, hypercholesterolemia and metabolic syndrome) in older people with intellectual disability: results of the HA-ID study. *Research in Developmental Disabilities, 33*(6), 1722–1731.

de Winter, C. F., Bastiaanse, L. P., Hilgenkamp, T. I. M., Evenhuis, H. M., & Echteld, M. A. (2012b). Overweight and obesity in older people with intellectual disability. *Research in Developmental Disabilities, 33*(2), 398–405.

de Winter, C. F., Echteld, M. A., & Evenhuis, H. M. (2014). Chronic kidney disease in older people with intellectual disability: results of the HA-ID study. *Research in Developmental Disabilities, 35*(3), 726–732.

de Winter, C. F., Hermans, H., Evenhuis, H. M., & Echteld, M. A. (2015). Associations of symptoms of anxiety and depression with diabetes and cardiovascular risk factors in older people with intellectual disability. *Journal of Intellectual Disability Research, 59*(2), 176–185.

Wisniewski, K. E., Wisniewski, H. M., & Wen, G. Y. (1985). Occurrence of neuropathological changes and dementia of Alzheimer's disease in Down's syndrome. *Annals of Neurology, 17*(3), 278–282.

World Health Organization. (2000). *Ageing and intellectual disabilities—Improving longevity and promoting healthy ageing: Summative report*. Geneva: World Health Organization.

World Health Organization. (2014). *The top 10 causes of death*. Retrieved from http://www.who.int/mediacentre/factsheets/fs310/en/.

Zaal, R. J., van der Kaaij, A. D. M., Evenhuis, H. M., & van den Bemt, P. M. L. A. (2013). Prescription errors in older individuals with an intellectual disability: prevalence and risk

factors in the healthy ageing and intellectual disability study. *Research in Developmental Disabilities, 34*(5), 1656–1662.
Zhu, J. L., Hasle, H., Correa, A., Schendel, D., Friedman, J. M., Olsen, J., et al. (2013). Hospitalizations among people with Down syndrome: a nationwide population-based study in Denmark. *American Journal of Medical Genetics Part A, 161*(4), 650–657.

CHAPTER SEVEN

Identifying and Addressing Disparities in Mortality: US and UK Perspectives

Emily Lauer*,[1], Pauline Heslop[§], Matthew Hoghton[¶]
*Center for Developmental Disabilities Evaluation and Research (CDDER), Eunice Kennedy Shriver Center, University of Massachusetts Medical School, Charlestown, MA, USA
[§]Norah Fry Research Centre, School for Policy Studies, University of Bristol, Bristol, UK
[¶]Clevedon Medical Centre, Clevedon Riverside Group, Clevedon, UK
[1]Corresponding author: e-mail address: Emily.Lauer@umassmed.edu

Contents

International Review of Research in Developmental Disabilities, Volume 48
ISSN 2211-6095
http://dx.doi.org/10.1016/bs.irrdd.2015.03.002

Abstract

Given the little available knowledge about population-level health for people with intellectual and developmental disabilities, mortality surveillance and case reviews represent important sources of health indicators for this population that can be used to understand and address health disparities and target population-level improvements. This chapter summarizes work conducted to date in the United States and England to review mortality for people with intellectual and developmental disabilities. It explores what is known about observed patterns in life expectancy and mortality across age, gender, and cause of mortality for this population. Existing evidence is reviewed regarding observed patterns of excess and premature mortality, mortality due to potentially preventable or avoidable causes, and health disparities. Lastly, the chapter covers challenges experienced to date in obtaining quality mortality data for this population, future implications for mortality surveillance, and future priorities for strategies to improve health and reduce disparities for this population.

1. INTRODUCTION

The past few decades have seen major changes in the treatment of people with intellectual and developmental disabilities in both the United States and England. From "dark ages of neglect and isolation" including eugenics programs in mainland Europe and care centered on separation and institutionalization in the United States and United Kingdom, relative "shining years" have emerged (Califano, 1977). In the 1950s and 1960s, the concept of normalization, which encourages attainment of a normal, community-based life experience for people with intellectual and developmental disabilities, spread from Danish legislation to Sweden and other countries, including the United States and United Kingdom through the work of Bengt Nirje. In the late twentieth century, the United States and United Kingdom led the world in legislation in support of the rights of people with disabilities, gradually transforming their lives. National support and recognition for this population began in the United States in the Kennedy administration (1960s), followed by the 1990 signing of the Americans with Disabilities Act and the 1995 passage of the United Kingdom Disability

Discrimination Act. These policy advances have led to transitions for the majority of people with these disabilities, from segregation in institutionalized settings to living in the community. As a result, people with these disabilities increasingly access generic community-based medical services and are more directly affected by community-based public health initiatives.

However, we have little knowledge about the health and associated needs of people with these disabilities at the population level. Early studies were generally limited to small institutionalized settings, or small groups of people with the same etiology of disability, e.g., Down syndrome. Few community-based studies exist, and those that do are often based on incomplete or biased representations of the population (e.g., recipients of public support services, people included on local registers). Additionally, people with intellectual and developmental disabilities are not well described in current national health surveillance efforts used to assess health and allocate resources for the general population (Bonardi et al., 2011). The 2002 US Surgeon General's report on the health of this population cited "enormous obstacles in seeking the kind of basic health care that many of us take for granted" and called for improvements to "American health research, the finest in the world, (which) has too often bypassed health and health services research questions of prime importance to persons with (intellectual disabilities)." As a result, we know little about leading health indicators for this population, hindering our ability to monitor and target population-level health strategies for this vulnerable population.

Obtaining better information about the health and needs of this population requires better and more comprehensive information collected on a routine basis. As a basic measure of health, vital statistics, including instances of mortality, represent practical and highly useful starting points for improved knowledge for a population such as this one with limited previous surveillance. Given the relative simplicity in measurement compared to other population measures, mortality is a powerful population-level indicator that can provide indices of disease burden and severity, health disparities and effects of public policies and medical and social care systems. Even in the general population, mortality surveillance is an important leading health indicator used to plan and allocate public- and individual-level health resources, and to identify targets for health and service improvement strategies (NHS Clinical Commissioning Group, 2013; Shaw, Thomas, Smith, & Dorling, 2008; US DHHS). Further, examination of mortality over time can demonstrate important changes in the health of a population and assess the impact of initiatives to improve the health and well-being of the population.

In addition to patterns in population-level mortality, another key aspect of mortality surveillance includes individual-level case reviews of deaths. Individual-level case reviews provide a complementary perspective to population trends and can help elucidate explanatory qualitative factors (Barbieri et al., 2013). Reviewing the circumstances and contributing factors of individual deaths facilitates the identification of potentially modifiable factors associated with deaths that may not be apparent in population-level surveillance. Multidisciplinary case reviews allow for factors across a multitude of levels to be understood in context and temporally to each other. These types of reviews can provide a rich source of information about legal, policy- and institutional-level barriers to quality care, and can illustrate positive examples of best practice.

Multiple groups have expressed support for the examination of mortality as a key health indicator for this population, both at the population-level and through individual case reviews. A recent report (2008) from the US Government Accountability Office (GAO) supported reviews and analysis of mortality for people with intellectual and developmental disabilities as one of several available mechanisms to ensure protection of this vulnerable population from harm and to address quality of care concerns. Since mortality review and surveillance was dependent on state discretion at the time, the report recommended that the Administrator of Centers for Medicare & Medicaid Services, the government entity that funds the vast majority of support services for this population, encourage US states to monitor and review mortality. In England following a set of case reports of deaths of people with learning disabilities (Mencap, 2007), the Department of Health (DH) established a Public Health Observatory for Intellectual Disabilities and commissioned a time-limited Confidential Inquiry into premature deaths of people with intellectual disabilities (CIPOLD). The lack of comprehensive mortality data has been identified as problematic by the English DH (Department of Health, 2013, 2014), and National Health Service (NHS) England has committed to monitoring excess under-60 mortality in people with intellectual disabilities (Department of Health, 2013) and establishing a national mortality review function for people with intellectual disabilities (NHS England, 2014).

This chapter will summarize work conducted to date in the United States and England to review mortality of people with intellectual and developmental disabilities and will explore what is known about observed patterns in life expectancy and across age, gender, and cause of mortality for this population. Existing evidence from the United States and United

Kingdom will be reviewed regarding observed patterns of excess and premature mortality, mortality due to potentially preventable or avoidable causes, and health disparities. Lastly, the chapter will cover challenges experienced to date in obtaining quality mortality data for this population, future implications for mortality surveillance, and future priorities for strategies to reduce health disparities for this population.

2. ASSESSING PATTERNS IN MORTALITY

In the United States and England, previous studies of mortality for this population are of limited generalizability, consisting of small institutionally based populations or up to a few hundred deaths of those living in the community. Studies tend to focus on mortality in specific disabilities (Esbensen, 2010; Esbensen, Seltzer, & Greenberg, 2007; Thorpe, Pahwa, Bennett, Kirk, & Nanson, 2012), changes in life expectancy (Janicki, Dalton, Henderson, & Davidson, 1999; Strauss, Brooks, Rosenbloom, & Shavelle, 2008), and causes of death (Glover & Emerson, 2013; Hollins, Attard, von Fraunhofer, McGuigan, & Sedgwick, 1998; Janicki et al., 1999). Because existing and well-established vital statistics programs in these two countries are unable to distinguish between trends in people with and without these disabilities, information must come from other sources—the existence of which may be subject to resource availability and political will. Some promising studies have emerged recently that examine larger and more representative populations including those based on local registers in the United Kingdom (Glover & Ayub, 2010; Glover & Emerson, 2013; Heslop et al., 2013) and state-based public service systems in the United States (e.g., Lauer, 2013a; Lauer et al., 2003—2012); however, their long-term existence is fragile as they tend to either be studies of limited duration (e.g., Heslop et al., 2013) or dependent upon resources of limited public programs. While these sources represent substantial improvements in population coverage, limitations still exist: people with mild intellectual and developmental disabilities and those arguably experiencing the largest barriers to medical and social care are among the least likely to be included. In addition, few sources are able to assess mortality patterns across factors related to known health disparities in the general population, such as ethnicity and socioeconomic status.

2.1 Overall Mortality

To assess overall mortality in people with intellectual and developmental disabilities, three basic measures will be reviewed: average life expectancy, crude mortality rate, and standardized mortality ratios (SMRs). Average life expectancy is estimated as the average age at death for the population. Crude mortality rate is a calculation of the number of deaths divided by the estimated size of the population. The resulting rate allows for comparison between populations of different size; the rate is described as "crude" because it is not adjusted for the distribution of mortality risk factors, such as age, in the underlying population. SMRs are an indirect method of comparison of mortality between populations where the mortality rate for the population of interest is divided by the mortality rate for the comparison population. The resulting ratio is a relative measure of mortality between the two populations that, similarly to the crude mortality rate, does not adjust for differences in the underlying distribution of mortality risk factors between the populations.

2.1.1 Life Expectancy

On average, life expectancy for people with intellectual and developmental disabilities has increased substantially over the last 50 years, similar to the general population. Data from the 1980s to 1990s demonstrate an improved average age at death from the late 50s to the mid-60s for this population in the United States and England (Carter & Jancar, 1983; Janicki et al., 1999). Improvements in life expectancy were driven by improvements in the health status of the general population, deinstitutionalization and benefits of living in a community setting, and improved access to medical care and interventions. Despite these improvements, even in the 1990s, people with intellectual and developmental disabilities were still at increased risk of death before the age of 50 than the general population (Hollins et al., 1998).

In the context of these vast improvements in life expectancy, it was suggested that life expectancy for this population would likely approach that of the general population (Fryers, 1986; Puri, Lekh, Langa, Zaman, & Singh, 1995). However, over 20 years since these findings, little change in the average age at death is observed. Recent data (2009) from three US state systems serving over 84,000 adults with intellectual and developmental disabilities showed an average age at death of between 58.7 and 62.0 years (Lauer & Bonardi, 2013) compared with the average age at death of US residents at birth (78.5 years) and US residents after 20 years (84.2 years) (Centers for Disease Control and Prevention, 2011b). Mortality data from 2010 in England show a median age at death of 56 years for people with intellectual disabilities, compared to 81 years in the general population (Emerson, Hatton, et al., 2012; Glover & Ayub, 2010). More recent data (2010–2011) from a portion of England show a median age at death of 64 years (IQR 52–75 years), with 22% of deaths occurring before the age of 50 years compared to only 9% in the general population (Heslop et al., 2014). Data over a 33-year period from the English city of Sheffield analyzed by Emerson, Glover, Hatton, and Wolstenholme (2014) found "little evidence of any closing of the gap in...life expectancy between people with intellectual disabilities and the general population" (Emerson et al., 2014, p. 94).

The lack of improvement in the average age at death for the population with intellectual and developmental disabilities since the early 1980s in the United States and England is likely influenced by variation in mortality risk within the population. For example, Glover and Ayub (2010) and Emerson, Hatton, et al., 2012 report variation in average age at death according to intellectual disability etiology and Heslop et al. (2014) found an inverse relationship between median age at death and severity of intellectual disability. Similarly, a US study of mortality in older adults with intellectual disabilities, as well as other studies, found differences in individual longevity within this population. Specifically, people with multiple comorbidities including neurological or physical impairments (Hitiris, Mohanraj, Norrie, & Brodie, 2007; Janicki et al., 1999; McGrother et al., 2006) or organic disability etiologies (Bittles et al., 2002) were more likely to die at earlier ages than the general population. Adults without these characteristics were more likely to have a life span similar to or higher than the general population (Janicki et al., 1999). Wide ranges in life span have also been observed in more recent data from US states and others, showing subsets of individuals with these disabilities living well into their 70s, 80s, and beyond (Connecticut DDS, 2011–2013; Heslop et al., 2014; Lauer, 2013a; Lauer et al., 2003–2012). Therefore, it appears that within the population with intellectual and developmental disabilities, life expectancies may be approaching that of the general population for subset(s) of this population.

As many of the mortality studies for this population occur in adults, average age at death may also be affected by higher rates of children with intellectual and developmental disabilities and substantial health complications surviving into adulthood. These adults may only survive into young adulthood, balancing out progressive improvements in life span for other portions of the population. Those disabilities of certain etiologies have experienced marked improvements in longevity, generally due to medical advances to mitigate health-related effects associated with the etiology. For example, over 50 years ago, average life expectancy for people with Down syndrome did not exceed about 25 years (Deaton, 1973; Penrose,

1949; Richards & Sylvester, 1969). A number of important changes have substantially increased the average life span of people with Down syndrome to upward of 50 years (Carter & Jancar, 1983; Janicki & Dalton, 1997), including surgical correction of congenital heart problems (Bittles et al., 2002; Goldman, Urbano, & Hodapp, 2011; Hayes et al., 1997), improved medical care (Zigman, 2013), and tendencies toward more community-based care (Yang, Rasmussen, & Friedman, 2002). However, people with Down syndrome still appear to experience a shorter life span than both the general population and other people with intellectual and developmental disabilities (Dupont, Vaeth, & Videbech, 1986; Eyman, Call, & White, 1991; Fryers, 1986; Janicki & Dalton, 1997).

2.1.2 Crude Mortality Rate

The surveillance and research available to date consistently suggests that people with intellectual or developmental disabilities experience higher crude mortality rates in the United States and England than in the general population. In 2009 data from three US state developmental disability services systems serving a combination of over 84,000 adults (aged 18 years or older), 1280 deaths occurred resulting in a crude adult mortality rate of 15.2 per thousand (Lauer & Bonardi, 2013).

2.1.3 Standardized Mortality Ratios

Comparisons of SMRs for people with intellectual and developmental disabilities show distinct areas of excess mortality in people in this population compared to the general population.

In past decades, multivariate survival analysis on the combined registers of two London districts revealed up to 18 times as many deaths in people with intellectual disabilities compared with the general population, and that half of all deaths occurred under the age of 50 (Hollins et al., 1998). In more recent data (1993–2006), Tyrer and McGrother (2009) found that mortality rates for adults with moderate to profound intellectual disabilities to be almost three times as high (SMR 2.77, 95% CI: 2.53–3.03) as the general population. Glover and Christie (2014) calculated adult SMR for two-fifths (39%; $n = 68$) of local area Partnership Boards from the 2013 English Joint Health and Social Care Self-Assessment on intellectual disability, finding a median SMR of 2.1 compared to the general population. In US data described above, comparison of the crude mortality rate to the general population yields an approximate SMR of 1.47 for adults (Lauer & Bonardi, 2013).

2.2 Mortality and Age

Examining mortality patterns across age groups can provide additional insight into age-related patterns beyond average life expectancy. Age-specific mortality rates within and between populations provide clues about where other factors, such as acute or chronic health conditions, may affect survival. Advancing age is an independent risk factor for mortality; in most industrialized countries, a nonlinear pattern exists between age and rate of mortality. Mortality rates in the general population across the life span in the industrialized nations of the United States and England generally follow a pattern of low mortality rates for children and young adults, with progressively larger increases with advancing age beyond 50 years. Typically, children under 1 year of age have a relatively higher mortality rate than older children, as children born with serious health conditions often have a lower chance of survival during this period. Figure 1 illustrates the typical patterns for mortality across the life span in the general population of the United States and England.

Survival across age groups is connected, and changes in infant and childhood health and survival for people with intellectual and developmental disabilities have affected the size and health of the population in subsequent years. The age-specific patterns of mortality in people with intellectual and developmental disabilities now tend to follow a similar nonlinear pattern observed in the general population, as shown in Figure 2. However, disparities persist as mortality rates begin to increase more rapidly across age groups starting at an earlier age (e.g., 40's—50's) than in the general population.

Emerson et al. (2014) analyzed data covering the English city of Sheffield over a 33-year period, finding a sustained reduction in age-standardized mortality rates for people with intellectual and developmental disabilities

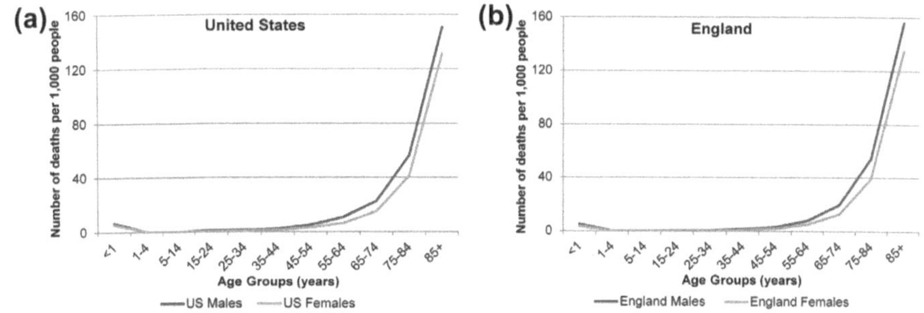

Figure 1 Mortality rates by age and gender for the United States and England general populations, 2011. *CDC (2014) and ONS (2014).*

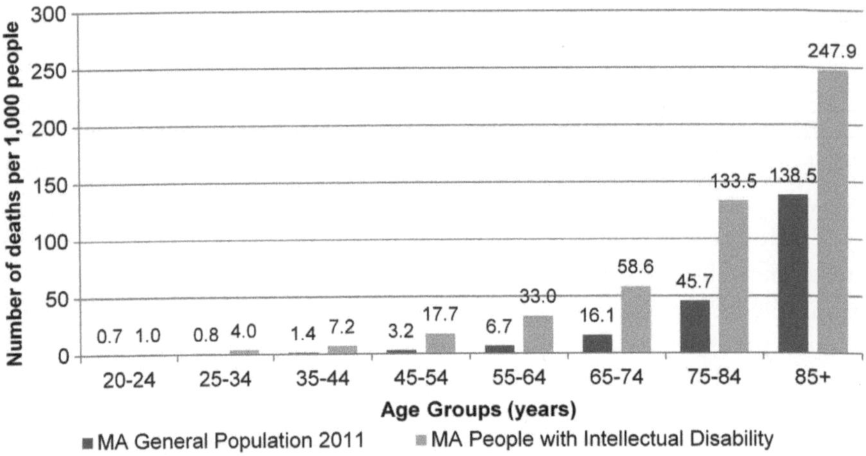

Figure 2 Mortality rate by age group for Massachusetts general population and adults with an intellectual disability (2011) served 2011. *CDC NCHS and Lauer (2013a).*

over the period, similar to the general population of England and Wales. However, they found an absolute gap in mortality rates remaining constant at an average of 776 excess deaths per 100,000, concluding the improvements had not been enough to eliminate the disparity from the general population patterns.

2.3 Mortality and Gender

Differences in gender-specific mortality patterns exist in both the United States and England general populations and the populations with intellectual and developmental disabilities. In the general population, male life expectancy is lower on average (US—76.0 years; UK—78.9 years) than for females (US—80.9 years; UK—82.7 years) (CDC, 2011b; ONS, 2014); men also experience higher mortality rates in older age groups than females as shown in Figure 1.

While gender differences in average age at death are also observed among people with intellectual and developmental disabilities, they differ somewhat from those in the general population. For example, in a large institution in Southwestern England in 1931–1935, Carter and Jancar (1983) described a difference in average age at death of about 7 years between genders (males: 15 years, females: 22 years). Later data suggest that the gap in life span between genders narrowed. In a 1976–1980 cohort, the gender difference fell to 1.5 years (males: 58.3 years, females: 59.8 years) (Carter & Jancar, 1983). In a US cohort of over 25,000 adults receiving public disability services, average age at death is at least 2 years lower in males than females

(Lauer, 2013a). In England during 2011–2012, males and females with intellectual and developmental disabilities had similar median ages of death (65 and 63 years, respectively) (Heslop et al., 2014).

While gender differences in average age at death for the population with intellectual and developmental disabilities are now small, differences in mortality rates persist. Mortality rates for females with these disabilities are generally higher than for males in the United States and England (Connecticut DDS, 2011–2013; Lauer, 2013a). For example, in the United States, the female adult mortality rate was 17.0 per thousand in 2010 and 19.6 per thousand in 2011, compared to a male adult mortality rate of 14.9 per thousand in 2010 and 17.5 per thousand in 2011 for people with intellectual and developmental disabilities (Lauer, 2013a).

In comparison to the general population, females with these disabilities experience greater disparity in mortality rate than do males. In a 1993–2010 study of adults (20-years old and older) identified as having an intellectual disability through a local register in England, the SMR for males was 2.2 (95% CI: 2.0–2.4) and was 2.8 (95% CI: 2.5–3.1) for females (Kiani et al., 2014). In England, Tyrer and McGrother (2009) reported SMRs for adults with moderate to profound intellectual disabilities of 2.28 for males and 3.24 for females over 1993–2006. CIPOLD in England found the age at death disparity, compared to the general population, to be 7 years greater for females (a disparity of 13 years for males versus 20 years for females) (Heslop et al., 2014).

Gender patterns may differ between people with intellectual and developmental disabilities and the general population in part because many of the major drivers of gender differences in the general population are observed less frequently in this population. General population gender differences are partially explained by increased risk factors for males including occupational risk factors (e.g., toxin or chemical exposure, accidental injuries in industries such as forestry, fishing, mining, construction, transportation) (US Bureau of Labor Statistics, 2014) and increased engagement in high-risk behaviors (e.g., smoking, motor vehicle speed and driving while intoxicated, and firearm use) (Lopez, 1983). Males in the general population have an injury-related mortality rate (both accidents and intentional injuries such as homicide) that is twice that of women's (CDC, n.d.; Gordis, 2004). In contrast, people with intellectual and developmental disabilities are less likely to be employed in the jobs that present significant occupational risks and engage in many of these behaviors. The reasons for the gender differences in people with intellectual or developmental disabilities are not completely understood, but are likely due to underlying differences in mortality risk factors such as prevalence and severity of chronic health conditions or health effects related to disability etiologies affecting one gender more than the other (e.g., Fragile X, autism, Down syndrome) (Shin et al., 2009). It is also possible that observed gender differences may be affected by selection biases in available data sources, such as differing reasons across gender for receipt of support services, or, in historical data, gender-related differences in which people with these types of disabilities were institutionalized.

2.4 Mortality and Cause of Death

Surveillance of trends within specific causes of death is a key component of examinations of mortality that directly informs estimates of morbidity and targets for public health efforts.

2.4.1 Immediate versus Underlying Cause of Death

In examinations of vital statistics, it is important to consider information about cause of death in the context of the source and coding of the underlying data. Since 1939, the United States and United Kingdom have used the same set of classifications for defining underlying cause of death categories (US Bureau of the Census, 1939), currently based on the 10th edition of the International Classification of Diseases. Additionally, the same report structure is used by both countries (WHO, 1992) to capture factors related to the cause of the death across multiple sections as shown in Figure 3.

This certificate contains fields to separately capture the manner of death (e.g., natural causes), a cascading list of causal factors, and other significant conditions contributing to the death. Causal factors are recorded as the immediate (final) cause of death, which is the injury, disease, or complication that directly precedes death, followed by conditions leading to the final cause and ending with the underlying cause of death. The underlying cause is defined as:

> *(a) the disease or injury which initiated the train of morbid events leading directly or indirectly to death or (b) the circumstances of the accident or violence which produced the fatal injury.*
>
> ***(WHO, 1992)***

While more than one cause of death may be listed on the US death certificate or England's Cause of Death certificate, it is the "underlying" cause which is used for vital statistics. While there are many challenges to the accuracy of death certificates (see *Accuracy of Death Certificates*), it is the best source of information available about why people die.

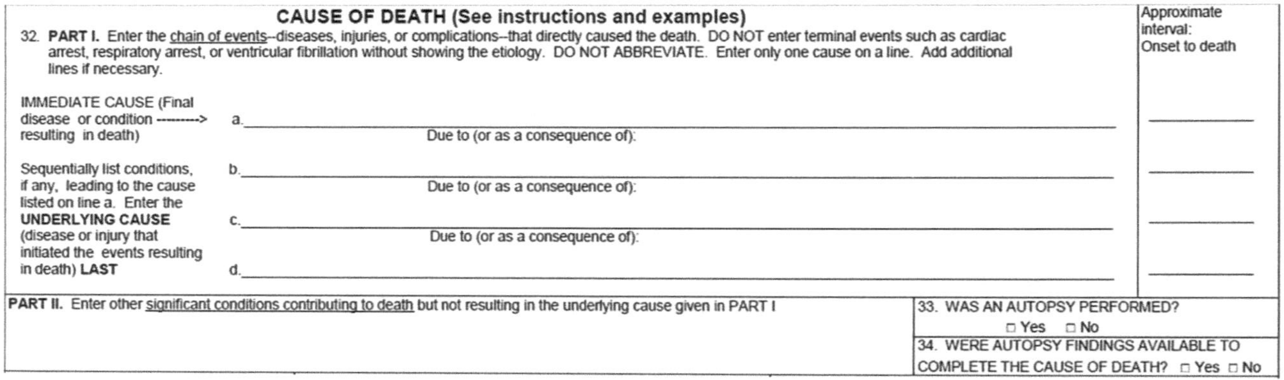

CAUSE OF DEATH (See instructions and examples)

32. **PART I.** Enter the chain of events--diseases, injuries, or complications--that directly caused the death. DO NOT enter terminal events such as cardiac arrest, respiratory arrest, or ventricular fibrillation without showing the etiology. DO NOT ABBREVIATE. Enter only one cause on a line. Add additional lines if necessary.

Approximate interval: Onset to death

IMMEDIATE CAUSE (Final disease or condition ---------> resulting in death) a.______________ ______

Due to (or as a consequence of):

Sequentially list conditions, if any, leading to the cause listed on line a. Enter the **UNDERLYING CAUSE** (disease or injury that initiated the events resulting in death) **LAST**

b.______________ ______

Due to (or as a consequence of):

c.______________ ______

Due to (or as a consequence of):

d.______________ ______

PART II. Enter other significant conditions contributing to death but not resulting in the underlying cause given in PART I

33. WAS AN AUTOPSY PERFORMED?
□ Yes □ No

34. WERE AUTOPSY FINDINGS AVAILABLE TO COMPLETE THE CAUSE OF DEATH? □ Yes □ No

Figure 3 Cause of death section of the US Standard Certificate of Death. *CDC (2003).*

2.4.2 Trends over Time in Causes of Death

Since the 1900s, trends in causes of death have undergone significant changes in the United States and England general populations, like much of the developed world. In the early twentieth century, about half of all deaths were due to infectious diseases, but now the vast majority of deaths are due to noninfectious causes such as chronic diseases (e.g., heart disease, cancer) and conditions that occur more frequently in older adults (e.g., stroke) (Armstrong, Conn, & Pinner, 1999). These changes were largely driven by improvements in the health of the population through advances in public health efforts including immunizations, improved nutrition, sanitation, and medical treatments such as antibiotics.

People with intellectual and developmental disabilities have also benefited from these public health and medical advances, as well as the development of treatments to mitigate health-related effects of certain etiologies of intellectual or developmental disabilities (e.g., correction of congenital heart conditions due to Down syndrome) (Janicki et al., 1999). As a result, similar to the general population, the most frequent causes of death have also shifted toward chronic conditions for large portions of people with intellectual and developmental disabilities (Heslop et al., 2014; Janicki et al., 1999).

2.4.3 Common Causes of Mortality in People with Intellectual and Developmental Disabilities

Presently in the United States and England, the most frequent underlying causes of death for people with intellectual and developmental disabilities are the same as for the general population, including heart disease, cancer, and respiratory diseases (Eyman et al., 1991; Glover & Ayub, 2010; Heslop et al., 2014; Janicki et al., 1999; Lauer & Bonardi, 2013; Puri et al., 1995; Tyrer & McGrother, 2009). This profile is similar to findings in other developed nations. However, these three causes account for a lower proportion of deaths of people with intellectual and developmental disabilities than for the general population, resulting in a more diffuse and varied profile of leading causes of death. Other causes of death, which can be relatively rare in the general population, appear more frequently in people with intellectual and developmental disabilities including neurological disorders (e.g., seizures, Alzheimer's disease), chronic and acute respiratory issues related to aspiration, accidental injuries due to falls, and gastrointestinal diseases (Eyman et al., 1991; Heslop et al., 2014; Janicki et al., 1999; Lauer & Bonardi, 2013; Puri et al., 1995; Tyrer & McGrother, 2009). This population may experience increased mortality risk related to disability etiology (e.g., syndromes with terminal effects, earlier onset and more rapid progression of Alzheimer's disease due to Down syndrome) (Patel, Goldberg, & Moss, 1993; Tyrer, Smith, & McGrother, 2007; Zigman, Schupf, Haveman, & Silverman, 1997) and from secondary factors (e.g., increased aspiration risk due to body habitus (physique) or swallowing disorders, potentially deleterious side effects of long-term antiepileptic medication use). Causes of death for this population may also be affected by important social support dimensions and the quality of medical care received, particularly for people that rely on others for assistance with their daily living activities (e.g., eating, bathing, access to medical treatment) (Hussain & Hyde-Bales, 2014).

An examination of cause-specific SMRs shows distinct areas of excess mortality in people with intellectual and developmental disabilities compared to the general population. Recent (2009) mortality data for a US cohort of over 84,000 adults (aged 18 years or older) from three state disability service systems demonstrate mortality patterns that roughly mirror the US population with some notable differences (Table 1) (Lauer & Bonardi, 2013). While these data may underrepresent people with mild intellectual disabilities and higher socioeconomic status, it include a large cohort of adults with varied levels of intellectual disability residing mostly in community-based settings. Cause-specific rates were similar to the general population for heart disease (SMR 1.1, 95% CI: 0.93−2.2), cancer (SMR 0.61, 95% CI: 0.51−1.8), and unintentional injuries (accidents) (SMR

Table 1 Cause-Specific Standardized Mortality Ratios, 2009

		Adults with ID: Adults in General Population	
US Rank	**Cause of Death**	**SMR**	**95% CI**
1	Heart disease	1.1	0.93−2.2
2	Cancer	0.61	0.51−1.8
5	Unintentional injuries (accidents)	1.2	0.94−2.6
6	Alzheimer's disease	3.5[a]	2.8−4.7
8	Influenza and pneumonia	5.8[a]	4.8−7.0
9	Kidney diseases	1.8[a]	1.3−3.2
11	Septicemia	3.2[a]	2.4−4.6
<16	Aspiration pneumonia	19.1[a]	15.9−20.3

Note: Certain top causes of death are not shown due to either a lack of sufficient detail to assess specified cause, or concerns about reliability of coding prevented comparison.

[a] $p \leq 0.01$.

Lauer and Bonardi (2013).

1.2, 95% CI: 0.94–2.6). However, significantly greater risk of death for people with intellectual and developmental disabilities was observed from Alzheimer's disease (SMR 3.5, 95% CI: 2.8–4.7), influenza and pneumonia (SMR 5.8, 95% CI: 4.8–7.0), septicemia (SMR 3.2, 95% CI: 2.4–4.6), and aspiration pneumonia (SMR 19.1, 95% CI: 15.9–20.3).

Areas of excess mortality for people with intellectual and developmental disabilities are similar in other studies in the United States and England. In a study of adults with moderate, severe, and profound intellectual disabilities in England, Tyrer and McGrother (2009) reported SMRs of 85.6 (95% CI: 62.7–114.2) for congenital anomalies, 16.3 (95% CI: 12.6–20.7) for diseases of the nervous system, 11.4 (95% CI: 4.6–23.5) for mental disorders other than dementia, 6.5 (95% CI: 2.2–13.6) for bronchopneumonia, 6.0 (95% CI: 3.6–9.5) for genitourinary diseases, and 4.64 (95% CI: 3.6–5.9) for other respiratory infections.

2.4.3.1 Cancer

Estimates of cancer-related mortality risk conflict across studies of people with intellectual and developmental disabilities, with findings of higher and lower overall risk compared to the general population and differences in occurrence by primary site and tissue type (Carter & Jancar, 1983; Evenhuis, 1997; Heslop et al., 2014; Hollins et al., 1998; Janicki et al., 1999; Lauer & Bonardi, 2013). Findings are likely to be affected by differences in underlying cancer risk overall and by type related to population characteristics (e.g., distribution of etiologies of disability, age distributions) and small sample sizes and/or skewed samples. However, colorectal cancer is frequently a leading type of cancer contributing to mortality in the United States and England for people with intellectual and developmental disabilities (Heslop et al., 2014; Lauer & Bonardi, 2013), as well as in the UK and US general populations (CDC, 2011b; ONS, 2014). Other leading cancers causing mortality in this population include cancers of the lung and the female breast (Lauer, 2013a; Lauer et al., 2003–2012; Tyrer & McGrother, 2009). Considering that screenings exist for both colorectal and breast cancer, improved medical care may be able to lessen cancer-related mortality risk for this population.

The medical literature points to potential predispositions for particular cancers in certain etiologies of intellectual and developmental disabilities (e.g., colorectal cancer) (Lucci-Cordisco et al., 2005; Patja, Eero, & Livanainen, 2001; Ross et al., 2005; Smith, Zhu, McAvoy, & Kuhn, 2006). In addition, this population is at risk of developing certain cancers at significantly younger ages than the general population (e.g., colorectal cancer starting at age 35

(Lucci-Cordisco et al., 2005)) with important implications for preventive screening guidance. Genetically based etiologies of intellectual and developmental disabilities appear to have the strongest predispositions for certain types of cancer, varied by genetic cause (Feliciano, 2012). Trisomy 21 (Down syndrome) has been associated with a greater risk of testicular and ocular tumors and leukemia, and a lower risk for many other types of cancers (Hasle, Clemmensen, & Mikkelsen, 2000; Hill et al., 2003; Patja et al., 2001; Satge et al., 1998). Rett's syndrome caries greater risk for certain types of bone cancer. Tuberous sclerosis presents increased risk for kidney and brain tumors (Al-Saleem et al., 1998).

Lifestyle factors or associated conditions that are more frequent in people with intellectual or developmental disabilities may also alter cancer risk. This population is less likely to experience certain environmental exposures (e.g., occupational) related to cancer risk. In relation to behavioral factors, people with moderate, severe, and profound intellectual disabilities may be less likely to use tobacco products lowering risks of lung cancer, and oropharyngeal (mouth/neck) cancers and less likely to be engaged in sexual activity lowering risk of human papillomavirus-related cancers (e.g., cervical). However, people with mild intellectual or developmental disabilities may engage in sexual activity at similar frequencies to the general population, but may have limited education about preventing the transmission of sexually transmitted diseases and lower cervical screening rates (Galea, Butler, Iacono, & Leighton, 2004; Greenwood & Wilkinson, 2013; Swango-Wilson, 2011). Certain conditions such as chronic gastrointestinal problems, including infections with bacteria commonly found in group living settings, may increase risk for stomach and colorectal cancer (Duff, Scheepers, Cooper, Hoghton, & Baddeley, 2001; Wallace, Webb, & Schluter, 2002).

2.4.3.2 Respiratory Diseases

Respiratory diseases, particularly respiratory infections, are a substantial source of mortality in people with intellectual and developmental disabilities. In particular, older people with intellectual and developmental disabilities appear to have both a higher risk of developing respiratory infections, and of dying from those infections (Chaney & Eyman, 2000). Community-acquired pneumonias tend to follow epidemiologic trends in the general population, but with many people with intellectual and developmental disabilities at increased risk of infection due to comorbid conditions, weakened immune systems, less ability to communicate signs and symptoms of illness, and living in congregate settings.

However, in contrast to the general population, pneumonia due to aspiration is also a substantial source of morbidity and mortality (Heslop et al., 2014; Hollins et al., 1998; Lauer & Bonardi, 2013; Tyrer & McGrother, 2009). Adults with intellectual and developmental disabilities in three US states were over 19 times more likely to die from aspiration pneumonia than the general population (Table 1). Aspiration pneumonia develops as a result of substances (secretions, food, vomitus) entering the lungs from swallowing disorders, choking while eating or from "silent" reflux from the stomach. In addition to irritating the lungs and/or bronchial tubes, this foreign matter can introduce bacterial or other infectious agents causing infection. People at the highest risk for aspiration pneumonia are those with dysmorphology of the oral cavity, abnormal swallowing due to neurological conditions or long-term medication side effects, poor oral health status, gastroesophageal reflux, or respiratory distress while eating or drinking (Hogg, Juhlberg, & Lambe, 2007; Patja et al., 2001; Rogers et al., 1994). In addition to acute infections, long-term damage to the lungs from chronic aspiration can result in chronic obstructive pulmonary disorders. Treatments for aspiration such as special positioning, modifications to food and beverage consistency, or surgical interventions (e.g., feeding tubes) may provide improvement in swallowing ability but are likely to provide incomplete protection (Marik, 2001).

Diagnosis of aspiration pneumonia can be complicated, particularly because the aspiration event is not generally witnessed (Marik, 2001). While testing can identify infectious agents, there is a lack of specificity between agents in relation to those uniquely associated with aspiration pneumonia. In addition, symptoms and progression can appear similar to community-acquired pneumonia. Therefore, aspiration pneumonias may be more likely to be coded as pneumonias due to undetermined cause unless there is definite diagnostic clarity of aspiration pneumonia or an observed choking episode.

2.4.3.3 Nervous Disorders: Seizures

Epilepsy occurs more frequently in people with intellectual and developmental disabilities than in the general population (Leung & Ring, 2013) with prevalence estimates of 25–50% (Kerr et al., 2009; Young et al., 2014) and 0.5–1.0% respectively (Forsgren, 2004; Joint Epilepsy Council, 2005; Rugg-Gunn & Sander, 2012). As the severity of the intellectual disability increases, so does epilepsy risk (Leung & Ring, 2013). Further, epilepsy in people with intellectual and developmental disabilities appears to be complex, with about half of those with epilepsy having treatment-resistant forms (Young et al., 2014).

Epilepsy, particularly when poorly controlled, presents a risk of sudden death. The increased prevalence and complexity in management of epilepsy appears to be reflected in a higher mortality burden for people with intellectual and developmental disabilities. While some variability exists, the majority of studies that consider mortality due to seizures in this population suggest that the presence of an intellectual disability may be an independent risk factor for death due to a seizure or sudden death in epilepsy, termed "SUDEP" (Kiani et al., 2014; Walczack et al., 2001; Young et al., 2014). SUDEP is a sudden and unexpected death of someone diagnosed with epilepsy while in reasonable health as defined by an advisory committee of the US Food and Drug Administration and Burroughs Wellcome. SUDEP can only be assigned to deaths occurring during normal activities and benign circumstances, without obvious medical causes, and not directly caused by the seizure or status epilepticus (Annegers, Coan, Hauser, & Leestma, 2000). Young et al. (2014) conducted a systematic review of risk factors for SUDEP, finding that of 23 studies that considered intellectual disability as a risk factor, 14 identified a risk factor for SUDEP. However, Young et al. (2014) caution that intellectual disability "though overrepresented in patients with epilepsy has not been looked at in any sufficient detail to enumerate its risk for SUDEP" (p. 4).

A study conducted from 1993 to 2010 in a portion of England examined mortality in a small subgroup of adults with epilepsy both with and without intellectual disabilities. Overall SMRs for people with epilepsy and intellectual disabilities were estimated to be 3.2 (95% CI: 2.7–3.8) for men and 5.6 (95% CI: 4.6–6.7) for women. SUDEP was the second most common cause of death for adults with intellectual disabilities and epilepsy after respiratory diseases with SMRs for SUDEP of 37.6 for men (95% CI: 21.9–60.2) and 52.0 for women (95% CI: 23.8–98.8) (Kiani et al., 2014), suggesting a high level of excess mortality due to SUDEP in adults with both conditions (Kiani et al., 2014). While this particular study experienced limitations due to sample size and limited case notes, other studies also suggest excess seizure-related mortality in people with intellectual disabilities and epilepsy (Heslop et al., 2014; Walczack et al., 2001). In the 2010–2011 CIPOLD in southwest England, 43% of decedents with intellectual disabilities had epilepsy and 39% received at least one (and up to seven concurrent) prescription medication for the management of epilepsy (Heslop et al., 2013). Of those with epilepsy, 73%, or about a third of all decedents, had a seizure in the past 5 years (Heslop et al., 2013). Even with the potential for misdiagnosis of epilepsy, the prevalence of recent seizures suggests that the actual prevalence of seizure disorders is quite high among decedents, and that challenges with the management of these disorders may not be uncommon.

However, challenges exist in the diagnosis of epilepsy both in the general population and for people with intellectual and developmental disabilities. The most information available about this issue appears to come from England where misdiagnosis in the general population was estimated to be at least 25% (All Parliamentary Committee on Epilepsy, 2007). Two main factors contribute to this misdiagnosis for people with intellectual and developmental disabilities: first, some seizure disorders are not well defined and mimic other conditions so seizure-like behaviors for people with intellectual and developmental disabilities may be misinterpreted by parents, paid caregivers, or health professionals. Second, variations in local service provisions for people with epilepsy may lead to differences in the accuracy of diagnosis (Morton & Appleton, 2002). For example, in a review of people in England with intellectual disabilities diagnosed with epilepsy only about 50% of epilepsy diagnoses were made by a seizure expert; less than 50% had an electroencephalography (EEG) to confirm seizure activity and even fewer had any type of brain imaging such as an X-ray, CT, or MRI scans (Reuber et al., 2008). Given the diagnostic challenges in people with intellectual and developmental disabilities, the lack of these practices presents particular concerns about diagnostic accuracy. Misdiagnosis does not appear to be limited to England, but may be lower in countries that more routinely use recommended procedures (e.g., EEG, brain imaging) to confirm diagnoses. A systematic review of the international literature shows that 32–38% of those with intellectual disabilities diagnosed with epilepsy either did not have epilepsy or had experienced nonepileptic events (Chapman et al., 2011).

In addition to the complexities around the diagnosis of epilepsy, challenges also exist in the confirmation of deaths as due to SUDEP. Identification of SUDEP is classified into four levels, depending on the strength of the evidence from an autopsy and other sources of information: (1) definite (requires an autopsy report), (2) probable, (3) possible (due to insufficient information about the circumstances of death), and (4) unlikely/not SUDEP (other causes of death are established) (Kiani et al., 2014). Because the diagnosis of SUDEP is one of exclusion, many uncertain cases exist (Nashef, Elson, Ryvlin, & Tomson, 2012; Shorvon & Tomson, 2011). In the CIPOLD, about 4% of deaths were due to SUDEP (Heslop et al., 2013).

However, epilepsy was questioned as the underlying cause of death in a number of deaths after detailed investigations and reviews of each death were conducted. Particular concerns were raised about the attribution of SUDEP in deaths for which no routine toxicology or biochemical screenings were conducted and that had no indication of seizure activity for over 10 years prior to death (Heslop et al., 2013).

2.4.3.4 Nervous Disorders: Dementia and Alzheimer's Disease

Evidence suggests an increased likelihood of developing dementia, including Alzheimer's disease, for people with intellectual disabilities, especially Down syndrome, compared to people without intellectual disabilities (Patel et al., 1993), presenting an increased source of morbidity and mortality (Tyrer, Smith, & McGrother, 2007). Some estimates suggest that of people with Down syndrome who live to the age of 60 years, at least half will develop Alzheimer's disease (Zigman et al., 1997). Additionally Alzheimer's and other types of dementia may develop at younger ages; Alzheimer's disease is reported to produce noticeable effects in people as young as 35-years old with Down syndrome (Burt et al., 1998; Mann, 1988; Wisniewski, Wisniewski, & Wen, 1985; Zigman, Schupf, Sersen, & Silverman, 1996). Clinically, people with Down syndrome and Alzheimer's diseases may be less likely to exhibit aggression, but more likely to have sleep disturbances, changes in mood, auditory hallucinations, and overactivity (Cooper & Prasher, 1998; Cosgrave, Tyrrell, McCarron, Gill, & Lawlor, 1999; Holland, Hon, Huppert, & Stevens, 2000). The higher prevalence and earlier onset of Alzheimer's disease in people with Down syndrome, together with the degenerative nature of the disease, are part of the reason for being a more frequent cause of death in this population.

Findings from limited available sources in the United States confer these patterns. As shown in Table 1, adults with intellectual and developmental disabilities receiving support services from US state agencies showed over three times the burden of mortality from Alzheimer's disease (Lauer & Bonardi, 2013). In addition, people in this cohort on average died at earlier ages from Alzheimer's disease than the general population. For example, an examination of top-ranked causes of death by 10-year age groups for one of these states showed Alzheimer's disease was the first or second most frequent cause of death for age groups of 45–54, 55–64, and 65–75 years, while it ranked lower for age groups older than 75 years (Lauer, 2013a); in the general population in the same state, it was not in the top three causes of death for any age group (Massachusetts DPH, 2010).

However, challenges with the reliability of diagnosis of dementia, including Alzheimer's disease, can affect mortality data. The diagnosis of Alzheimer's disease in people with intellectual and developmental disabilities is more challenging than for the general population. People with these disabilities have a wide range of variability in baseline cognitive functioning which can make obtaining baseline levels of cognitive functioning against which to assess change more difficult. In addition, different diagnostic and methodological procedures are used in the field. Diagnosis of dementia in people with Down syndrome "remains clinically integrative based on history, physical examination and brief cognitive testing" (Feldman et al., 2008) and the lack of a gold standard by which to diagnose dementia in people with intellectual disabilities means that clinicians should exercise caution in diagnosing it (Burt et al., 1996). Due to limited formal diagnostic information, clinicians may be forced to depend largely on informant reports, which may assess symptoms differently from how an individual might assess symptoms and focus on behaviors that more directly impact on their own lives (Nieuwenhuis-Mark, 2009).

Shifts in mortality reporting also affect mortality data for dementia, including Alzheimer's disease. In the United States (Healy, 2013; Moschetti, Cummings, Sorvillo, & Kuo, 2012) and Europe (Brunnström & Englund, 2009; Harteloh, de Bruin, & Kardaun, 2010), there is evidence of an increased likelihood of reporting dementia, including Alzheimer's disease, as an underlying cause of death for people who die of complications due to advanced states of these diseases. Previously, mortality reporting was more likely to report more immediate causes of death, such as pneumonia or congestive heart failure, as underlying causes for these types of death. As a result, Alzheimer's disease may have been underreported as an underlying cause of death. However, there appears to be growing recognition and emphasis among physicians in recognizing and reporting the contributions of Alzheimer's disease and other sources of dementia as the underlying causes of these deaths (Healy, 2013). Consequently, this trend, together with a growing understanding of the relationship between Down syndrome and dementia (Dalton, 1995; Duggan, Lewis, & Morgan, 1996; Zigman, 2013; Zigman et al., 1996), increases the likelihood that Alzheimer's disease will be appropriately recorded as an underlying cause of death for people with intellectual and developmental disabilities in the United States (Janicki et al., 1999).

2.4.3.5 Injuries

People with intellectual and developmental disabilities have similar or slightly higher rates of death due to unintentional injuries (accidents) (e.g.,

Table 1), and lower rates of intentional injuries such as those due to homicide or suicide. However, the profile of causal factors of unintentional injuries and relationship with age tend to vary greatly from the general population. People with intellectual or developmental disabilities, particularly those with more severe disabilities, are less likely to engage in high-risk behaviors (such as use of firearms, tobacco, alcohol, and drugs) and correspondingly less likely to experience injuries from them (Kastner, Nathanson, & Friedman, 1993; Janicki et al., 1999; Tyrer & McGrother, 2009). As discussed previously (see Mortality and Gender), they are also less likely to experience occupational exposure to external agents or risk of occupation-related unintentional injuries.

Instead, people with intellectual and developmental disabilities are much more likely to experience unintentional injuries related to their disabilities, including choking and aspiration, and falls. As discussed previously in relation to aspiration pneumonia, many people with intellectual or developmental disabilities are at increased risk for aspiration due to swallowing disorders, physical and positional challenges, and long-term side effects of some psychotropic medications. In addition, behavioral issues may increase the risk of choking or aspiration such as tendencies to eat rapidly and/or incompletely chew food before swallowing, and the ingestion of nonfood items (pica). Factors such as poor oral hygiene can complicate this risk.

In relation to falls, people with intellectual and developmental disabilities have a risk of falling that is estimated to be three times higher than the general population and exceeds that of the elderly (Finlayson, Morrison, Jackson, Mantry, & Cooper, 2010; Willgoss, 2010). About half of people with intellectual and developmental disabilities fall over the course of a year, and about one-third of those falls are injurious (Finlayson et al., 2010; Wagemans & Cluitmans, 2006; Willgoss, 2010). Increased fall risk also presents at much younger ages in the population with intellectual and developmental disabilities; injuries from falls have been found to be more common in young people with intellectual disabilities (aged 5–29) than in the general population and more than 60% of injuries in this younger age group were due to falls (Sherrard, Tonge, & Ozanne-Smith, 2001). In these youths, the rate of hospitalizations for injuries was twice that of the general population, with the profile of injuries more closely resembling younger children in the general population (Sherrard et al., 2001). Numerous factors affect falls risk in this population including impaired mobility, ataxia and abnormal gait, epilepsy, urinary incontinence, side effects of psychotropic medications (particularly antiepileptics), and untreated visual deficits (Finlayson et al., 2010; Willgoss, 2010).

3. POTENTIALLY MODIFIABLE DETERMINANTS OF MORTALITY

3.1 Premature Mortality in People with Intellectual Disabilities

The concept of premature mortality is considered an important measure of the burden of a population's health because many of these deaths may be considered preventable. There are a number of methods that are used to calculate premature mortality including crude, age-specific or age-adjusted death rates, life expectancy, probability of survival, and years of potential life lost (Gardner & Sanborn, 1990; Wheller, Baker, & Griffiths, 2006). Many of these measures rely on a threshold age below which deaths are considered premature. There is debate over the appropriate age limit used to define premature mortality with these methods; in the United States, ages of 65, 75, or even 85 years are among those typically used (Dranger & Remington, 2004). While there is utility in dissecting mortality statistics into deaths and associated morbidity that may be preventable, use of a solely age-based strategy serves as a blunt methodology for this purpose that may not be very meaningful for a population such as those with intellectual and developmental disabilities.

3.1.1 Challenges with Traditional Measures

For many of the people with intellectual and developmental disabilities, the etiology of their disability can cause associated health conditions which affect the expectations of their life span. Regardless of other factors such as the access to and quality of health care, individual-level behaviors, etc., the life expectancy for these people may be substantially lower than the general population. Therefore, the application of a traditional age-related measure of premature death (e.g., benchmark of age 75) would prove rather meaningless for any subset of the population with intellectual and developmental disabilities where the etiology of the disability would result in a life expectancy below this benchmark. For example, it is unusual for someone born with Batten disease to live beyond their 30s, but using a threshold age for prematurity, everyone with Batten disease would be considered to die prematurely, irrespective of the age at which they die and whether they outlive the natural life expectancy for that condition. Similarly, probability of survival estimates are usually derived from life tables drawn from the general population which are not always appropriate for people with intellectual and developmental disabilities given the possible coexistence of life-limiting and/or genetic conditions. It may be possible to calculate the probability of survival to a given age for a particular condition if condition-specific life tables were available (e.g., for Down syndrome) but complications arise in calculating the probability of survival when Down syndrome coexists with dementia and/or congenital heart disease, or any other condition.

In most available data sources of mortality surveillance for the population of people with intellectual and developmental disabilities, it is not feasible to accurately distinguish between those for whom general population estimates are appropriate and those for whom they are not. Yet understanding and gaining an accurate measurement of premature mortality remains extremely important for the population with intellectual or developmental disabilities. More accurate methods, and ones that are not based solely on age cutoffs, are needed to more meaningfully assess premature mortality and by extension preventable mortality. In fact, these types of methods will likely yield more informed estimations of premature mortality for all populations.

3.2 Preventable and Amenable Mortality

Interest in the causes of avoidable death has primarily been based on the work of Rutstein et al. (1976) who sought to measure outcomes of medical care and to identify areas where the quality of health care could be improved. Rutstein published lists of diseases that caused "unnecessary and untimely" premature deaths. Subsequent studies of avoidable mortality have been based on modified versions of these original lists (Charlton & Velez, 1986; Mackenbach, Bouvier-Colle, & Jougla, 1990) to reflect advances in medical treatment and social changes affecting definitions of what is regarded as "avoidable." These definitions may differ between societies, will change over time and may affect different ages depending on the condition in question (Kamarudeen, 2010). Most recently, the UK ONS engaged in a consultation exercise and developed a set of national indicators of avoidable mortality (Office for National Statistics, 2011). Deaths that are avoidable include:

- Amenable mortality: conditions amenable to medical intervention, such as appendicitis
- Preventable mortality: causes of death that could have been prevented through effective public health policy or social intervention, such as smoking cessation measures or road traffic calming.

For some causes of deaths, examination of age-specific proportion of deaths is recommended because although a particular condition could be considered to be avoidable, not every death caused by the condition may be preventable, taking into account the age of the patient, the extent of disease progression at diagnosis, or the existence of complex impairments or multiple comorbidities (Office for National Statistics, 2006).

The CIPOLD study in England (Heslop et al., 2013) used this categorization to assess the extent of premature deaths in people with intellectual disabilities in England. Overall, 48.5% of the deaths of people with intellectual disabilities were avoidable, compared with 24% in the general population. The same proportion of deaths (21%) were preventable by effective public health measures in the cohort of people with intellectual disabilities as in the general population; however, the proportion of deaths of people with intellectual disabilities that were amenable to good quality care was three times that of the proportion in the general population (37.5% compared to 13%).

The concept of avoidable mortality can be complicated because some people with intellectual disabilities have a predisposition to conditions that are related to the cause of their disability; for example, leukemia is more common in children with Down syndrome than in the general child population. Adjustments may therefore need to be made to the proportion of deaths from particular causes that are considered to be avoidable in people with intellectual disabilities. An alternative would be to use avoidable causes of death that are universal regardless of whether the person has an intellectual or developmental disability, which is the approach taken in the US. Healthy People Targets, a set of established benchmarks that can be measured within and between States (US DHHS).

Thus, while some causes of premature mortality in people with intellectual and developmental disabilities may be associated with the cause of the person's developmental or intellectual disability and challenging to mitigate, others may have modifiable determinants either unique to this population or similar to the general population. Discerning which causes are avoidable (either preventable or amenable) in a systematic fashion is likely to yield a better understanding of modifiable determinants or contributing factors that lead to or increase the risk of death.

3.2.1 Risk Factors for Premature Mortality

A complex range of factors influence our health, as summarized by Dahlgren and Whitehead (1991), ranging from biological differences caused by genetic inheritance, through to individual lifestyle factors, the ways in which we are connected in our communities and the broader socioeconomic, cultural, and environmental conditions of the society in which we live. Apart from biological differences caused by genetic inheritance, other influences on health are modifiable by social processes and can be the source of health inequalities. A number of studies have focused on the range of individual and socioeconomic risk factors for premature mortality in people with intellectual and developmental disabilities.

3.2.1.1 Biological Factors

People with moderate to profound intellectual disabilities are more likely to die from congenital abnormalities than people in the general population (Forsgren, Edvinsson, Nystrom, & Blomquist, 1996; Freilinger et al., 2010; Tyrer & McGrother, 2009). In addition, some specific aspects of physiological functioning have been associated with increased risk of premature mortality.

Having limited mobility has been identified as a predictor of premature mortality in people with intellectual and developmental disabilities by a range of studies. Eyman, Grossman, Chaney, and Call (1990), found that people with profound and sometimes multiple disabilities had a shorter life expectancy than those who were independently mobile, and that this was the strongest predictor of survival in the cohort studied. Being nonmobile was identified with a sevenfold and being partially mobile with a twofold increased risk of death compared with being fully mobile in a longitudinal study of adults with intellectual disabilities in England over a 19-year period (Tyrer, Smith, McGrother, & Taub, 2007). Mobility was also a significant risk factor in people with cerebral palsy in Strauss's study in California (Strauss, Shavelle, Reynolds, Rosenbloom, & Day, 2007). Those with severe cerebral palsy with the poorest mobility (unable to lift their heads in the prone position) had approximately four times the mortality of those with the best motor function (could roll or sit independently).

Eyman et al. (1990) reported that being tube fed was the second most significant predictor of premature mortality in (young) people with intellectual and developmental disabilities. This was supported by Cohen, Asor, and Tirosh (2008) who followed up 1000 children aged 6 months to 22 years with neurodisabilities from 1975 to 1985, reporting that restricted mobility and assisted feeding were significant risk factors of early death when compared to an age-matched group without neurodisability.

It is likely that some of these individual factors are related to the person having severe or profound intellectual disabilities and that it is combinations of characteristics that are at play. Hogg et al. (2007), for example, reported that in a cohort of people with profound and multiple intellectual disability in receipt of support services in Scotland, motor (in)competence emerged as the only significant predictor of nonsurvival when all other potential contributory factors were accounted for in a logistic regression analysis.

3.2.1.2 Social Factors

There is a wide literature about the contribution of social factors to inequalities in health of people with intellectual and developmental disabilities (e.g., Allerton, Welch, & Emerson, 2011; Emerson, Baines, et al., 2012; Krahn, Hammond, & Turner, 2006; Ouellette-Kuntz, 2005; Van Schrojenstein Lantman-De Valk, 2005). The causal framework for this is explained by Krahn et al. (2006) as being a "cascade of disparities" (p. 70) that ultimately leads to poor health outcomes. The illustrative model developed by Krahn (see Krahn & Fox, 2014, p. 4) starts with higher rates of adverse health conditions, which cascade into disparities in attention to health needs, disparities in preventive care and health promotion practices, disparities in equitable access to health care, and finally onto poorer health outcomes.

More recently, there has been an increased scrutiny of the particular role that access to, and quality of, health care services contributes to premature mortality in this population group. In the United Kingdom, Mencap (2007) highlighted the circumstances leading to death of six people with intellectual disabilities while in the care of the NHS, and concluded that "institutional discrimination" had led to these deaths. Subsequent investigations into deaths by the organization confirmed this perspective (Mencap, 2012). CIPOLD also provided evidence of the substantial contribution of factors relating to the provision of care and health services to the health disparities between people with and without intellectual disabilities (Heslop et al., 2013, 2014). Contributory factors to premature deaths for people with intellectual disabilities included problems with advanced care planning and the provision of proactive rather than reactive care; the ability of health and care services to respond in a timely way to changing support needs; adherence to legislation about the provision of "reasonable adjustments" for disabled people, and to legislation about the assessment of capacity and decision-making; living in inappropriate accommodation for one's needs; caregivers not feeling listened to; and delays in the diagnosis and treatment of illness. CIPOLD also reported that adults with a close friend or partner were significantly less likely to die from a cause of death amenable to good quality care than were other people with intellectual disabilities.

In the United States, the State of Connecticut report about contributory factors associated with mortality of people with intellectual disabilities identified the placement and quality of care of people with intellectual disabilities in generic care homes, the lack of competent health care coordination and assertive advocacy, and the need for constant vigilance and good communication as being key factors in relation to early deaths (McGaughey, 2012). In Massachusetts, mortality reviews have highlighted the contribution of deaths from injuries due to falls as contributing to excess mortality in people with intellectual and developmental disabilities (Lauer, 2013a). In addition, increased prevalence of poor health-related behaviors such as poor diet and physical activity contribute to obesity-related health effects in this population (Robertson et al., 2000; Tyrer & McGrother, 2009).

4. REFLECTIONS ON CURRENT CHALLENGES

There are clearly many challenges to accurately measuring premature mortality in people with intellectual disabilities, and taking remedial action in response to this. The World Health Organization (WHO) Constitution states that "the highest standards of health should be within reach of all, without distinction of race, religion, political belief, economic or social condition" (WHO, 2006, p. 1) but evidence pertaining to people with intellectual and developmental disabilities does not suggest that this is being realized. Current and future efforts in identifying and eliminating excess mortality in this population need to take into account, and successfully address a number of challenges that have been identified as being important to overcome.

4.1 The Quality of Available Mortality Data

The main source of vital statistics data about mortality is the official Medical Certificate of the Cause of Death in the United Kingdom and the death certificate in the United States (both are referred to here as death certificates). One of the purposes of the death certificate is to provide information at population level about the relative contributions of different diseases to mortality. This is used for "monitoring the health of a population, designing and evaluating public health interventions, recognizing priorities for medical research and health services, planning health services and assessing the effectiveness of these services" (ONS, 2005). In most developed nations with well-established vital statistics systems, mortality data from death certificates can provide useful insights into trends in cause of death and where efforts to reduce premature deaths could best be targeted. However, death certificates do have a number of limitations, particularly in relation to reliability and validity. Problems with data quality are likely to exist in all mortality data, but can particularly affect information for people with intellectual and developmental disabilities.

4.1.1 Accuracy of Death Certificates

In both the United States and United Kingdom, death certificates are completed by the medical doctor who cared for the person during the illness that led to their death. The certifying doctor should be familiar with the person's medical history and treatment regimen, and should have access to medical records pertaining to the individual. However, inaccuracies in reporting causes of death on these certificates can manifest in a number of ways. First are temporal differences and trends in reporting certain causes of death—for example, in the United Kingdom, old age or senility was accepted as the sole cause of death in some circumstances in people over the age of 70, but this was changed to a threshold age of 80 in 2009.

Secondly, a number of studies have highlighted problems with the completeness of death certificates (Sehdev & Hutchins, 2001). Common problems regarding the completeness of recording include incomplete sequencing of events leading to death, omitting causes of death, or reporting nonspecific causes of death that are in need of further explanation (Jordan & Bass, 1993).

Third is the issue of inaccuracies in the causes of death recorded on certificates (Sehdev & Hutchins, 2001). These are largely due to misattributing a cause of death to another disease, or reporting a cause of death instead of a mode of death. Gordis (2004) suggested that higher rates of validity exist for certain causes of death, such as cancer, than for other causes. In deaths caused by conditions that were not considered terminal, a known and recent injury, or in situations where an autopsy was not conducted, rates of validity in the cause identified on the death certificate is generally lower. Further, for deaths where the cause is not clear, some physicians list a mode of death as a cause—for example, incorrectly reporting a cause of death as "cardiopulmonary arrest," which does not provide any causal information related to why the heart and/or lungs stopped functioning (Sehdev & Hutchins, 2001).

Some errors in death certificates can be attributed to the lack of proper training for physicians on death certificate completion, unfamiliarity of the patient by the physician charged with completing the death certificate, the physician being unfamiliar with the person's medical history, or the need for further investigations to determine the underlying cause (Drummond, Wise, Matthias, Zvarich, & McGarvey, 2010; Landes & Peek, 2013; Sehdev & Hutchins, 2001).

4.1.1.1 The Accuracy of Death Certificates for People with Intellectual and Developmental Disabilities

In addition to the issues outlined above in relation to the general population, additional inaccuracies in death certificates may occur for people with intellectual and developmental disabilities when their disability itself is incorrectly cited as the cause of death. For example, it is not unusual for "mental retardation" to be listed on death certificates of people with intellectual and developmental disabilities (Landes & Peek, 2013; Lilienfeld & Stolley, 1994). The following are examples of comparisons between external records and actual death certificates of decedents with intellectual and developmental disabilities in the United States between 2000 and 2010:

- *For an 86-year-old man "Unspecified mental retardation" was listed as the primary cause of death, with no other causes or contributing conditions listed. The man actually died from an upper and lower GI bleed.*
- *For a 62-year-old woman, the death certificate listed the cause of death as "Down Syndrome." The woman had late-stage renal cancer and was receiving hospice services at the time of her death.*
- *For an 86-year-old man, the cause of death was listed as "failure to thrive." The man was in hospice for end-stage leukemia, which was the actual underlying cause of death.*

Lauer (2013b).

Recording of intellectual and developmental disability as a causal factor on death certificates occurs most frequently when diagnostic ambiguity exists because of incomplete medical histories; this then leads to an increased tendency for "diagnostic overshadowing" or the reliance on a more obvious condition such as the intellectual disability as the cause of death (Landes & Peek, 2013; Tyrer & McGrother, 2009). Decedents with ambiguity resulting from both incomplete medical history and diagnostic uncertainty, or decedents whose death was caused by external causes (injury, poisoning, etc.) were at the highest risk for this type of coding error. In addition, Landes and Peek (2013) found that people with intellectual disabilities who died in locations where their medical documentation was unlikely to be available (such as an emergency room) were at an increased risk of having erroneous information recorded than those who died at other locations.

It is recognized that intellectual and developmental disability should not be listed as a causal factor for any death (Baird & Sadovnick, 1990; Tyrer & McGrother, 2009), but guidance on the completion of US death certificates indicates that "mental retardation" may be listed as the underlying cause of death if the underlying cause of death is not known (CDC, 2011a). Landes and Peek (2013) pose the important question of "why at any time is the physician allowed to utilize a diagnosis code for a disability as an underlying cause of death, which represents a disease, injury, accident or act of violence?" (p. 1189). Rather, intellectual disability should be listed in Part II of the death certificate ("other significant conditions contributing to death but not resulting in the underlying cause") so that this coding error does not misinform public health care policy for people with intellectual and developmental disabilities (Hoel, Ron, Carter, & Mabuchi, 1993; Landes & Peek, 2013; Lloyd-Jones, Martin, Larson, & Levy, 1998; Tyrer & McGrother, 2009).

4.1.1.2 Limitations of the Use of Underlying Causes of Death

While the use of a single underlying cause of death offers some advantages for the provision of consistent and comparable vital statistics, this restriction also presents some limitations. The publication of vital statistics that only present a single underlying cause of death, and not any immediate or contributory causes, limits our ability to understand patterns of the sequence of events leading to death and ways of mitigating the effects of contributory causes. The effects of the selection of a single cause of death for vital statistics have become even more problematic as an increasing number of people have multimorbidity (more than one long-term condition) at the time of their death. In England, the number of people with three or more long-term conditions is predicted to rise from 1.9 million in 2008 to 2.9 million in 2018 (Department of Health, 2012) and higher rates have been reported in people with intellectual and developmental disabilities than in the general population (McCarron et al., 2013).

A second issue regarding the use of a single underlying cause of death in vital statistics is that the impact of some causes of death in a population may be underestimated. For example, in the past two decades, the number of deaths reported due to Alzheimer's disease has been increasing, in part due to a growing recognition of Alzheimer's disease as an underlying cause of death. As a consequence, the more immediate related conditions, such as aspiration of solids or liquids due to losing the ability to swallow, appear to become less frequently reported as a cause of death.

4.1.1.3 Autopsies or Postmortem Investigations

Autopsies are useful to confirm clinical findings, provide additional information related to cause of death, and identify conditions that were undiagnosed prior to death. The importance of autopsy is demonstrated by the extensive literature that exists about the frequency with which autopsies, when performed, reveal clinically significant diagnoses missed before death (Shojania, Burton, McDonald, & Goldman, 2003). For example, a study in a Boston hospital over three decades (1960–1980) found Type 1 errors (revealing major diagnosis that, if known, might have led to a change in therapy or prolonged survival) in about 10% of autopsies, and Type II errors (revealing missed diagnoses that did not affect survival but were nonetheless clinically important) in an additional 12% of autopsies (Shojania et al., 2003).

In the United States, there are two types of autopsies: (1) hospital or clinical autopsies, which family or physicians can request to clarify the cause of a person's death or to assess care and (2) Medicolegal autopsies which legal officials order in order to further investigate the circumstances surrounding a death (Hoyert, 2011). In the United States, the proportion of deaths that have an autopsy has declined significantly—prior to 1970, autopsies were conducted for between 40% and 60% of deaths but the proportion has more recently dropped to 5–10% of deaths (Nemetz et al., 2006; Shojania & Burton, 2008). This is, in part, due to the elimination of the requirement for at least 20% of deaths to have autopsies by the US Hospital Accreditation Board because of the emergence of more sophisticated (and reimbursable) molecular-based diagnostic testing, less of a focus on the autopsy as being clinically informative, and a reluctance to ask families to consent to an autopsy (Shojania & Burton, 2008). This mandate has now been discontinued, largely because hospitals were unselectively using autopsies to meet target rates without utilizing the information obtained to assess and improve the quality of hospital care.

In the United Kingdom, there is a legal duty for certain deaths to be referred to a coroner, who then decides whether further investigation, including autopsy, should take place. Over the last 15 years, the proportion of autopsies ordered by coroners has reduced from 60% to an average of 42% in 2011 (Ministry of Justice, 2012). In a review of the quality of 1691 autopsy reports, a quarter (23%) were considered to be of good or excellent quality, half (52%) were satisfactory, and a quarter (25%) were of poor or unacceptable quality (National Confidential Inquiry into Patient Outcome and Death, 2006).

Information about the availability and quality of autopsies for people with intellectual and developmental is very limited. A 1980 study suggested autopsies were ordered less frequently for people with intellectual and developmental disabilities than those without (Lilienfeld & Stolley, 1994), a fact that seemed to be borne out by Kiani et al. (2014) who reported little detailed documentation on the circumstances leading up to deaths and an absence of autopsies in people with intellectual and developmental disabilities who had died from probable sudden unexpected death in epilepsy. The CIPOLD study into premature deaths of people with intellectual disabilities in England, however, found no discernible pattern regarding the severity of intellectual disability and whether or not an autopsy was performed (Heslop et al., 2013).

4.2 The Quality of Available Demographic Data

There are a number of reasons driving the lack of identification of people with intellectual and developmental disabilities in vital statistics: a lack of consistency in the identification of people with intellectual and developmental disabilities; multiple coding options for the existence of intellectual and developmental disabilities; incomplete and incompatible registers of people with intellectual disabilities and developmental disabilities; a lack of recording of intellectual and developmental disabilities on death certificates; and few large scale, sufficiently powered, studies of people with intellectual and developmental disabilities sufficient to draw robust conclusions.

4.2.1 Challenges in Defining and Capturing Level of Disability

A broad agreement about the definition of "intellectual and developmental disabilities" exists, although the terminology used to describe this does differ between countries—for example, the terms learning disabilities (United Kingdom), developmental disabilities (United States and Canada), and mental disability (Canada) are sometimes used interchangeably with the term "intellectual disabilities" or "intellectual and developmental disabilities." Essentially, the term "intellectual and developmental disabilities" is understood to refer to a state of:

- significant limitations of cognitive (reasoning, learning, problem solving) and adaptive (conceptually, socially, and practically) functioning
- which affect areas of major life activity and the capacity to live independently as an adult
- which originated before the person reached adulthood (18—22 years of age)
- and which are likely to be lifelong in nature.

In the United Kingdom, the "social" model of disability has been adopted in policy, thus the criteria above relate to the impairment of a person; their disability would depend on the extent to which environmental factors support the person's full participation and inclusion in society.

How to operationalize such a definition, and use it to identify people with intellectual and developmental disabilities for epidemiological purposes is rather more problematic, as there is no clear dividing line between those who do or do not have some degree of impairment. At a local level, administrative databases in some countries identify people with intellectual and developmental disabilities who access services, although eligibility criteria for such services varies, and many people, particularly those with mild or moderate disabilities, are unlikely to be included (Bonardi et al., 2011). At a national level too, problems exist. In the United States, for example, funding and provision of most services (education, health, and social services) are under state jurisdiction and there is no adequate national data set(s) for this population. In England, registers held by local authorities count the number of children with special educational needs, whose primary need is because of intellectual disabilities, and by primary care doctors (GPs) of people with intellectual disabilities registered with their practice, but there is a considerable disjoint between the registers (Emerson & Glover, 2012). Given the difficulties in identifying and recording people with intellectual and developmental disabilities at either local or national levels, it is little wonder that identifying this population in national vital statistics is not usually possible.

4.2.2 Identification of People with Intellectual and Developmental Disabilities through Death Certificates

It is also not possible to fully identify the population with intellectual or developmental disabilities solely through death certificates. In a comprehensive review of coding of death certificates over a 2-year period in England, Glover and Ayub (2010) found that only 22% of people with intellectual and developmental disabilities could be identified as such from their death certificates alone. Adults with profound and multiple intellectual disabilities more frequently (53%) had intellectual disability listed on their death certificate than did those with severe (26.5%), moderate (28%), or mild intellectual disabilities (9.5%). These findings were supported by the CIPOLD study of premature deaths in people with intellectual disabilities in England which found that 23% of people with intellectual disabilities could be identified from their death certificate alone.

Glover and Ayub (2010) identified 48 ICD-10 codes for conditions usually associated with intellectual and developmental disabilities, 76 ICD-10 codes for conditions sometimes associated with intellectual and developmental disabilities, and 58 codes for conditions rarely associated with intellectual and developmental disabilities. The codes most frequently used in death certificates for intellectual and developmental disabilities were "development disorder of scholastic skills, unspecified," and "Down Syndrome" but the sheer array of different codes that could be used illustrate how difficult it would be to easily extract data pertaining to particular codes and to fully understand them. Due to such difficulties in identifying people with intellectual and developmental disabilities in death certificates, Hollins et al. (1998) had, more than 10 years previously, suggested that modification should be made to the death certificate form to include a section that indicated diseases or conditions present at death, but which did not contribute to the death, so that examination of the presence of a range of chronic conditions including intellectual and developmental disabilities, could be made.

4.3 The Value of Individual Case Reviews

Routine death registration does not capture all relevant factors that might contribute to understanding mortality in people with intellectual and developmental disabilities. Individual case review systematically gathers comprehensive data about the potential contributory factors to death, identifies remediable factors, and makes recommendations for system improvements to avoid premature deaths (Fraser, Sidebotham, Frederick, Covington, & Mitchell, 2014). Such individual case reviews can also identify evidence of good practice and effective policies or systems that should be expanded.

The specific purpose of an individual case mortality review can vary, depending on the needs of the organization. In some cases, the purpose of the review may be clinically focused, such as in hospital-based reviews used to determine cause of death in complicated clinical cases or the contributory factors related to medical errors. In other cases, the purpose of mortality review may be to examine wider factors in relation to a death, including a focus on social services and care provision. In order to assure a valid review process, it is essential that all relevant information about the death and the circumstances leading to death are available to the reviewer, including the death certificate, any autopsy or toxicology reports, the person's medical history, and records from any health or social care services used.

In the United States, some state-based service systems have their own reporting forms for deaths, which capture additional information about health-related conditions and life experiences prior to death that could be relevant to the cause of death. Annually, such data are currently collected, analyzed, and publicly reported for state service recipients in certain US states (e.g., Massachusetts, Connecticut) with the possibility of adopting such an approach in additional states. In addition, multidisciplinary mortality reviews occur for a selection of cases, examining case records and circumstances of death. A similar, but more intensive approach was taken by the CIPOLD study in England, which reviewed the individual circumstances leading to death of people with intellectual and developmental disabilities (and a comparator group of people without intellectual disabilities) through interviews and analysis of case record.

The value adopting such an approach to reviewing deaths has been well documented in relation to deaths of children (CYMRC, 2011; Fraser et al., 2014; Quan, Pikey, Gomez, & Bennett, 2011). For adult populations, the use of such approaches underpins many of the national confidential inquiries in England—focusing on specific causes of death (e.g., National Confidential Enquiry into Patient Outcome and Death), conditions (e.g., National Inquiry into deaths from asthma), or causes of death by people with specific conditions (e.g., National Confidential Inquiry into Suicide and Homicide by People with Mental Illness). Most such inquiries involve the detailed assessment of individual cases by a panel of experts in order to determine any contributory factors leading to the person's death. Confidentiality of patients, practitioners, and locations is ensured by anonymization of data, and aggregated findings are used to develop recommendations to improve patient safety or quality of care. In 2006, Rankin et al. conducted a study of the potential impact on clinical practice of participating in a confidential inquiry and concluded that such an approach could be a valuable learning experience for practitioners, which motivates change in their own clinical practice and that of their colleagues (Rankin, Bush, Bell, Cresswell, & Renwick, 2006). These findings are echoed by Heslop and Marriott (in press) who discussed how taking part in a detailed review of the circumstances leading to the death of a person with intellectual and developmental disabilities has had an impact on those participating in the process of the work in five key ways: by raising their awareness about relevant legislation and guidelines, by providing professionals with an opportunity to consider the whole person and their health and social care needs in a way that had not been done previously, by reinforcing the importance of accurate documentation and sharing of information, by reflecting on the ways in which the end of life care could be better managed, and by identifying outstanding training needs. In addition, collation of data from individual case reviews influenced change at wider local, regional, and national levels, including being instrumental in NHS England acknowledging premature mortality of people with intellectual and developmental disabilities as an area of concern and introducing a placeholder indicator (which represents a commitment to develop an indicator) in the NHS Outcomes Framework to capture and monitor data about excess mortality in this population (Department of Health, 2011).

5. FUTURE PRIORITIES

The evidence outlined in this chapter indicates substantial gaps in our knowledge, at the population level, about mortality of people with intellectual and developmental disabilities. At its root, there appears to be a major stumbling block—the identification of people with intellectual and developmental disabilities in national population-level data sets. In order to fill in existing data gaps, addressing this must be a clear priority. However, this chapter has also documented a wealth of evidence about current inequalities in health in people with intellectual and developmental disabilities, and our second priority must be to address these in practice. Our final priority must be the collection of internationally comparable data about mortality in order to have sufficiently large, robust data sets to be able to draw firm conclusions about excess mortality and its causes in this population. It is to these key priorities that we now turn.

5.1 The Identification of People with Intellectual and Developmental Disabilities in National Population-Level Data Sets

We have already seen that people with intellectual and developmental disabilities are largely invisible in national data sets, and, more importantly, data about them as a discrete subpopulation are usually impossible to extract. They are "out of sight" in this respect, and thus largely "out of mind." Given this, the importance of effective record linkage cannot be understated and appears to be the most fruitful way forward (Heslop et al., 2013; Ouellette-Kuntz et al., 2009; Tyrer & McGrother, 2009).

There are a number of approaches to data linkage that could be considered:

1. *Merging health and nonhealth administrative data sets of people with intellectual and developmental disabilities with national mortality data.*

Improvements in technology, data storage and retrieval, data governance, privacy measures, and analytic techniques make data linkage between existing data sets an increasingly promising option (Urbano, 2013). It is feasible to produce reliable information about mortality by merging administrative databases of people with intellectual and developmental disabilities (e.g., those on a GP register, or those in receipt of services) with national mortality data. This would link information provided on a death certificate (date of birth and death, gender, causes of death, place of death) with known people with intellectual and developmental disabilities in order that standardized information about a clearly defined population of people with intellectual and developmental disabilities could be reported. In England, the Minister of State for Care and Support, Norman Lamb, has made it clear that he expects data linkage between registers of people with intellectual disabilities held by GPs and national mortality data to go ahead (Department of Health, 2013), and while theoretically possible, delays in processing requests and information governance concerns have proved to be difficult obstacles to overcome during the past 2 years.

2. *Utilizing nonservice-related data to capture information about a wider group of people with intellectual and developmental disabilities.*

   A second option is to link more general data identifying people with intellectual and developmental disabilities with national mortality data. In the United States, for example, it may be possible to explore mortality for more complete populations of people with intellectual disabilities using medical claims data to identify people with intellectual disabilities that are not state service recipients and to link this to vital statistics databases. Although this has not been trialed, Massachusetts, for example, has a comprehensive claims database and could be a candidate for piloting such a process.

Pooling data across different registers and operational databases can lead to a number of challenges, due to the potential inconsistency of such registers, particularly in relation to how intellectual and developmental disability is defined and people are identified (Emerson & McGrother, 2011). The clear and consistent identification of people with intellectual and developmental disabilities in specific and nonspecific databases is central to this, despite some concerns about such "labeling" and the preference for a focus on "need for assistance" rather than that a person has intellectual disabilities per se (Australian Bureau of Statistics 2011, 2012). In addition, the need to conduct such studies in a systematic way that is internationally comparable is important.

5.2 Addressing Current Inequalities in Health in People with Intellectual and Developmental Disabilities

Our second priority must be to address the current inequalities in health and health outcomes that we already know about in relation to people with intellectual and developmental disabilities. We have already seen the potential value of individual case review (above) in changing attitudes and practice in relation to mortality of people with intellectual and developmental disabilities, and initiatives to look at the microlevel in addition to addressing gaps in mesolevel data are in urgent need. The purpose of any such initiative should be to drive improvement in service delivery, by clarifying the contribution of various amenable factors in relation to a person's death, and making adjustments to local practice that address modifiable factors. The US Government Accountability Office (2008) recommended that:

> *...publicly reporting information about mortality review findings helps to ensure transparency in the mortality review process and demonstrates to the public areas where the agency should direct its efforts to improve the quality of care. (p. 28)*

By collating information from detailed individual case reviews, local and regional and national patterns can then be established. This "bottom-up" approach has a number of advantages—Rodway, Windfur, Kapur, Shaw, and Appleby (2014) suggest that it is a rich source of locally relevant information that can lead to immediate changes in local practice if a formal component of "reflective learning" is included. However, such an approach is resource-intensive, and unless well coordinated can result in the production of unstandardized information that is difficult to collate in a meaningful way. It therefore best sits as supplementary to the collection of national-level data about mortality of people with intellectual and developmental disabilities.

5.3 The Collection of Internationally Comparable Data about Mortality

We have already highlighted challenges to the collection and analysis of comprehensive, robust data about people with intellectual and developmental disabilities at national level. The imperative, however, must be to work collaboratively and in partnership across national boundaries. It is vital that equivalent definitions and methods are used to collect internationally comparable data, including a common definition of "intellectual and developmental disabilities" and harmonious mortality data.

The benefits to this are likely to be substantial. By having available internationally comparable data about the age and cause of death of people with intellectual disabilities, we will be able to (1) have more robust data about less common conditions associated with intellectual and developmental disabilities, (2) identify areas of lower cause-specific burdens and successful interventions to share lessons across countries, and (3) better understand the major causes of death of people with intellectual and developmental disabilities to target preventative measures.

There already exists considerable enthusiasm by international colleagues to ensure that comparable data are collected and used to monitor and reduce health inequalities experienced by this population. As a first step, an international seminar series has been established to facilitate continued collaboration (see: http://www.bristol.ac.uk/sps/seminars/international/). In addition to this, information is also needed about mortality of people with intellectual disabilities in developing countries, especially those in Africa, Latin America, and South Asia where population-based epidemiological studies are largely lacking and cultural approaches to people with intellectual and developmental disabilities are more varied.

This chapter has summarized what we know to date, mainly in the United States and England, about mortality of people with intellectual and developmental disabilities and where there are gaps in our current knowledge about the age and cause of death. We find those with milder impairments are largely hidden from data sources but nevertheless extremely vulnerable to early death. We have a long way to go before we have sufficiently robust national and international data about mortality of people with intellectual and developmental disabilities, and routine surveillance of deaths in this population is used as an opportunity for reflective practice and enhanced learning. We have no time to waste.

REFERENCES

Al-Saleem, T., Wessner, L. L., Scheithauer, B. W., Patterson, K., Roach, E. S., Dreyer, S. J., et al. (1998). Malignant tumors of the kidney, brain, and soft tissues in children and young adults with the tuberous sclerosis complex. *Cancer, 83*, 2208–2216.

All Parliamentary Committee on Epilepsy. (2007). *The human and economic cost of epilepsy in England*. Leeds: Joint Epilepsy Council of the UK and Ireland.

Allerton, L. A., Welch, V., & Emerson, E. (2011). Health inequalities experienced by children and young people with intellectual disabilities: a review of literature from the United Kingdom. *Journal of Intellectual Disabilities, 15*(4), 269–278.

Annegers, J. F., Coan, S. P., Hauser, W. A., & Leestma, J. (2000). Epilepsy, vagal nerve stimulation by the NCP system, all-cause mortality, and sudden, unexpected, unexplained death. *Epilepsia, 41*, 549–553.

Armstrong, G. L., Conn, L. A., & Pinner, R. W. (1999). Trends in infectious disease mortality in the United States during the 20th century. *The Journal of the American Medical Association (JAMA), 281*, 61–66.

Australian Bureau of Statistics. (2011). *How Australia takes a census* (Catalogue No. 2903.0). Canberra: Commonwealth of Australia. Retrieved from http://www.ausstats.abs.gov.au/Ausstats/subscriber.nsf/0/B7AA16E5542280AFCA25787F00137F7C/$File/29030_2011_for_web.pdf.

Australian Bureau of Statistics. (2012). *Census of population and housing: Consultation on content and procedures, 2016* (Catalogue No. 2007.0). Canberra: ABS. Retrieved from http://www.abs.gov.au/AUSSTATS/abs@.nsf/Latestproducts/2007.0Appendix22016#assist.

Baird, P. A., & Sadovnick, A. D. (1990). Underlying cause of death in Down syndrome: accuracy of British Columbia death certificate data. *Canadian Journal of Public Health, 81*, 456–461.

Barbieri, J. S., Fuchs, B. D., Fishman, N., Cutilli, C. C., Umscheid, C. A., Kean, C., et al. (2013). The mortality review committee: a novel and scalable approach to reducing inpatient mortality. *Joint Commission Journal on Quality and Patient Safety, 39*(9), 387–395.

Bittles, A. H., Petterson, B. A., Sullivan, S. G., Hussain, R., Glasson, E. J., & Montgomery, P. D. (2002). The influence of intellectual disability on life expectancy. *The Journals of Gerontology Biological Sciences & Medical Sciences, 57*(7), M470–M472.

Bonardi, A., Lauer, E., Mitra, M., Bershadsky, J., Taub, S., & Noblett, C. (2011). *Expanding surveillance of adults with intellectual disability in the US.* Retrieved January 8, 2015, from http://shriver.umassmed.edu/sites/shriver.umassmed.edu/files/documents/Recommendations%20for%20Expanding%20Surveillance%20of%20Adults%20with%20Intellectual%20Disability%20in%20the%20United%20States%20(PDF).pdf.

Brunnström, H. R., & Englund, E. M. (2009). Cause of death in patients with dementia disorders. *European Journal of Neurology, 16*, 488–492.

Bureau of Labor Statistics, US Department of Labor. (September 11, 2014). *National census of fatal occupational injuries in 2013.* Retrieved January 2, 2015, from http://www.bls.gov/news.release/pdf/cfoi.pdf.

Burt, D. B., Chen, Y. W., Loveland, K. A., Lewis, K. R., Lesser, J., Cherry, L., et al. (1996). Dementia in adults with Down syndrome: report from a longitudinal study. In *Paper presented at the annual convention of the American Association on Mental Retardation.*

Burt, D. B., Loveland, K. A., Primeaux-Hart, S., Chen, Y. W., Phillips, N. B., Cleveland, L. A., et al. (1998). Dementia in adults with Down syndrome: diagnostic challenges. *American Journal of Mental Retardation, 103*(2), 130–145.

Califano, J. (1977). *Letter to President John F. Kennedy accompanying the tenth annual report of the President's Committee of Mental Retardation.*

Carter, G., & Jancar, J. (1983). Mortality in the mentally handicapped: a 50-year survey at the Stoke Park group of hospitals (1930–1980). *Journal of Mental Deficiency Research, 27*, 143–156.

Centers for Disease Control and Prevention, National Center for Health Statistics. (2003). *US Standard Certificate of Death.* Retrieved from http://www.cdc.gov/nchs/data/dvs/DEATH11-03final-ACC.pdf.

Centers for Disease Control and Prevention, National Center for Health Statistics. (2011a). *Instructions for classifying the underlying cause-of-death, ICD-10.* Retrieved December 31, 2014, from http://www.cdc.gov/nchs/data/dvs/2a2011.pdf.

Centers for Disease Control and Prevention, National Center for Health Statistics, National Vital Statistics System. (2011b). *Deaths: Final data for 2009* (National Vital Statistics Reports, 60(3)). Retrieved December 31, 2014, from http://www.cdc.gov/nchs/data/nvsr/nvsr60/nvsr60_03.pdf.

Centers for Disease Control and Prevention, National Center for Health Statistics. (2014). *CDC WONDER online database.* Retrieved January 8, 2015, from http://wonder.cdc.gov/ucd-icd10.html.

Centers for Disease Control and Prevention, National Center for Health Statistics. (n.d.) Annual mortality statistics for US population. www.cdc.gov.

Chaney, R. H., & Eyman, R. K. (2000). Patterns of mortality over 60 years among persons with mental retardation in a residential facility. *Mental Retardation, 38*, 289–293.

Chapman, M., Iddon, P., Atkinson, K., Brodie, C., Mitchell, D., Parvin, G., et al. (2011). The misdiagnosis of epilepsy in people with intellectual disabilities: a systematic review. *Seizure, 20*, 101–106.

Charlton, J. R. H., & Velez, R. (1986). Some international comparisons of mortality amenable to medical intervention. *British Medical Journal, 292*, 295–300.

Child and Youth Mortality Review Committee. (2011). *Special report: Unintentional suffocation, foreign body inhalation and strangulation*. Wellington: CYMRC.

Cohen, A., Asor, E., & Tirosh, E. (2008). Predictive factors of early mortality in children with developmental disabilities: a case-comparison analysis. *Journal of Child Neurology, 23*(5), 536–542.

Connecticut Department of Developmental Services. (2011–2013). *Mortality annual report FY 2009, FY 2011, and FY 2012*. Retrieved from http://www.ct.gov/dds/lib/dds/health/reports/mortality_report_fy_11.pdf http://www.ct.gov/dds/lib/dds/health/reports/mortality_report_fy_12.pdf.

Cooper, S. A., & Prasher, V. P. (1998). Maladaptive behaviours and symptoms of dementia in adults with Down's syndrome compared with adults with intellectual disability of other aetiologies. *Journal of Intellectual Disability Research, 42*(4), 293–300.

Cosgrave, M. P., Tyrrell, J., McCarron, M., Gill, M., & Lawlor, B. A. (1999). Determinants of aggression, and adaptive and maladaptive behaviour in older people with Down's syndrome with and without dementia. *Journal of Intellectual Disability Research, 43*(5), 393–399.

Dahlgren, G., & Whitehead, M. (1991). *Policies and strategies to promote social equity in health. Background document to WHO-strategy paper for Europe*. Stockholm: Institute for Futures Studies. Retrieved January 8, 2014, from http://www.iffs.se/wp-content/uploads/2011/01/20080109110739filmZ8UVQv2wQFShMRF6cuT.pdf.

Dalton, A. J. (1995). Alzheimer disease: a health risk of growing older with Down syndrome. In L. Nadel, & D. Rosenthal (Eds.), *Down syndrome: Living and learning in the community* (pp. 58–64). New York: Wiley-Liss.

Deaton, J. G. (1973). The mortality rate and cause of death among institutionalized Mongols in Texas. *Journal of Mental Deficiency Research, 17*, 117–122.

Department of Health. (2011). *The NHS outcomes framework 2012/13*. Retrieved January 8, 2015, from https://www.gov.uk/government/uploads/system/uploads/attachment_data/file/213711/dh_131723.pdf.

Department of Health. (2012). *Long-term conditions compendium of information* (3rd ed.) Retrieved January 8, 2015, from https://www.gov.uk/government/publications/long-term-conditions-compendium-of-information-third-edition.

Department of Health. (2013). *Government response to the confidential inquiry into premature deaths of people with learning disabilities*. Retrieved December 29, 2014, from https://www.gov.uk/government/uploads/system/uploads/attachment_data/file/212077/Government_Response_to_the_Confidential_Inquiry_into_Premature_Deaths_of_People_with_Learning_Disabilities_-_full_report.pdf.

Department of Health. (September 2014). *Premature deaths of people with learning disabilities: Progress update*. Retrieved December 29, 2014, from https://www.gov.uk/government/uploads/system/uploads/attachment_data/file/356229/PUBLISH_42715_2902809_Progress_Report_Accessible_v04.pdf.

Dranger, E., & Remington, P. (2004). *YPLL: A summary measure of premature mortality used in measuring the health of communities*. Madison, WI: University of Wisconsin Population Health Institute. Issue Brief 5(7).

Drummond, M. B., Wise, R. A., Matthias, J., Zvarich, M. T., & McGarvey, P. (2010). Accuracy of death certificates in COPD: analysis from the TORCH trial. *Journal of Chronic Obstructive Pulmonary Disease, 7*, 179–185.

Duff, M., Scheepers, M., Cooper, M., Hoghton, M., & Baddeley, P. (2001). Helicobacter pylori: has the killer escaped from the institution? A possible cause of increased stomach cancer in a population with intellectual disability. *Journal of Intellectual Disability Research, 45*, 219–225.

Duggan, L., Lewis, M., & Morgan, J. (1996). Behavioral changes in people with learning disability and dementia: a descriptive study. *Journal of Intellectual Disability Research, 10*, 311–321.

Dupont, A., Vaeth, M., & Videbech, P. (1986). Mortality and life expectancy on Down's syndrome in Denmark. *Journal of Mental Deficiency Research, 30*, 111–120.

Emerson, E., Baines, S., Allerton, L., & Welch, V. (2012). *Health inequalities and people with learning disabilities in the UK*. London: Improving Health and Lives Learning Disabilities Observatory, Public Health England.

Emerson, E., & Glover, G. (2012). The "transition cliff" in the administrative prevalence of learning disabilities in England. *Tizard Learning Disability Review, 17*(3), 139–143.

Emerson, E., Glover, G., Hatton, C., & Wolstenholme, J. (2014). Trends in age-standardised mortality rates and life expectancy of people with learning disabilities in Sheffield over a 33-year period. *Tizard Learning Disability Review, 19*(2), 90–95.

Emerson, E., Hatton, C., Robertson, J., Roberts, H., Baines, S., & Glover, G. (2012). *People with learning disabilities in England 2011: Services and supports*. Durham: Improving Health and Lives: Learning Disabilities Observatory.

Emerson, E., & McGrother, C. (2011). *The use of pooled data from learning disabilities registers: A scoping review*. Durham: Improving Health and Lives: Learning Disabilities Observatory.

Esbensen, A. J. (2010). Health conditions associated with aging and end of life of adults with Down syndrome. *International Review of Research in Mental Retardation, 39*, 107–126.

Esbensen, A. J., Seltzer, M. M., & Greenberg, J. S. (2007). Factors predicting mortality in midlife adults with and without Down syndrome living with family. *Journal of Intellectual Disability Research, 5*, 1039–1050.

Evenhuis, H. (1997). Medical aspects of ageing in a population with intellectual disability: III. Mobility, internal conditions and cancer. *Journal of Intellectual Disability Research, 41*, 8–19.

Eyman, R. K., Call, T. L., & White, J. F. (1991). Life expectancy of persons with Down syndrome. *American Journal of Mental Retardation, 95*, 603–612.

Eyman, R. K., Grossman, H. J., Chaney, R. H., & Call, T. L. (1990). The life expectancy of profoundly handicapped people with mental retardation. *The New England Journal of Medicine, 323*, 584–589.

Feldman, H. H., Jacova, C., Robilard, A., Garcia, A., Chow, T., Borrie, M., et al. (2008). Diagnosis and treatment of dementia: 2 diagnosis. *Canadian Medical Association Journal, 178*, 825–836.

Feliciano, P. (August 7, 2012). *Epigenetic convergence in intellectual disability and cancer?* (Web Log Post). Retrieved from http://blogs.nature.com/freeassociation/2012/08/epigenetic-convergence-in-intellectual-disability-and-cancer.html.

Finlayson, J., Morrison, J., Jackson, A., Mantry, D., & Cooper, S. A. (2010). Injuries, falls and accidents among adults with intellectual disabilities. Prospective cohort study. *Journal of Intellectual Disability Research, 54*(2), 966–980.

Forsgren, L. (2004). Epidemiology and prognosis of epilepsy and its treatment. In S. Shorvon, E. Perrucca, D. Fish, & E. Dodson (Eds.), *The treatment of epilepsy* (pp. 21–42). Oxford: Blackwell Publishing.

Forsgren, L., Edvinsson, S. O., Nystrom, L., & Blomquist, H. K. (1996). Influence of epilepsy on mortality in mental retardation: an epidemiologic study. *Epilepsia, 37*, 956–963.

Fraser, J., Sidebotham, P., Frederick, J., Covington, T., & Mitchell, E. A. (2014). Learning from child death review in the USA, England, Australia and New Zealand. *Lancet, 384*, 894–903.

Freilinger, M., Bebbington, A., Lanator, I., de klerk, N., Dunkler, D., Seidl, R., et al. (2010). Survival with Rett syndrome: comparing Rett's original sample with data from the Australian Rett Syndrome database. *Developmental Medicine and Child Neurology, 52*, 962–965.

Fryers, T. (1986). Survival in Down's syndrome. *Journal of Mental Deficiency Research, 30*, 101–110.

Galea, J., Butler, J., Iacono, T., & Leighton, D. (2004). The assessment of sexual knowledge in people with intellectual disability. *Journal of Intellectual and Developmental Disability, 29*(4), 350–365.

Gardner, J. W., & Sanborn, J. S. (1990). Years of potential life lost (YPLL)—what does it measure? *Epidemiology, 1*(4), 322–329.

Glover, G., & Ayub, M. (2010). *How people with learning disabilities die*. Durham: Improving Health and Lives: Learning Disabilities Observatory.

Glover, G., & Christie, A. (2014). *Joint health and social care self-assessment framework 2013: Detailed report on number questions*. London: Public Health England. Retrieved from https://www.improvinghealthandlives.org.uk/gsf.php5?f=312890.

Glover, G., & Emerson, E. (2013). Estimating how many deaths of people with learning disabilities in England could be prevented by better care. *Tizard Learning Disability Review, 18*(3), 146–149.

Goldman, S. E., Urbano, R. C., & Hodapp, R. M. (2011). Determining the amount, timing and causes of mortality among infants with Down syndrome. *Journal of Intellectual Disability Research, 55*, 85–94.

Gordis, L. (2004). *Epidemiology* (3rd ed.). Philadelphia: Elsevier Health Sciences.

Greenwood, N. W., & Wilkinson, J. (2013). Sexual and reproductive health care for women with intellectual disabilities: a primary care perspective. *International Journal of Family Medicine, 2013*. http://dx.doi.org/10.1155/2013/642472.

Harteloh, P., de Bruin, K., & Kardaun, J. (2010). The reliability of cause-of-death coding in the Netherlands. *European Journal of Epidemiology, 25*, 531–538.

Hasle, H., Clemmensen, I. H., & Mikkelsen, M. (2000). Risks of leukemia and solid tumors in individuals with Down's syndrome. *Lancet, 355*, 165–169.

Hayes, C., Johnson, Z., Thornton, L., Fogarty, J., Lyons, R., O-Connor, M., et al. (1997). Ten-year survival of Down syndrome births. *International Journal of Epidemiology, 26*, 822–829.

Healy, M. (April 8, 2013). Margaret Thatcher's dementia: cause of death or unrelated factor? *Los Angeles Times*. http://articles.latimes.com/2013/apr/08/news/la-heb-thatcher-dementia-cause-death-20130408.

Heslop, P., Blair, P., Fleming, P., Hoghton, M., Marriott, A., & Russ, L. (2013). *Confidential inquiry into premature deaths of people with learning disabilities (CIPOLD)*. Bristol: Norah Fry Research Centre.

Heslop, P., Blair, P. S., Fleming, P., Hoghton, M., Marriott, A., & Russ, L. (2014). The confidential inquiry into premature deaths of people with intellectual disabilities in the UK: a population-based study. *Lancet, 383*, 889–895.

Heslop, P. & Marriott, A. Making a difference—the impact of the confidential inquiry into premature deaths of people with learning disabilities. *British Journal of Learning Disabilities*, in press.

Hill, D. A., Gridley, G., Cnattingius, S., Mellemkjaer, L., Linet, M., Adami, H. O., et al. (2003). Mortality and cancer incidence among individuals with Down syndrome. *Archives of Internal Medicine, 163*, 705–711.

Hitiris, N., Mohanraj, R., Norrie, J., & Brodie, M. J. (2007). Mortality in epilepsy. *Epilepsy & Behavior: E&B, 10*, 363–376.

Hoel, D. G., Ron, E., Carter, R., & Mabuchi, K. (1993). Influence of death certificate errors on cancer mortality trends. *Journal of the National Cancer Institute, 85*, 1063–1068.

Hogg, J., Juhlberg, K., & Lambe, L. (2007). Policy, service pathways and mortality: a 10-year longitudinal study of people with profound intellectual and multiple disabilities. *Journal of Intellectual Disability Research, 5*(51), 366–376.

Holland, A. J., Hon, J., Huppert, F. A., & Stevens, F. (2000). Incidence and course of dementia in people with Down's syndrome: findings from a population-based study. *Journal of Intellectual Disability Research, 44*(2), 138–146.

Hollins, S., Attard, M. T., von Fraunhofer, N., McGuigan, S., & Sedgwick, P. (1998). Mortality in people with learning disability: risks, causes, and death certification findings in London. *Developmental Medicine & Child Neurology, 40*(1), 50–56.

Hoyert, D. L. (2011). The changing profile of autopsied deaths in the United States, 1972–2007. *NCHS Data Brief, 67*, 1–8.

Hussain, T., & Hyde-Bales, K. (2014). *Independent investigation into the death of C.S.* London: Verita.

Janicki, M. P., & Dalton, A. J. (1997). *Mortality and morbidity of a group of older adults with Down syndrome.* Unpublished paper (New York State Institute for Basic Research in Developmental Disabilities, 1050 Forest Hill Road, Staten Island, NY 10314, USA).

Janicki, M. P., Dalton, A. J., Henderson, C. M., & Davidson, P. W. (1999). Mortality and morbidity among older adults with intellectual disability: health services considerations. *Disability and Rehabilitation, 21*(5–6), 284–294.

Joint Epilepsy Council. (2005). *Epilepsy prevalence, incidence and other statistics.* Retrieved December 31, 2014, from http://jointepilepsycouncil.org.uk.

Jordan, J. M., & Bass, M. J. (1993). Errors in death certificate completion in a teaching hospital. *Clinical Investigations in Medicine, 16*, 249–255.

Kamarudeen, S. (2010). Amenable mortality as an indicator of healthcare quality—a literature review. *Health Statistics Quarterly, 47*, 1–15.

Kastner, T., Nathanson, R., & Friedman, D. L. (1993). Mortality among individuals with mental retardation living in the community. *American Journal of Mental Retardation, 98*, 285–292.

Kerr, M., Scheepers, M., Arvio, M., Beavis, J., Brandt, C., Brown, S., et al. (2009). Consensus guidelines into the management of epilepsy in adults with an intellectual disability. *Journal of Intellectual Disability Research, 53*, 687–694.

Kiani, R., Tyrer, F., Jesu, A., Bhaumik, S., Gangavati, S., Walker, G., et al. (2014). Mortality from sudden unexpected death in epilepsy (SUDEP) in a cohort of adults with intellectual disability. *Journal of Intellectual Disability Research, 58*(6), 508–520.

Krahn, G. L., & Fox, M. H. (2014). Health disparities of adults with intellectual disabilities: what do we know? what do we do? *Journal of Applied Research in Intellectual Disabilities, 27*(5), 431–446.

Krahn, G. L., Hammond, L., & Turner, A. (2006). A cascade of disparities: health and health care access for people with intellectual disabilities. *Mental Retardation and Developmental Disabilities Research Review, 12*, 70–82.

Landes, S. D., & Peek, C. W. (2013). Death by mental retardation? the influence of ambiguity on death certificate coding error for adults with intellectual disability. *Journal of Intellectual Disability Research, 57*(12), 1183–1190. http://dx.doi.org/10.1111/j.1365-2788.2012.01614.x.

Lauer, E. (2013a). *2010 & 2011 mortality report, Massachusetts department of developmental disabilities.* Boston: Massachusetts Department of Developmental Disabilities. Retrieved January 6, 2015, from http://www.mass.gov/eohhs/consumer/disability-services/services-by-type/intellectual-disability/newsroom/quality-assurance/mortality-reports.html.

Lauer, E. (2013b). Death certificates of people with an intellectual disability, Unpublished raw data.

Lauer, E., & Bonardi, A. (November 2013). Utility of mortality surveillance in adults with intellectual and developmental disabilities. In *Presented at the American Public Health Association 141st annual meeting & expo, Boston, MA.*

Lauer, E., et al. (2003–2012). *Annual mortality reports (2002–2009), Massachusetts department of developmental disabilities*. Boston: Massachusetts Department of Developmental Disabilities. Retrieved January 6, 2015, from http://www.mass.gov/eohhs/consumer/disability-services/services-by-type/intellectual-disability/newsroom/quality-assurance/mortality-reports.html.

Leung, H. T. T., & Ring, H. (2013). Epilepsy in four genetically determined syndromes of intellectual disability. *Journal of Intellectual Disability Research, 57*(1), 3–20.

Lilienfeld, D. E., & Stolley, P. D. (1994). *Foundations of epidemiology* (3rd ed.). New York: Oxford University Press.

Lloyd-Jones, D. M., Martin, D. O., Larson, M. G., & Levy, D. (1998). Accuracy of death certificates for coding coronary heart disease as the cause of death. *Annals of Internal Medicine, 129*(12), 1020–1026.

Lopez, A. D. (1983). The sex mortality differential in developed countries. In A. D. Lopez, & L. T. Ruzicka (Eds.), *Sex differentials in mortality: Trends, determinants and consequences* (pp. 53–120). Canberra: Australian National University Press.

Lucci-Cordisco, E., Zollino, M., Baglioni, S., Mancuso, I., Lecce, R., Gurrieri, F., et al. (2005). A novel microdeletion syndrome with loss of the MSH2 locus and hereditary non-polyposis colorectal cancer. *Clinical Genetics, 67*(2), 178–182.

Mackenbach, J. P., Bouvier-Colle, M. H., & Jougla, E. (1990). "Avoidable" mortality and health services: a review of aggregate data studies. *Journal of Epidemiology and Community Health, 44*, 106–111.

Mann, D. M. A. (1988). Alzheimer's disease and Down's syndrome. *Histopathology, 13*, 125–127.

Marik, P. E. (2001). Aspiration pneumonitis and aspiration pneumonia. *The New England Journal of Medicine, 344*(9), 665–671.

Massachusetts Department of Public Health, Bureau of Health Information, Statistics, Research & Evaluation. (August 2010). Top ten leading underlying causes of death by age, Massachusetts 2008. In *Massachusetts deaths 2008* (p. 43). Retrieved January 2, 2015, from http://www.mass.gov/eohhs/docs/dph/research-epi/death-report-08.pdf.

McCarron, M., Swinburne, J., Burke, E., McGlinchey, E., Carroll, R., & McCallion, P. (2013). Patterns of multimorbidity in an older population of persons with an intellectual disability: results from the intellectual disability supplement to the Irish longitudinal study on aging (IDS-TILDA). *Research in Developmental Disabilities, 34*(1), 521–527.

McGaughey, J. (2012). Connecticut's system for reviewing the deaths of individuals with intellectual disabilities: lessons learned from 10 years of mortality reviews and investigations. In *Hartford: Office of protection and advocacy for persons with disabilities*.

McGrother, C. W., Bhaumik, S., Thorp, C. F., Hauk, A., Branford, D., & Watson, J. M. (2006). Epilepsy in adults with intellectual disabilities: prevalence, associations and service implications. *Seizure, 15*, 376–386.

Mencap. (2007). *Death by indifference*. London: Mencap.

Mencap. (2012). *Death by indifference: 74 deaths and counting. A progress report 5 years on*. London: Mencap.

Ministry of Justice. (2012). *Coroners statistics 2011 England and Wales*. Retrieved January 8, 2015, from https://www.gov.uk/government/uploads/system/uploads/attachment_data/file/217475/coroners-bulletin-2011.pdf.

Morton, R., & Appleton, R. E. (2002). Misdiagnosis of epilepsy. *British Medical Journal, 324*(7347), 1219.

Moschetti, K., Cummings, P., Sorvillo, F., & Kuo, T. (2012). Burden of Alzheimer's disease-related mortality in the United States 1999–2008. *Journal of the American Geriatric Society, 60*, 1509–1514.

Nashef, L., Elson, L. S., Ryvlin, P., & Tomson, T. (2012). Unifying the definitions of sudden expected death in epilepsy. *Epilepsia, 53*(2), 227–233.

National Confidential Inquiry into Patient Outcome and Death. (2006). *The coroner's autopsy: Do we deserve better?* Retrieved December 31, 2014, from http://www.ncepod.org.uk/2006Report/Downloads/Coronial%20Autopsy%20Report%202006.pdf.

Nemetz, P. N., Tanglos, E., Sands, L. P., Fisher, W. P., Jr., Newman, W. P., 3rd, & Burton, E. C. (2006). Attitudes toward the autopsy—an 8-state survey. *MedGenMed, 8*(3), 80.

NHS Clinical Commissioning Group. (2013). *CCG outcomes indicator set.* Retrieved January 8, 2015, from http://www.england.nhs.uk/ccg-ois/.

NHS England. (2014). *Putting patients first: The NHS England business plan for 2014/15—2016/17.* Retrieved December 29, 2014, from http://www.england.nhs.uk/wp-content/uploads/2014/04/ppf-1415-1617-wa.pdf.

Nieuwenhuis-Mark, R. E. (2009). Diagnosing Alzheimer's dementia in Down syndrome: problems and possible solutions. *Research in Developmental Disabilities, 30,* 827—838.

Office for National Statistics (UK). (2005). *Guidance for doctors certifying cause of death.* London: General Register Office.

Office for National Statistics (UK). (November 2006). *Measuring premature and avoidable mortality: ONS proposals for national indicators.* Retrieved January 6, 2015, from http://www.ons.gov.uk/ons/about-ons/get-involved/consultations/archived-consultations/2006/measuring-premature-and-avoidable-mortality/index.html.

Office for National Statistics (UK). (February 2011). *Definitions of avoidable mortality.* Retrieved January 6, 2015, from http://www.ons.gov.uk/ons/about-ons/get-involved/consultations/archived-consultations/2011/definitions-of-avoidable-mortality/index.html.

Office for National Statistics (UK). (September 25, 2014). *National life tables, United Kingdom, 2011—2013.* Retrieved January 2, 2015, from http://www.ons.gov.uk/ons/dcp171778_377972.pdf.

Ouellette-Kuntz, H. (2005). Understanding health disparities and inequities faced by individuals with intellectual disabilities. *Journal of Applied Research in Intellectual Disabilities, 18,* 113—121.

Ouellette-Kuntz, H., Shooshtari, B., Temple, B., Brownell, M., Burchill, C., Yu, C. T., et al. (2009). Estimating administrative prevalence of intellectual disabilities in Manitoba. *Journal on Developmental Disabilities, 15,* 69—80.

Patel, P., Goldberg, D., & Moss, S. (1993). Psychiatric morbidity in older people with moderate and severe learning disability. II: the prevalence study. *British Journal of Psychiatry, 163,* 481—491.

Patja, K., Eero, P., & Livanainen, M. (2001). Cancer incidence among people with intellectual disability. *Journal of Intellectual Disability Research, 45*(4), 300—307.

Penrose, L. S. (1949). The incidence of mongolism in the general population. *Journal of Mental Science, 95,* 685—688.

Puri, B. K., Lekh, S. K., Langa, A., Zaman, R., & Singh, I. (1995). Mortality in a hospitalized mentally handicapped population: a 10-year survey. *Journal of Intellectual Disability Research, 39,* 442—446.

Quan, L., Pikey, D., Gomez, A., & Bennett, E. (2011). Analysis of paediatric drowning deaths in Washington State using the child death review (CDR) for surveillance: what CDR does and does not tell us about lethal drowning injury. *Injury Prevention, 17*(Suppl.), i28—33.

Rankin, J., Bush, J., Bell, B., Cresswell, P., & Renwick, M. (2006). Impacts of participating in confidential enquiry panels: a qualitative study. *British Journal of Obstetrics and Gynaecology, 113,* 387—392.

Reuber, M., Gore, J., Wolstenhome, J., Jonas, P., Frankson, C., Murray, C., et al. (2008). Examining a community model of epilepsy care for people with learning disabilities. *Seizure, 17,* 84—91.

Richards, B. W., & Sylvester, P. E. (1969). Mortality trends in mental deficiency institutions. *Journal of Mental Deficiency Research, 13*, 276–292.

Robertson, J., Emerson, E., Gregory, N., Hatton, C., Turner, S., Kessissoglou, S., et al. (2000). Lifestyle related risk factors for poor health in residential settings for people with intellectual disabilities. *Research in Developmental Disabilities, 21*(6), 469–486.

Rodway, C., Windfur, K., Kapur, N., Shaw, J., & Appleby, L. (2014). National learning disability review development project. Stage 1—Options development report. In *Manchester: National confidential inquiry into suicide and homicide by people with mental illness*. Retrieved January 9, 2015, from http://www.hqip.org.uk/assets/National-Team-Uploads/CORP/Options-Appraisals-Report-on-the-development-of-a-Learning-Disabilities-Mortality-Review-Function-2014.pdf.

Rogers, B., Stratton, P., Msall, M., Andres, M., Champlain, M. K., Koerner, P., et al. (1994). Long-term morbidity and management strategies of tracheal aspiration in adults with severe developmental disabilities. *American Journal of Mental Retardation, 98*(4), 490–498.

Ross, J. A., Blair, C. K., Olshan, A. F., Robison, L. L., Smith, F. O., Heerema, N. A., et al. (2005). Periconceptional vitamin use and leukemia risk in children with Down syndrome: a children's oncology group study. *Cancer, 104*(2), 405–410.

Rugg-Gunn, J. F., & Sander, W. J. (2012). Management of chronic epilepsy (Clinical Research Ed.). *British Medical Journal, 345*, e4576.

Rutstein, D. D., Berenberg, W., Chalmers, T. C., Child, C. G., Fishman, A. P., & Perrin, E. B. (1976). Measuring the quality of healthcare: a clinical method. *New England Journal of Medicine, 294*, 582–588.

Satge, D., Sommelet, D., Geneix, A., Nishi, M., Malet, P., & Vekemans, M. (1998). A tumor profile in Down syndrome. *American Journal of Medical Genetics, 78*, 207–216.

Sehdev, A. E., & Hutchins, G. M. (2001). Problems with proper completion and accuracy of the cause-of-death statement. *Archives of Internal Medicine, 161*(2), 277–284.

Shaw, M., Thomas, B., Smith, G. D., & Dorling, D. (2008). *The grim reaper's road atlas: An atlas of mortality in Britain*. Bristol: Policy Press.

Sherrard, J., Tonge, B. J., & Ozanne-Smith, J. (2001). Injury in young people with intellectual disability: descriptive epidemiology. *Injury Prevention, 7*, 56–61.

Shin, M., Besser, L. M., Kucik, J. E., Lu, C., Siffel, C., Correa, A., &, The Congenital Anomaly Multistate Prevalence and Survival (CAMPS) Collaborative. (2009). Prevalence of Down syndrome among children and adolescents in 10 regions of the United States. *Pediatrics, 124*(6), 1565–1571.

Shojania, K. G., & Burton, E. C. (2008). The vanishing nonforensic autopsy. *The New England Journal of Medicine, 358*(9), 873–875.

Shojania, K. G., Burton, E. C., McDonald, K. M., & Goldman, L. (2003). Changes in rates of autopsy-detected diagnostic errors over time: a systematic review. *The Journal of the American Medical Association (JAMA), 289*, 2849–2856.

Shorvon, S., & Tomson, T. (2011). Sudden unexpected death in epilepsy. *The Lancet, 378*, 2028–2038.

Smith, D. I., Zhu, Y., McAvoy, S., & Kuhn, R. (2006). Common fragile sites, extremely large genes, neural development and cancer. *Cancer Letters, 232*(1), 48–57.

Strauss, D., Brooks, J., Rosenbloom, L., & Shavelle, R. (2008). Life expectancy in cerebral palsy: an update. *Developmental Medicine & Child Neurology, 50*, 487–493.

Strauss, D., Shavelle, R., Reynolds, R., Rosenbloom, L., & Day, S. (2007). Survival in cerebral palsy in the last 20 years: signs of improvement? *Developmental Medicine & Child Neurology, 49*, 86–92.

Swango-Wilson, A. (2011). Meaningful sex education programs for individuals with intellectual/developmental disabilities. *Sexuality and Disability, 29*(2), 113–118.

Thorpe, L., Pahwa, P., Bennett, V., Kirk, A., & Nanson, J. (2012). Clinical predictors of mortality in adults with intellectual disabilities with and without Down's syndrome. *Current Gerontology and Geriatrics Research, 2012.* http://dx.doi.org/10.1155/2012/943890.

Tyrer, F., & McGrother, C. (2009). Cause-specific mortality and death certificate reporting in adults with moderate to profound intellectual disability. *Journal of Intellectual Disability Research, 53*, 898–904.

Tyrer, F., Smith, L. K., & McGrother, C. W. (2007). Mortality in adults with moderate to profound intellectual disability: a population-based study. *Journal of Intellectual Disability Research, 51*(7), 520–527.

Tyrer, F., Smith, L. K., McGrother, C. W., & Taub, N. A. (2007). The impact of physical, intellectual and social impairments on survival in adults with intellectual disability: a population-based register study. *Journal of Applied Research in Intellectual Disabilities, 20*, 360–367.

US Bureau of the Census. (1939). *Manual of the international list of causes of death (fifth revision) and joint causes of death (fourth revision).* Washington: US Government Printing Office.

US Department of Health and Human Services, Office of Disease Prevention and Health Promotion. Healthy People 2020. Washington, DC.

US Government Accountability Office. (2008). Medicaid home and community-based waivers: CMS should encourage states to conduct mortality reviews for individuals with developmental disabilities. In *Report to the ranking member, US Committee on Finance, US Senate. (GAO-08–529).* Retrieved from http://www.gao.gov/new.items/d08529.pdf.

US Surgeon General. (2002). Closing the gap: a national blueprint to improve the health of persons with mental retardation. In *Report of the surgeon general's conference on health disparities and mental retardation.*

Urbano, R. C. (2013). Using secondary datasets to understand persons with developmental disabilities and their families. In R. C. Urbano (Ed.), *International review of research in developmental disabilities.* Waltham, MA: Academic Press.

Van Schrojenstein Lantman-De Valk, H. M. J. (2005). Health in people with intellectual disabilities: current knowledge and gaps in knowledge. *Journal of Applied Research in Intellectual Disabilities, 18*, 325–333.

Wagemans, A. M. A., & Cluitmans, J. J. M. (2006). Falls and fractures: a major health risk for adults with intellectual disabilities in residential settings. *Journal of Practice in Intellectual Disabilities, 3*(2), 136–138.

Walczack, T. S., Leppik, I. E., D'Amelio, M., Parick, J., So, E., Ahmen, P., et al. (2001). Incidence and risk factors in sudden unexpected death in epilepsy: a perspective cohort study. *Neurology, 56*, 519–525.

Wallace, R. A., Webb, P. M., & Schluter, P. J. (2002). Environmental, medical, behavioural and disability factors associated with *Helicobacter pylori* infection in adults with intellectual disability. *Journal of Intellectual Disability Research, 46*, 51–60.

Wheller, L., Baker, A., & Griffiths, C. (2006). Trends in premature mortality in England 1950–2004. *Health Statistics Quarterly, 31*, 34–41.

Willgoss, T. G. (2010). Falls in people with learning disabilities: what are the risk factors and prevention strategies? *Nursing Times, 106*(46).

Wisniewski, K. E., Wisniewski, H. M., & Wen, G. Y. (1985). Occurrence of neuropathological changes and dementia of Alzheimer's disease in Down's syndrome. *Annals of Neurology, 17*, 278–282.

World Health Organization. (1992). *International statistical classification of diseases and related health problems: 10th revision* (Vol. 2). Geneva: World Health Organization.

World Health Organization. (2006). *Constitution of the World Health Organisation.* Basic documents, 45th ed., Supplement. Geneva: WHO. Retrieved from http://www.who.int/governance/eb/who_constitution_en.pdf.

Yang, Q., Rasmussen, S. A., & Friedman, J. M. (2002). Mortality associated with Down's syndrome in the USA from 1983 to 1997: a population-based study. *Lancet, 359*, 1019–1025.

Young, C., Shankar, R., Palmer, J., Craig, J., Hargreaves, C., McLean, B., et al. (2014). Does intellectual disability increase sudden unexpected death in epilepsy (SUDEP) risk. Retrieved January 2, 2015, from *Seizure, 25*, 112–116. http://dx.doi.org/10.1016/j.seizure.2014.10.001.

Zigman, W. B. (2013). Atypical aging in Down syndrome. *Developmental Disabilities Research Reviews, 18*, 51–67.

Zigman, W., Schupf, N., Haveman, M., & Silverman, W. (1997). The epidemiology of Alzheimer's disease in mental retardation: results and recommendations from an international conference. *Journal of Intellectual Disability Research, 41*, 76–80.

Zigman, W. B., Schupf, N., Sersen, E., & Silverman, W. (1996). Prevalence of dementia in adults with and without Down syndrome. *American Journal of Mental Retardation, 100*, 403–412.

INDEX

Note: Page numbers followed by "*f*" indicate figures and "*t*" indicate tables.

L

M

CONTENTS OF PREVIOUS VOLUMES

VOLUME 1

VOLUME 2

VOLUME 3

VOLUME 4

VOLUME 5

VOLUME 6

VOLUME 7

VOLUME 8

VOLUME 9

VOLUME 10

VOLUME 11

VOLUME 12

VOLUME 13

VOLUME 14

VOLUME 15

VOLUME 16

VOLUME 17

VOLUME 18

VOLUME 19

VOLUME 20

VOLUME 21

VOLUME 22

VOLUME 23

VOLUME 24

VOLUME 25

VOLUME 26

VOLUME 27

VOLUME 28

VOLUME 29

VOLUME 30

VOLUME 31

VOLUME 32

VOLUME 33

VOLUME 34

VOLUME 35

VOLUME 36

VOLUME 37

VOLUME 38

VOLUME 39

VOLUME 40

VOLUME 41

VOLUME 42

VOLUME 43

VOLUME 44

VOLUME 45

VOLUME 46

VOLUME 47

FSC
www.fsc.org
MIX
Papier | Fördert gute Waldnutzung
FSC® C083411

Kolibri 360 GmbH
Ferdinand-Jühlke-Straße 7
99095 Erfurt, Deutschland
produktsicherheit@kolibri360.de